Peacekeeping in Albania and Kosovo

Peacekeeping in Albania and Kosovo

Conflict response and international intervention in the Western Balkans, 1997–2002

Daan W. Everts

I.B.TAURIS
LONDON • NEW YORK • OXFORD • NEW DELHI • SYDNEY

I.B. TAURIS
Bloomsbury Publishing Plc
50 Bedford Square, London, WC1B 3DP, UK
1385 Broadway, New York, NY 10018, USA

BLOOMSBURY, I.B. TAURIS and the I.B. Tauris logo are trademarks of
Bloomsbury Publishing Plc

First published in Great Britain 2020

Copyright © Daan W Everts, 2020

Daan W Everts has asserted his right under the Copyright, Designs and Patents Act, 1988, to be identified as Author of this work.

Cover design by Adriana Brioso

All rights reserved. No part of this publication may be reproduced or transmitted in any form or by any means, electronic or mechanical, including photocopying, recording, or any information storage or retrieval system, without prior permission in writing from the publishers.

Bloomsbury Publishing Plc does not have any control over, or responsibility for, any third-party websites referred to or in this book. All internet addresses given in this book were correct at the time of going to press. The author and publisher regret any inconvenience caused if addresses have changed or sites have ceased to exist, but can accept no responsibility for any such changes.

A catalogue record for this book is available from the British Library.

A catalogue record for this book is available from the Library of Congress.

ISBN: HB: 978-1-8386-0448-6
PB: 978-1-8386-0447-9
ePDF: 978-1-8386-0450-9
eBook: 978-1-8386-0449-3

Typeset by Deanta Global Publishing Services, Chennai, India

To find out more about our authors and books visit www.bloomsbury.com and sign up for our newsletters.

Every dog will have its day, so will the underdog – *Swami Vivekananda*

Bigotry is the last refuge of scoundrels – *Paul Krugman paraphrasing Samuel Johnson's famous quote of 1776*

We should understand that we are not each other's enemies but that we have a common enemy – those at the top – *'Encyclopedia for the Living', Serb-Albanian co-production by Zlatko Pakovic, Belgrade, and Jeton Neziraj, Pristina.*

Contents

Foreword viii
Preface xi
Map xiii
Context xiv

1 Albania: Recoil from the abyss 1
2 The unstoppable war 35
3 Ethnic revenge 61
4 International protectorate I: Starting from scratch 83
5 International protectorate II: Preparing for the next phase 121
6 Transition to self-rule I: Preparing a constitution and central elections 151
7 Transition to self-rule II: Handing over governance 181
8 Concluding remarks: Lessons not learned 205

List of abbreviations 221
Sources consulted 224
Index 226

Foreword

The end of the Cold War – symbolized by the fall of the Berlin Wall in 1989 – seemed to many the beginning of a new, hopeful era of growing trust and cooperation between nations, resulting in greater security and stability. Promotion and defence of common basic rights and values became the order of the day. Francis Fukuyama, the American historian, announced 'the End of History', implying an end to ideological competition. The earlier 'convergence' theory of Jan Tinbergen, Netherlands' foremost economist and first-ever recipient of the Nobel Prize for Economics, seemed prescient and validated: East and West were coming together, capitalism and communism meeting each other halfway. This euphoria also extended to supranational and intergovernmental institutions. The European Union was on a determined path towards expansion and deepening, the Council of Europe (CoE) was consolidating its role as custodian of the human rights commitments by its member states, and the Organization for Security and Cooperation in Europe (OSCE) was basking in glory for its success in fostering dialogue both between and within participating states. Through its network of national Helsinki Committees – covering the northern hemisphere from Vancouver to Vladivostok – it was actively promoting and defending basic democratic and human rights 'on the ground'. The end of the Cold War also implied fundamental change for the two opposing military alliances. The Warsaw Pact was dissolved altogether; the North Atlantic Treaty Organization (NATO) succeeded in extending its *raison d' être* by redefining its mission, including support for peacekeeping efforts worldwide.

The euphoria was not to last long. Realities on the ground, including human mindsets, were not as malleable as hoped for. In Europe the Western Balkans became the first 'unfrozen' theatre where the clash between vested interests and claims for reforms became unmanageable and turned vicious. Fierce nationalism and ethnic strife led to wars, with unspeakable consequences in terms of human debasement and suffering. Joint intergovernmental responses to such outbursts of violence, or the crises that preceded them, had been legitimized in principle by the United Nations Charter of 1945. While economic and geopolitical interests were always important if not decisive factors driving such multinational action – in line with the age-old adage 'What is in it for me' – the post-Cold War 'universalization' of basic democratic and human rights introduced the new notion of 'humanitarian interventions'. This referred to benevolent interventions aimed at furthering or restoring basic rights for vast groups of people who are systematically denied these rights. While still serving the (self-) interest of the interveners in terms of global security, this new type of intervention is distinctly different from those that are mainly driven by geopolitical and/or economic considerations. The international interventions, including military action, in the Western Balkans in the 1990s, aimed at ending armed conflicts, correspond to this new type of intervention.

Given the vast differences in conflicts, it is obvious that interventions are not alike. By now the international community has built up a considerable caseload of such multinational ventures, small and big. The results have been very mixed, with failures probably preponderant. Given the enormous consequences of foreign intervention, not only for the country at stake but also for the intervening countries, utmost care and prudence is needed in their preparation, execution and termination. In this regard I can only underwrite what Daan Everts, the author who served as Head of Mission for the EU, NATO and OSCE in several crisis situations, advocates: empathetic realism. Without empathy – reaching the hearts and minds of people affected, to use an old but still valid cliché – any foreign intervention is bound to fail. Similarly, unrealistic targets and planning can only lead to shortcomings and disillusion all around. Being 'empathetically realistic', we may avoid or at least minimize the risks of ill-advised incursion, inadequate handling of the evolving situation and unsatisfactory termination.

The Albanian and Kosovo interventions described in this book provide a very useful insight into how the international dynamics in humanitarian interventions play out on the ground. Both Albania and Kosovo have remarkable post-conflict experiences to offer. In both cases the joint stabilization and reconstruction efforts, despite the inevitable setbacks and downsides, have laid the foundation for European integration – in the security interest of all of Europe. Judging from my own experience at the helm of the OSCE and NATO I can only subscribe to the author's analysis of the need for an inclusive, persistent but realistic approach. Anno 2019, with populism, ethnophobia and autocratic tendencies on the rise and various crises looming around the world, such an approach is direly needed, indeed, when embarking on new interventions.

Jaap de Hoop Scheffer   The Hague, 25 November 2019

Minister of Foreign Affairs of The Netherlands (2002–2004)
Chairman-in-Office of the OSCE (2003)
Secretary General of NATO (2005–2008)

Preface

This book is in response to the urgings of friends, colleagues and many interlocutors to recount the experiences of an 'insider' of two remarkable, international interventions in the Western Balkans, namely in Albania and Kosovo. As a Netherlands diplomat I have had the special privilege to be involved in the work of four prominent international organizations: the United Nations (UN), the European Union (EU), the Organization for Security and Cooperation in Europe (OSCE) and the North Atlantic Treaty Organization (NATO). Working for the OSCE and UN in Albania and Kosovo was particularly challenging because of the outsized responsibilities that had befallen the OSCE, as the key player in these two post-conflict reconciliation and rehabilitation efforts.

As Head of Mission, I was in a vantage position to witness from within the dynamics of international 'meddling' in internal affairs. Despite not being an avid notetaker myself and despite being far too absorbed in daily work, I did religiously oversee the daily, weekly and monthly reports sent by my office to the OSCE headquarters in Vienna. In addition, Spot Reports were prepared on incidents and occurrences that required special or immediate attention. All this material was available at the OSCE Archives in Prague for me to consult in the course of writing.

The societal turbulence that unavoidably characterizes post-crisis situations makes it often difficult to stay above the fray and carefully weigh all the factors that come into play. The lapse of twenty years allows the events to be reviewed and assessed with the benefit of hindsight as well as of insights coming from other sources and my own subsequent mission experiences. I have tried to describe and analyse them in fairness, cognizant of the perspectives from different sides. Impartiality does not mean, however, bland neutrality and indifference. Instead, I believe, one should strive to be on the 'just side' and recognize rights and wrongs as they occur, irrespective of who they are attributed to. This is particularly challenging in Kosovo where Albanian and Serb versions of historical, recent and current developments are often diametrically opposed. I am under no illusion that my attempted moral and intellectual rectitude will not bring me scorn from both sides.

Collegial inputs from many sides have helped me greatly in finalizing the text. Among the many, I should specially mention Ismije Beshiri, for her detailed knowledge about Albania and Kosovo, Miriam Cias, for relentlessly going over draft texts, and Hans Weerstra, for his scrutiny of readability. Alice Nemcova was crucially helpful in providing access to documents in the OSCE Archives in Prague. Of course, the post-hoc reflections and conclusions are solely my own.

I should add a word on the use of language when spelling the names of places and regions. I have applied the most common English denominations for countries and main cities as used in professional publications – hence, Kosovo instead of Kosova and Tirana instead of the Tirane or Pristina instead of Pristhine. As regards names of places in Kosovo I have followed the current, politically correct practice and, while cumbersome, have used the Albanian and Serbian version jointly, for instance Peja/Pec or Skenderaj/Srbica, except where the two spellings are almost identical like with Prizren, Gjilane or Leposavic.

Map

Map of Albania/Kosovo/Serbia ©Erik Eshuis Infographics.

Context

International interventions in conflict-ridden societies have left a trail of debacles. Often they primarily served the national interest of the intervening nation(s) wishing to access material resources or obtaining geopolitical advantage. In other, more benign cases they served 'enlightened self-interest', with a higher cause at stake as well. To pick only one self-evident example from the vast trove of historical cases: the US intervention to come to the rescue of Nazi-occupied democracies in Europe belongs to the loftier category, while its more recent, ill-advised and ill-fated incursion in Iraq clearly does not.

Ever growing interdependence between states intensified awareness of the need for multinational cooperation to uphold the rule of law and prevent escalation of peace-threatening conflicts. Chapter VII of the United Nations Charter, adopted in 1945, even mandates multilateral *military* intervention in case a state's internal development threatens international peace and security. Since then, joint intervention to redress national developments that endanger international security has become justifiable – if authoritatively mandated. Moreover, in 2005 all Heads of State and Government, at a UN World Summit, affirmed the Responsibility to Protect populations from genocide, ethnic cleansing, and crimes against humanity. This 'R to P' (or R2P), as it is often referred to, also includes the responsibility of the international community to protect in case an individual State flagrantly fails to protect its population.

Of all the regions in the world, the Western Balkans certainly has had more than a fair share of strife, military incursions and occupations. Surrounded by the great Austrian-Hungarian, Russian and Ottoman empires, it was at the crossroads of multiple trade routes and home to different and overlapping ethnic and religious communities: Slavs and Albanians, predominantly, and Orthodox Christians, Roman Catholics and Muslims plus a sprinkling of Jews.

As such it was a ready theatre for political intrigue, conflict and territorial ambitions of forces from both within and outside. The conquest of the region by the Ottomans in the late-fourteenth- and early-fifteenth-centuries was followed by nearly 500 years of occupation, albeit relatively benign. Their empire slowly declined in the nineteenth century, with new national states emerging, and was definitively ended by two brutal Balkan Wars in 1912 and 1913. Although rebellion by Kosovo Albanians was at the onset of the first, it was Serbia, Bulgaria, Greece and Montenegro that ended up with most of the territorial spoils. The Albanian nationhood aspirations were curbed by the then dominant European powers, through their London Conference in 1912–13. The newly proclaimed state of Albania was restricted to narrowly defined borders, comprising less than half of what was then predominantly Albanian-inhabited territory – a root cause for continuous ethnic strife until the present day.

More war and occupation followed in 1914 with the First World War, again originating in the Western Balkans, while the region also bore the full brunt of the Second World War. The Cold War era after 1945 brought four decades of relative stability. Internal dissent was kept in check by tight, centralized rule in the Socialist Federal Republic of Yugoslavia, under Josip Broz Tito, and even more so in autocratic, communist Albania under Enver Hoxha. However, the fall of the Berlin Wall in 1989 and the collapse of the Soviet Union also ended the status quo in the Western Balkans. The Titoist promise of peaceful, multiethnic coexistence in Yugoslavia could no longer be sustained. Nationalist sentiments, stirred up by unscrupulous leaders, civic and religious, created ethnic division and enmity beyond repair. Poor European Union diplomacy, reflecting internal divisions, did not help to prevent the tensions growing out of control. Armed struggles for national independence followed in Slovenia, Croatia and Bosnia and Herzegovina in succession, with a horrendous impact on interethnic relations. It was only a combination of political and military pressure from outside, with UN involvement and a decisive role played by the USA, that put an end to the internecine Yugoslav wars as marked by the Dayton Peace Agreement of 1995.

It was, alas, not the end of Balkan violence. Two new crises emerged that caused international alarm and new foreign intervention. Chaos in post-communist Albania with the imminent threat of civil war in 1997 triggered a European intervention by a 'coalition of the willing' that was to help restore order and stability. In Kosovo an even greater threat to regional peace and stability developed. Years of ethnic discrimination and oppression had brought civil resistance, guerilla activity and, in response, armed retaliation with massive ethnic cleansing. Prolonged but irresolute diplomatic efforts produced no result. Amid controversy, a 'humanitarian intervention' was launched, in 1999, to impose a solution by force.

The Albania and Kosovo cases are the subject of this book. Both belong, in the view of the author, to the 'enlightened self-interest' category of foreign interventions, even if vastly different in scale, scope and intensity as well as international repercussions. Although separate in time and geography, they were closely linked since both involved Albanian populations sharing a long history, common culture, close kinship and personal networks. In both cases the Organization for Security and Cooperation in Europe played a vital role, which makes it the prime institutional focus of this book. Founded in 1975 during the Cold War and headquartered in Vienna, the OSCE brought together participating states from Vancouver to Vladivostok with the intent to foster security through dialogue, building mutual confidence and promoting basic human, social and economic rights. It is credited with having contributed to the thaw in the frosty East–West relations that resulted in the fall of the Berlin Wall and the collapse of the Soviet bloc. With the end of the Cold War the OSCE's *raison d' être* became less self-evident. It was therefore keen to expand its role and assist in raising democratic and human rights standards, notably in the new democracies 'East of Vienna'. To this end it deployed long-term missions at the country level. It had instituted a rather unique system of mutually reviewing the record of basic rights in its participating states. In practice, this turned out to be more of an examination of the new than the established democracies. This asymmetry was still acceptable in the 1990s with the newly independent states of the former Soviet Union – including Boris Yeltsin's still vulnerable Russia – and the newly emerging Balkan states seeking their democratic legitimacy. The (temporary) triumph of liberal democracy even produced an unprecedented agreement in the early 1990s – known as the Moscow mechanism – that permitted a majority of OSCE participating states to proactively subject a partner state to an international investigation in case of serious violations of basic rights.[1]

The two international interventions in Albania and Kosovo are described – with the benefit of ample hindsight – 'from within' an OSCE and, in the case of Kosovo also, a UN setting. As the former Head of the OSCE Missions in both Tirana and Pristina, and member of the lead UN team in the latter, the author was part of the international efforts *in situ* to engage and reconcile the different interests at play. The focus is on the work done under the mandate of the OSCE, notably with regard to basic democratic and human rights, reconciliation, institution building, media development and elections. Most of the text is devoted to the Kosovo case because it is far more complex than the Albanian intervention. Also, emotions related to its origin, course and consequences ran, and still run, inordinately high. Chauvinism, prejudice, misinformation and propaganda are blurring the Kosovo picture even today.

In providing an 'inside story', the author also dwells on the human factor and shares – in some detail when warranted – the daily 'handiwork' of generally well-meaning but not infallible international mission members. He takes issue with unrealistic ambitions, inflated expectations (and egos), under-rated challenges and, as a result, the deceptions that all international interventions invariably entail. The book is a plea for empathetic realism.

Note

1 The mechanism was invoked only a few times and de facto abandoned in later years when resurgent national pride – first of all in Vladimir Putin's new Russia – started to forestall multinational censure.

1

Albania
Recoil from the abyss

A country in turbulence

There it was, vaguely in the distance, that unknown country, Albania. I could see it through the open door of the helicopter that brought us from Italy to Tirana. The view was partially blocked by a heavily armed soldier, his machine gun readied for any problems during the approach. 'Us' was a small group of officials from the European Union and the Organization for Security and Cooperation in Europe (OSCE) on a brief 'fact-finding' mission. We were to work out the international response to the chaos that had engulfed the country. It was March 1997. As the mountainous outlines came closer, I recalled from my student days, in the 1960s, that Albania under Enver Hoxha had been voted 'most admired country' in Europe by fellow students in the Netherlands. Those were the days when naïve Maoism was en vogue among the restive, leftist student population. I had counted myself among them, still under the spell of Herbert Marcuse from my year of study at Brandeis University and before Simon Leys had unmasked totalitarian communism with his 'Ombres Chinoises'. Since then the Albanian people had done their own act of unmasking, in 1990, by forcing an end to the dictatorial regime left by Enver Hoxha. Decades of isolation and one-party rule, however, had made the path towards a more open and democratic society very thorny.

The new Albania we were rapidly approaching, had imploded in the two preceding months. Simmering civilian discontent had reached boiling point with the collapse of financial pyramid schemes that had robbed the savings of almost every Albanian family. A complete breakdown of law and order followed, with riots, governmental disarray, large-scale theft of arms, rampant crime and violence, and people desperately trying to flee the country. The cultural North–South divide along ethnographic lines (Tosks in the South, Ghegs in the North) became more manifest with the Southerners openly rebelling. A state of emergency was declared, but the army and police had basically dissolved leaving the space to armed bands. All-out civil war threatened.

In the first week of March, with the situation spinning out of control, the sitting president Sali Berisha and the main opposition parties had embarked on consultations to end the crisis. Berisha, a medical doctor and former member of the communist Workers Party, had supported the founding of the ruling Democratic Party (DP) by the end of 1990, and been its undisputed leader ever since. The main opposition party was the Socialist Party (SP), whose leader Fatos Nano had been imprisoned by the Berisha government in 1994 on rather spurious charges. Nano – Albania's last communist prime minister, albeit briefly – had been elected leader when Hoxha's Workers Party had reformed itself into a 'European-style' Socialist Party in 1991. Considered a political prisoner, he had remained in charge of the party. As the two dominant players in the Albanian political theatre – also opposite in character: the authoritarian, disciplined, but rigid, Berisha from the rural North versus the slick, indulgent urbanite Nano from the South – there was little love lost between them. They would remain locked in battle for many years to come. Given their enmity, it helped that widely respected and less flamboyant representatives of the Opposition, such as Rexhep Meidani and Neritan Ceka, initiated the talks with Berisha. Meidani was the SP General Secretary and an academician of integrity, while Ceka was an archaeologist and leader of the Democratic Alliance, a centrist party he co-founded with other dissident DP members when they broke ranks with an increasingly autocratic Berisha in 1992.

Internationals to the rescue

With these talks underway, the 'international community' – one of the most used and abused clichés in international diplomacy – finally saw reason to become more actively involved in the ever-deepening crisis. The Presidency of the European Union, in the person of the Netherlands foreign minister Hans van Mierlo, visited Tirana on 7 March to press – vainly – for a broad-based reconciliation government and new elections. More effective was the mediation by Austria's former prime minister, Franz Vranicki, who arrived one day later on behalf of the OSCE as a Special Envoy. The combined efforts led to a '9 March Agreement', signed by ten political parties, that established a broad-based Government of National Reconciliation and called for new elections. Shortly thereafter, the political prisoners, including Fatos Nano, were set free. The unrest, however, was still far from over. Violence continued, especially in the South, with crime and politics intertwined. By mid-March, Berisha and the new caretaker government under SP prime minister Bashkim Fino asked for outside military assistance.

It was at this juncture that the EU/OSCE fact-finding mission took place, bringing me to Tirana for the first time. It was also then that I first met Berisha personally. Clearly no longer in sole control of the situation, he was considerably more subdued and modest than his reputation had suggested. The mission, headed by my colleague from the Dutch Foreign Affairs Ministry, Jan d'Ansembourg – Jan Dans (Dancing John) to his friends – concluded that no international aid, humanitarian and otherwise, would be effective if air- and seaports were not secured against attacks and pillage. Hence the recommendation for a military intervention, limited in scope. There was, however, no international eagerness to step on the Albanian hornet's nest. The EU was internally too divided to mount a military force, with empathetic southern member states pitted against reluctant northern ones. As the US considered the Albanian crisis an internal affair that was best addressed in a European context, neither NATO nor UN were permitted to become militarily engaged. Thus it befell the OSCE to take charge. On the 27 March its Permanent Council in Vienna agreed to support participating states to send forces to Albania, provided it had UN concurrence. This came in the form of a UN Security Council Resolution 1011 the next day. The resolution authorized a 'temporary and limited multinational protection force', acting under Chapter VII of the UN Charter. Italy, as the most affected nation, was mandated to create this force, under the code name ALBA, with ten other volunteering countries together forming a 'Coalition of the Willing'. A major consideration for Italy to be the lead nation was, of course, its need to stop the exodus of Albanians to its shores. They numbered 13.000 already by the end of March and brought back bad memories of an earlier, huge and frantic, inflow of Albanians in 1990 after the collapse of the communist regime. Alongside the military ALBA, the OSCE was to provide the guidance for international civilian support. To this end it established a permanent mission, overseen by Vranicki in Vienna, that itself should focus on the areas of democratization, media, human rights and elections. Since Albania thought the very word 'Mission' to be derogatory to its international image, the new office would go under the name 'OSCE Presence in Albania'.

To the OSCE – always eager to prove its *raison d' être* as a European security organization – this was a welcome call. Given its role of custodian in the area of basic democratic and human rights, the OSCE did have an institutional, moral authority. This 'natural' authority would turn out to be a great asset in the operational work of the OSCE on the ground. In the wake of ALBA, the OSCE Presence in Albania was gradually being built up, under the close supervision of Vranicki in Vienna. I was at that time still based in Sarajevo, heading the European Community Monitoring Mission for the former Yugoslavia. This ECMM (later renamed EUMM) oversaw the implementation of the 1995 Dayton Peace Accords that had ended the Yugoslav wars. Because Albanian instability also posed a threat to the wider region, I was authorized to explore expanding the ECMM's coverage to include Albania. This provided me with the welcome opportunity to become more familiar with the country I would soon be heading for.

ALBA started deployment in mid-April. It was to provide a secure environment for international aid delivery and the parliamentary elections that had been agreed upon. Its original mandate was three months, later extended by another three months to allow for an orderly retreat. Although the forces were sometimes described as 'armed tourists' because they were strictly prohibited from acting as policemen, ALBA definitely contributed to the much needed stability. The limited scope and numbers (6000 military), the short duration, the unity of (Italian) command and the fact that the force was widely welcomed by an anxious population, all contributed to its relative success. As such it compares well with other international interventions in the Balkans and elsewhere. It also enabled the elections to take place, after long interparty tussling, by the end of June. The SP won convincingly and Fatos Nano became the new prime minister in a SP-led government. Sali Berisha protested against the outcome of the elections and decided, with his DP party, on an indefinite boycott of the newly elected Parliament. He did resign as president, though, to make place for Rexhep Meidani. With the elections over, a new government in place and the 'international community' definitely on board, a new chapter in Albania's volatile post-communist history had begun.

In a bizarre little sideshow, a remnant group of Albanian monarchists had foisted, by way of referendum, an additional choice on the June election ballot papers: whether or not to restore the monarchy. Nostalgic about the pre-Second World War times of King Zog, the monarchists sought to lift his son, Leka, to the throne through a popular vote. The old Zog, from a beylik family of landowners in the North, had been successively a minister of interior, prime minister and president before he elevated himself to royal status in 1925. He had a mixed record as far as governance was concerned. His rule, supported by the Italians who treated Albania as a quasi-colony, was dictatorial although he did establish the structure of a constitutional monarchy. Some parts of his legacy were quite positive: he contributed to the unification of the country, established a strong national police force, eliminated serfdom (!) and abolished Islamic law in favour of a Western-style civil code (copying Turkey's Ata Turk). Although he called himself the 'King of Albanians', meaning to include also those outside Albania proper, his early relations with Kosovo Albanians were anything but monarchic. He sided with the Serbs after the First World War in repressing the local, Albanian resistance – by so-called *Kacak* rebel bands – to Serb rule in Kosovo.

(Speaking of strange bedfellows, even remnants of the anti-Bolshevik Russian White Army, headquartered in Serbia under General Wrangel, joined that anti-Albanian fight.) To his credit, he opened Albania's borders to Jewish refugees fleeing Nazi Germany in the 1930s – just like Sephardic Jews had found refuge in Albanian lands when expelled from Spain and Portugal in the fifteenth century. Zog was also a survivor: fifty-five assassination attempts and 200 cigarettes a day did not bring him down. He fled the country under Italian occupation in 1941, only to return posthumously in 2012 when his remains were reburied in Tirana. His throne had been formally abolished by the victorious communists in 1946.

'Crown Prince' Leka was raised abroad and had later made his residence in South Africa. He had never set foot on Albanian soil and his command of the Albanian language was poor. Over two metres tall, he cut quite a towering figure. Other than being named the king in exile by his expatriate following, there was not much that was majestic about him. Rumours had him involved in the arms trade, for which he had faced arrest in South Africa. He returned to Tirana ahead of the elections, which his followers had succeeded to include a referendum on the monarchy as well. During a meeting with him he did not particularly impress me. I was still acting in my capacity as head of the European monitors. The setting was simple: a plainly furnished room in a modest villa, a housekeeper serving coffee. Leka's knowledge of the country, its recent history and current challenges seemed sparse. So was his vision for a future Albania. When I had a chance later to mention his name to Queen Beatrix of the Netherlands, she rolled her eyes demonstratively. It was clear that Leka, or Zog for that matter, was not taken seriously and certainly not considered a peer in European royal circles. The election results showed two-thirds of the voters against restoration of the monarchy. Leka called the outcome rigged – against all evidence. In a rather silly 'show of force', he walked down Tirana's main Skanderbeg avenue in military fatigues, brandishing two revolvers, with a bunch of followers. He was quickly stopped by the police and guided away, off the streets of Tirana and not much later out of Albania. In absentia he was found guilty of organizing an armed uprising, but in 2002 was amnestied and allowed to return to Tirana where he died in 2011.

The 'Presence' established

Now that the OSCE had more or less established itself, the Austrian Chairmanship of the OSCE asked me to head its mission in Albania, still called the 'Presence', in the fall of 1997. By that time I had visited Albania several times and become intrigued by the country, the people, their hospitality and keen interest in international contacts. Seldom would a foreigner feel so welcome as in those days in Albania. Whether drinking coffee or eating burek in the omnipresent cafés in Tirana or in the countryside, people invariably came up to inquire and chat. Often they had already settled the bill without your knowing, by way of saying 'thank you for your presence in Albania'. This deep-rooted hospitality is something still to be encountered in present days. Nearly twenty years later I experienced this in an innocent but telling way: being early for an official meeting, I was accosted by a few students when passing a high school in a remote and poor rural area. In no time the group swelled to some twenty girls and boys, all eager to volunteer English answers to my many questions. Suddenly one of them stopped the lively exchange to ask me whether they could get me something to drink. It needed an insistent NO to persuade them to continue the conversation.

There was another Albanian characteristic that appealed to me. After having witnessed so much ethnic and religious strife in the war-torn former Yugoslavia, I found the ethnic and religious climate in Albania remarkably open-minded and untroubled. Not surprising, perhaps, with a fifteenth-century patron-hero, Skanderbeg, the self-declared Lord of Albania who switched from Christianity to Islam in 1423 only to revert to Christianity twenty years later when he led the rebellion against the Ottoman rule. And also not surprising given the tolerant role, past and present, of the Sufi-related Bektashi movement. Tirana had become the headquarters of Bektashism in 1925 when Turkey banned this Islamic order. It survived the 1967 prohibition of religious practice by Enver Hoxha (although he himself was of Bektashi stock). Its moderating influence in today's secularized Albania (and Kosovo, I may add) is still noticeable. Further, and remarkable, proof of Albania's religious tolerance was the way it had offered a safe haven to many persecuted Jews before, and even during, the Second World War when it was under Italian occupation. It was the only European nation that saw its Jewish population grow, from 80,000 to 300,000 by the end of the war.

Having come to like much about Albania from my several visits, I had no hesitation in accepting the job offer. My ready acceptance had a slightly sentimental touch to it. Some eighty years before, in 1913, the same 'international community', in those days meaning the main European powers, had also decided to deploy an international military mission in Albania. Its purpose was to bolster the newly independent Albania that Albanian nationalists had proclaimed on the ruins of the Ottoman empire, in November 1912. These same powers had selected a German prince to head the new state. The idea was that a European-supported monarchy could consolidate the statehood of Albania vis-à-vis outside regal predators such as Greece, Bulgaria, Serbia and Montenegro. That the international overlords decided to delimit this new state – with around 750,000 inhabitants – to only part of the much larger territory inhabited by 1.2 million Albanians would become the root cause of ethnic strife and conflict in the Western Balkans that continues to the present day.

The 1913 predecessor

Given its neutral stance at the time, with international tensions on the rise, the Netherlands was requested to help organize a police force to bring law and order in the newly created state that was still under attack from its hostile neighbours. A small band of Dutch military was entrusted with this task, probably the first modern peacekeeping mission in the Balkans, if not Europe. It was headed by General De Veer, a traditional, not very imaginative officer. The best known among this group was a lieutenant colonel, Lodewijk Thomson, who attained hero status after he was killed in the course of duty. Thomson had already acquired a reputation in the Netherlands as a vocal protagonist of radical, military reform in favour of a more democratic, conscription-based army. He had been a member of parliament after having served as a military observer in South Africa, at the time of the Boer War, and following deployment in the Atjeh war in the then Netherlands Indies. Much more ambitious than de Veer, he projected the image of being the *de facto* leader of the mission. The new Head of State – Mbret for the Albanians – whom the European powers had installed, also had a small Dutch connection. Prince Wilhelm zu Wied was a distant relative of the then Queen Wilhelmina of the Netherlands. So, taking on the OSCE assignment in Albania felt to me like following up on earlier Dutch efforts in peacekeeping and nation building in the very same geographical area.

The early-twentieth-century Dutch-led police mission was short-lived and not a great success. Among the Albanian nationalists there was opposition to the foreign rule and armed skirmishes were the order of the day. The evil character in this drama was Esad Pasha Toptani. Although a minister in the Mbret cabinet, he conspired with the new Ottoman leaders, the Young Turks, to undercut him and establish his own fiefdom in northern Albania. (A relative of the later King Zog, and known for his lavish lifestyle, he was assassinated in Paris in 1922.) Colonel Thomson lost his life during an attack on Durres. His body was repatriated and transported to his burial place in Groningen with full military honours and an outpour of public admiration. Later research revealed that his violent death was probably more accidental than heroic. It occurred when, after a bout of boisterous drinking, he ventured out in the middle of the night and was struck by either a stray bullet or sniper fire.[1]

Shortly thereafter, with the outbreak of the World War, the whole mission was aborted. Prince zu Wied beat a hasty, ignominious retreat. Although his tenure was indistinctive, with no memento left in place in Albania, he did achieve some local recognition back in The Hague. A handsome pavilion at the beach of Scheveningen still bears his name. (Little had I known about him and his brief Balkan venture when in earlier years I had regularly walked my granny's poodle past this building ….) Thomson's name, on the other hand, still lives on in Albania and the Netherlands. Fan Noli – Albania's famous literary, religious and political figure, founder of the Albanian Orthodox Church and short-time prime minister in 1924 – devoted, in 1914, a poem, 'Thomson and the Dragon', to his service and untimely death. In this poem, Noli castigates his compatriots for betraying the 'war hero from afar who sacrificed his life for us' in the fight against 'the Ottoman dragon'. In The Hague a square and street were named after Thomson. It was eighty-five years later, on the occasion of an agreement between the Netherlands and Albania on military cooperation, that I was present at the unveiling of his bust in Tirana as well as its identical twin in Groningen, the place of his military roots, and burial. Sabri Godo – historian and widely respected *eminence grise* of Albanian politics whom I was to meet regularly during my time in office – sometimes referred to me, jokingly, as 'our new Colonel Thomson' to which I would steadfastly reply: 'Rather not, given his fate'.

The new beginning

The modest 'headquarters' of the OSCE Presence in Tirana were housed in a villa at the edge of the infamous block of residences where in the old days the communist nomenklatura had been residing, comfortably and safely, inaccessible to ordinary mortals. In a small, adjacent park the three busts of the Frasheri brothers – members of the patriotic Prizren League in Kosovo in the 1870s, intellectual forefathers of Albanian nationhood – languished under official neglect. In the midst of the block was Enver Hoxha's villa, then in a state of disrepair with a garden overgrown with weeds. Across from the block was the new, Austrian-run Rogner hotel, which was, for the lack of competition in those days, the favourite meeting place of the local elite, expats, visiting dignitaries and anyone who wanted to be seen and appear important. It served as the location for some key encounters in later years that shaped the course of political events. I had made my domicile in this hotel, as this freed me from daily household chores and the frequent but unpredictable water and electricity cuts. Its ground-floor bar and restaurant opened up to a semicircular, outdoor terrace bordering a beautiful, shaded garden that offered plenty of opportunity for discreet talks. An extra bonus was its in-house ensemble that delighted the guests with authentic Albanian music in the evening. We were even treated occasionally to 'a capella', polyphonic singing from the South, another unique Albanian phenomenon. Many years later, when returning to a rapidly modernizing Tirana, I found these 'landmarks' – Rogner hotel, the Frasheri brothers and Hoxha's villa – virtually unchanged: even after twenty years Rogner was still the same rustic, beautifully landscaped oasis, the Frasheri brothers were still standing in relative anonymity, while Hoxha's villa continued its slow decay amid an unkempt garden. All of this in a bustling, glaring environment of new high-rises, cafés and trendy shops.

The main political issue in the early days of the OSCE Presence was, of course, the continuing boycott of the Parliament by the Democratic Party, still in denial over the June elections result. In an effort to help overcome the political impasse, I sought help from outside. Knowing the Albanian respect for international parliamentary bodies – which they had so proudly joined as a new member – I contacted the OSCE Chairman, the Polish Foreign Minister Geremek who held stellar pro-democracy credentials. I suggested that we try to mobilize the OSCE Parliamentary Assembly, the Council of Europe Parliamentary Assembly and the European Parliament to jointly come to the rescue of Albania's parliamentary process. In what was a novelty at the time, we succeeded in getting all three parliaments to agree on a joint mission to Tirana. It took place in January 1998, received vast publicity and provided the much needed impetus. It was unusually frank in its assessment, so much so that a local paper wrote that 'the Europeans have finally learned to speak Albanian'.

The tripartite mission confirmed the legitimacy of the (outcome of the) June 1997 elections, rejected the call for fresh elections and called on the DP to return to Parliament. It stressed the need for a new Constitution and endorsed the procedure chosen – through a parliamentary commission rather than a specially elected Constitutional Assembly as Berisha had insisted. Cleverly, it also suggested international monitoring of the Parliament so as to reassure the DP about the due democratic procedures and leave no more excuse for the boycott. To the pleasant surprise of all around, the DP responded positively by announcing its intention to return to the political process. We, in turn, quickly set up a project of monitoring the Parliament, bringing in expertise from abroad (including the Dutch Parliament), providing equipment and assigning additional OSCE staff to the task. Through its constant monitoring and regular reporting, the project proved helpful in improving parliamentary practices, so much so that twenty years later I still found the project to be alive and kicking, with the same solid June Taylor in charge who had taken over the job in 1999.

Border inspection in the north

It was one morning in early March 1998, when a phone call caused considerable excitement in the OSCE office. 'The Prime Minister is on the line,' exclaimed my Albanian assistant. Normally we would get a call from his staff when there was a message to be communicated. I took the call wondering what kind of emergency had brought Fatos Nano to pick up the phone himself. It did not take long to learn that he needed our help urgently. There had been reports of large-scale weapons smuggling from the north of Albania into the western part of Kosovo, where since earlier that year the Kosovo Liberation Army (UCK by its Albanian initials) had stepped up their armed rebellion against Serbian rule. As we shall see in later chapters, the Milosovic regime had stripped Kosovo of its autonomous status within Yugoslavia in 1990 and had turned it into a mere province of Serbia, subject to direct and harsh rule from Belgrade. The Kosovo Albanians, some 80 per cent of the population, were set to restore, as a minimum, autonomy and, ultimately, attain independence. Attempts to reach political accommodation by non-violent means – led by Ibrahim Rugova, the man with the distinguishing scarf – had only met with Serbian intransigence, despite American and European mediating efforts. This lack of any progress had led to calls for more militant resistance and the emergence of the Kosovo Liberation Army.

Against this backdrop, Prime Minister Nano had been confronted by Western governments with Serbian accusations that arms were being massively trafficked from the Albanian north-eastern provinces into Kosovo by KLA fighters, in collusion with local authorities. Also, it was alleged that the KLA was running recruitment and training camps in the border areas. Nano had rejected these accusations. In order to prove them wrong, he had agreed to organize an international inspection of the border area. As the OSCE had a field office in a nearby area, it was agreed that it should make a quick assessment of the local situation. Hence the early morning personal call: Could I as Head of the OSCE Office organize a reconnaissance trip and report back after on-site inspection and interviews? It was to be done in three days, as soon as possible. A government helicopter would be made available. He would not take NO for an answer. Nor would I give him one

– being always keen to show our readiness to be a 'helpful Presence'. By that time we had established ourselves firmly as a prominent multinational Presence, with six field offices spread evenly over the country and totalling about twenty-five international staff, supported by many more dedicated local staff.

We had two military advisers on the staff, seconded by the Dutch government, so obviously I turned to them to help organize the emergency assignment. Bad surprise: they would not hear of it and advised me not to go. The helicopter, in their view, was a totally unreliable Chinese chopper long past its final date of use. They flatly refused to join and board 'a flying coffin'. Speak of Dutch courage! The task was about to be aborted when Ismije Beshiri came to the rescue. A German political adviser of Macedonian–Albanian stock, she strongly felt the mission could not honourably reject the official request and offered to go in my place. This was too much for me to accept and thus it happened that it was the two of us, accompanied by a volunteer from my former European Monitoring Mission, who scaled the high mountains on the way to the north-east. The assurances of the Albanian pilots that this Chinese helicopter had a perfect record of survival, gave us only slight comfort. It dated from the communist time of Enver Hoxha when he bonded with China and defiantly declared that 'we and the Chinese are a billion strong' – the same Hoxha who had pocked the countryside with 700,000 mini bunkers to withstand a nuclear attack. Many of them still stand as ugly reminders of his paranoia. Rumour had it that Hoxha forced the designer-builder to prove the quality of his product by standing inside a bunker while it was pounded by heavy artillery fire. To his credit, though, Hoxha also had an eye for the environment, instructing his citizens to clear their immediate surroundings of debris and garbage once a week, and, environmentalist avant la lettre, ordering them 'to attack the mountains' by planting hundreds of thousands of trees – not unlike his political friend Mao who had ordered every Chinese to go out and kill flies. Unfortunately, the tree planting did not have a lasting effect, as later Albania has seen many of its trees (illegally) felled and plastic garbage become a widely present eyesore.

The helicopter lived up to its local reputation. We flew to Bajram Currie to talk to the provincial authorities, we went to Tropoja where we saw the site where a small band of KLA had camped the previous night, we saw a train of donkeys carrying goods uphill towards Kosovo, we flew further south to Kukes to ask around with villagers and the local police and, of course, we spoke at length to our mission members in nearby areas. The conclusion was not difficult to reach. Surely, there was active sympathy for the KLA in this part of the country and surely there was readiness to support them. And yes, given the length of the border and the great distances (50 km!) between border posts, control by the poorly equipped border police was far from tight. On the other hand, the rough, mountainous terrain without roads was difficult to cross, while on the other side of the border, the Serb forces were well lined up with radio communication and night vision equipment, rocket launchers and helicopters. It was, in short, quite likely that arms and ammunition would find their way across, but nothing hinted at any type of large-scale movements of arms. About the training camps also we heard nothing – directly or indirectly from our field mission members and others we interviewed – that would indicate the kind of facilities alleged. Upon completion of the visit, we returned safely by the same helicopter and filed our report to general satisfaction. The PM was happy … and the two military advisers left the mission.

As a result of the report, we did reinforce our Presence in the north-east area with two additional teams and also arranged for considerable extra equipment for the border police. We returned for an extensive follow-up visit two months later, and reported similar conclusions: '*The number and location of Border Crossing Points (few and far between) and the limited capacity for continuous and intensive border control do allow for illegal border crossing, particularly at night. Active official dissuasion by the Albanian (central) Government (especially through the deployment of special forces not from the area) and the risks posed by the greatly stepped up FRY (Federal Republic of Yugoslavia) police and military presence, however, make large-scale movements of arms and men unlikely. The possession of weapons, while rampant, is very dispersed, leaving large-scale purchasing, storage and transportation improbable and – with increasing military, police and international presence – almost impossible to conceal.*' The same report stated that '*no indications exist of guerilla training camps on the Albanian side of the border. With our ever-increasing network of local contacts – at homes and in the omnipresent local cafés – it seems impossible that such *activity could take place in any systematic or significant way without it having come to our attention*'.[2]

In retrospect, I won't rule out that we may have underestimated the number of weapons that could be moved using small-scale transport over an extended period of time. And probably the shipments did increase later in the year when the fighting in Kosovo became more intense and KLA was in control of some of the adjacent Kosovo areas. We suspected at the time that the larger quantities of arms had found their way to Kosovo earlier, in the aftermath of the 1997 riots in Albania when depots were ransacked and an estimated million weapons stolen and trafficked. This large-scale acquisition of arms from Albanian stocks was, indeed, acknowledged by KLA-spokespersons many years later.

The good old Chinese helicopter crossed my path once more, one year later. As a result of ethnic cleansing – about which there will be much more in the following chapters – a massive exodus of Kosovo Albanians out of Kosovo was underway in the spring of 1999. The Dutch public television sent a crew to report on the emergency situation at the Morina border crossing near Kukes, on the road from Kosovo's Prizren.

They sought my help to reach the place and, mindful of the proverbial Dutch stinginess, I opted for the services of the old Chinese machine. Same crew, same shabby appearance. Twan Huys, the Dutch reporter, did not bat an eye seeing the prehistoric contraption and soon we were airborne. Then the storm unleashed – there was lightning and pouring rain all around us, with hardly any visibility. We were on our way up to go over the Dajti mountain – its summit not much lower than the helicopter's maximum altitude – and we grew seriously worried. Fortunately, the pilot shared the feeling and made a hasty return, thus helping the reporter to continue his budding career and become one of the Netherlands' foremost TV personalities. The same Twan, by the way, crossed my path in Afghanistan in 2006 when the international intervention there had not yet turned sour. As NATO's ambassador I managed to arrange a visit to a heavily guarded prison outside Kabul. We were not supposed to film inside, but somehow got tacit permission to do so provided it was done inconspicuously. The prison director took a risk here but felt that it was important for the outside world to see the miserable conditions he had to supervise. We got some compelling footage of prisoners who had been kept in what were little better than dungeons, on vague charges and without trial for many months. The televised report created quite a stir back home. The director was not there anymore when I inquired about the place a few months later … another example of good intentions and bad consequences.

Helicopters, of course, were the preferred means of transportation given the poor state of the roads. At OSCE we would normally move around in our white four-wheel drives, but for long distances we could count on aircraft made available by friendly nations or organizations. Thus it was an American helicopter that brought Robert Frowick and me to the rather unruly north-east. Bob was an American ambassador from the US State Department and an old OSCE friend from Sarajevo and Skopje. We were to visit a small village that had seen two of its sons murdered by a criminal gang. We were supposed to demonstrate the international interest in establishing the rule of law and boosting the morale of the police. Not an easy task in this mountainous region where *kulas* – fortified dwelling towers – still dotted the countryside and the *Kanun* of Leke Dukagjini still ruled. The Kanun is the customary law of northern Albania, with a strict code of conduct, including the strictly prescribed blood revenge and its counterpart, the compelling notion of *besa* (truce and protection).[3] The OSCE had had its own close encounters with armed bandits in the area, in one of which a driver had been wounded and our vehicle stolen. Apart from its lawlessness, and no doubt related to it, the region was known for its widespread poverty. How dire the circumstances were, became clear when we entered a simple peasant abode to offer condolences to the bereaved family. Their only possibility to offer post-funeral hospitality was by sharing their cigarettes. There was no way that we, both non-smokers, could refuse.

Trouble in the South

If the north-east was a permanent security concern, so was one peculiar spot in the south, the village of Lazarat. Strategically located on a hill not far from the border crossing of Kakavija, it overlooked the main road to Greece.

Predominantly Muslim and Democrat Party-aligned in a religiously mixed and Socialist Party-dominated environment, it was known for being a lawless place where the police did not dare to enter. To lovers of comic strips, it bore a likeness to the Gallic village of Asterix surrounded by hostile Romans. Reality was anything but comical, however. Lazarat had a history of crime linked to drug smuggling, trafficking of illegal immigrants and armed robbery. I recall a report from our Field Office in nearby Girokaster noting that over a half-year period, more than 200 armed robberies had taken place. When one serious incident threatened to trigger a violent confrontation with state forces, the OSCE Presence was asked to offer 'our good offices' to defuse the situation. A district official and his nephew had been kidnapped and held for ransom, with a road blockade erected and manned by armed villagers. Against official advice we went unescorted into the village, in the company of a courageous official from Tirana. We were cordially received by some village elders, of course over coffee and rakija. We listened to their grievances: no income opportunities, no bus service, no telephone lines, no recreation facilities for their youth. We pledged to take up their plight with the central Government. I promised to spend some of our discretionary funds from friendly donors such as Norway and the Netherlands on needed facilities like a soccer field and water supply. The request to approach a Dutch town with a view to establish a (presumably lucrative) formal bond of friendship I politely held off – knowing very well the slim chance of finding any takers given Lazarat's reputation.

Our well-meaning intervention did create some goodwill but no lasting effects. In subsequent years Lazarat developed into a huge – and hugely profitable – centre of cannabis, with links to European markets through Albanian–Italian mafia channels. It became known as Europe's Cannabis Capital, supposedly employing in its top year as many as 3,000 seasonal labourers from outside and producing an estimated 900 metric tonnes of cannabis, with a street value of over a billion of euros. This anomaly could not continue, obviously, with Albania drawing closer to the EU politically and economically. In 2014, under strong European pressure, the Government sent in hundreds of police who overwhelmed the armed gangs and destroyed their production and storage facilities. Among the weapons seized were mortar grenades and a rocket launcher. Predictably, rather than putting an end to the illegal practice, this clampdown led to a subsequent diversification of the cannabis production over many other areas in Albania. Much to the chagrin of the 'international community' – although they were colluding by providing seeds and markets – but to the delight of traffickers, real estate agents and related business as well as many poor farmers who found a welcome, extra source of income.

Goodwill projects

The mandate of the OSCE Presence was sufficiently general to allow for many initiatives, even when not directly linked to the core business: democratization, rule of law and human rights, civil society development, elections. Thus we also addressed more pedestrian challenges, which helped to popularize the OSCE's role in Albania. People often turned to us when they thought that foreign eyes and ears could help to solve a problem. One of the minor initiatives was an attempt to salvage the Tirana zoo. Ever since my arrival in December 1997, a few office enthusiasts and I used to regularly run around the artificial lake on the outskirts of Tirana, stones in hand to fend off stray dogs. It was flanked by a forest on one side and a few scattered houses, a botanical garden and a zoo on the other. The zoo was in a lamentable state. Not surprising, of course, in an impoverished state where people are more concerned about basic needs than animal welfare. Lack of funds had led to ever-deteriorating conditions: the sheds were dilapidated, fences broken or removed, walking paths overgrown with weeds and many cages in shambles. A few animals had survived the years of official neglect. Among them was an old lion – probably a present to Hoxha from one of his very few, foreign ruling friends. The bare living space measured only a few square metres. To our horror, the neighbour in an equally cramped space was his soon-to-be meal, an understandably traumatized donkey. It was clear that these conditions did not even meet sub-animal standards. We solicited some local interest in reviving the place and established a link with a private zoo in the UK for further support. While the initiative did lead to some early improvements – the lion and its live food were separated, for example – the zoo never quite made it to 'European standards'. Fifteen years later it was still voted to be among the six saddest zoos in the world and accusations of animal cruelty and substandard conditions recurred regularly. It had become, however, a popular family destination again and hope for better days ahead was never given up.

The old botanical garden was in no better shape. It had basically ceased to exist except for some scattered beds of roses and a nice tree-lined, pot-holed road unto the centre. With local volunteers, we managed to arrange for some restoration in the form of new fencing, weeding and planting. Its survival was endangered not so much by lack of public funding as by private greed to occupy this prime public property for illegal construction. Money and influence – corruption in other words – did combine to encroach on the adjacent areas, but miraculously the garden withstood the threat. The next fifteen years saw the garden gradually revive on at least half of its acreage; the other half remained undeveloped but at least did not fall victim to illegal privatization. More instant was the success of the 'Tidy Tirana' campaign that our Presence launched, with strong support from the then president Meidani and Prime Minister Nano. The ubiquitous presence of plastic and other garbage defacing the public space was an annoyance to many of Tirana's citizens, certainly those who remembered Hoxha's yard-cleaning orders. We offered rewards to primary schools that collected garbage in bags which had been distributed beforehand. The action received ample media attention and met with enthusiastic response. Politicians helped in collecting the huge number of full bags that were deposited at the large square in front of the central University building for final disposal. A similar civic project helped to quickly raise funds and restore the amphitheatre in the park.

More macabre was the issue we stumbled upon when visiting a jail in the coastal town of Vlora. Reviewing the prison conditions with the warden, we saw in one of the cells a man wearing an iron helmet, who was chained to the wall. He had been convicted of murder and was awaiting the appeal process. Apparently there were five such cases of pre-trial, death row imprisonment. One of them had been in such a condition for twenty-two months. Appalled, I fired off a letter to Deputy Prime Minister Ilir Meta, asking for a more humane treatment with at least the helmet and manacles removed. The response was as quick as underhanded. The medieval practice was stopped right away. It had probably been a legacy from Hoxha times that had gone on as a matter of routine – which, of course, did not make it any more bearable for the victim.

Speaking about helmets, another more lighthearted moment springs to mind. I had to go regularly to Vienna to report to the OSCE Permanent Council on the developments in Albania and the dynamics of the mission. Albania's Permanent Representative to the OSCE, Roland Bimo, was one of the most esteemed council members who could always be relied upon for intelligent and fair comments. The meetings took place in the Hofburg, in a wing of the classicist Neue Burg building. The central balcony of that building is notorious: here Hitler had bathed in the adulation of tens of thousands of cheering Austrians after he had achieved the 'Anschluss', the merger of Austria with Nazi Germany. The Neue Burg houses a terrific collection of musical instruments but an impressive assortment of ancient weapons as well. Among the latter is the helmet of Skanderbeg, Albania's heroic fifteenth-century patron. Would it not be a just act on my part, if I surreptitiously exchanged the helmet for a copy and brought the original back to the country where it belonged? After all it was a clear case of 'Raubkunst' – looted art – so I would only be righting a cultural wrong. Such an audacious act would surely earn me accolades from the Albanians! I had doubts, however, whether my diplomatic immunity would protect me. So, after long deliberation, I decided to better leave it to proper, official negotiations. As far as I know the old helmet is still resting in its foreign home …

The coup attempt

The scariest episode that we faced – and probably the scariest event in Albania's post-communist history – was a coup attempt in September 1998. It had been an unruly period, with Sali Berisha and militants of his Democrat Party unwilling to play the role of a loyal opposition. They organized frequent demonstrations demanding the resignation of Nano's Government. In August the Government had added fuel to the agitation by arresting prominent DP members on the egregious charge of crimes against humanity for their role in the 1997 pyramid riots. Then came, on 12 September, the murder of Azem

Hajdari, a famous, albeit controversial, DP member from the north, and his bodyguard. He had been a leader of the student protests and one of the co-founders of the DP back in 1990, and had remained a hot-headed member ever since. He had survived an assassination attack a year before. The exact circumstances of his death were unclear (later it was linked to a clan feud), but Berisha was quick to blame it on government conspiracy and used the occasion to up the ante.

I had met Hadjari shortly before in my office, when he had complained, more aggressively than convincingly, about police harassment. After his death I went to see his widow to offer my condolences and support. She was remarkably composed in those trying days. As she was concerned about the future of her young son, we arranged some official help for his continued studies. I felt sorry for her, about the way the DP tried to exploit her grief by enlisting her (passive) presence at protest rallies. Similarly, I felt uneasy about the way the DP used a venerable, long-term political prisoner from Hoxha's time, Pjeter Abnori, for party political gains rather than leaving him at peace in his role as an elderly, respectable national figure. Interestingly, I met an almost identical Mandela-of-sorts later in Kosovo, in the person of Adem Demaci who had also served nearly thirty years in jail and was more respected for his courageous past than for his contemporaneous views. In turn, they both reminded me of the fate that had befallen the prominent Yugoslav partisan-writer-politician Milovan Djilas, the first communist dissident of stature. An early Leninist radical, he ended up as a social democrat imprisoned by his one-time comrade Tito. He remained a national pariah after his release, while being an international celebrity. All three survivors, I felt, were deserving of more recognition and respect. As the Dutch (biblical) saying goes: *profeten in eigen land worden niet geeerd* (prophets go unrecognized in their own country). In the case of Demaci, though, I should add the nuance that he was honoured with a state funeral and national mourning when he died in 2018.

With the benefit of hindsight, I have often been tempted to think that if people like Demaci and the later, reformed Djilas, with their moral fortitude and inclusive attitude, had been allowed more prominence and clout in the early 1990s, the chances of averting the Kosovo war and its horrendous violence and aftermath might have been better.

In the morning after Hajdari's murder the situation rapidly escalated. A crowd of DP supporters, fired on by Berisha's accusations of government complicity, took to the streets in an aggressive fashion. In response President Meidani appeared on television calling for the arrest of Hajdari's murderers and appealing for calm. By then word had spread that weapons were being brought into Tirana from the north, the DP's stronghold. A vigil for the dead was held during the night in anticipation of the memorial that the DP had scheduled for the following day. I vividly remember the tense atmosphere. Anxiety was tangible all around. The new day saw a rapidly growing crowd filling the main Skanderbeg square. After a few hours of rising anger it started to move, with the coffins, not to the graveyard for burial, but down the boulevard towards the Prime Minister's office. Soon the crowd was controlling the streets and storming various official buildings, including the Parliament. The government panicked. Ministers hurriedly fled their offices. Prime Minister Nano was unreachable (rumours had it that he had left for Greece with a suitcase full of cash). With a few OSCE staff members I tried to have a first-hand look at the turmoil, but we became trapped in an unfriendly crowd and were forced to retreat to the office. When shots were fired in the immediate vicinity, we were instructed by our security guards to lie low on the floor and stay away from the windows.

In the midst of it all I tried to call the PM's office, but to no avail. Official life seemed to have ground to a halt. I then called the president's residence to check with President Meidani, whose calm and rational demeanour could always be relied upon. This time, however, even he seemed rattled by events. Basically he told me that the government was out of control and that there was little hope for a return to normalcy. I remember telling him that the 'international community' would not condone a violent takeover and, rather preposterously, urged him 'to hang in there'. I managed to get through to the local radio and to broadcast the same message: the outside world strongly denounced the violence and would not support any political outcome resulting from it. In the streets the situation worsened. An armed group of militants had taken control of the television station. Others had succeeded in intimidating soldiers at an army barrack unit and taking possession of two tanks. I went live on the radio again, this time more directly addressing Berisha and asking him to stop the escalation, give up the tanks and return to democratic means of dissent. I told him in so many words that his behaviour would be severely condemned by all of Europe, including the Christian Democrat parties that he had been so eagerly trying to befriend. Being in the midst of the turmoil I had had no chance to check with the OSCE headquarters, but I learned later that similar messages had reached him from different capitals abroad.

For several hours a very uneasy stalemate ensued. Then, slowly but surely, the Ministry of Defence – directed by Deputy Minister Ndre Legisi, rather than the Minister himself who apparently remained shell-shocked – started to roll back the rebellion. Soon the TV building was the last holdout, with an adamant self-appointed leader – Berisha's bodyguard Haxhia – refusing to give up. In fact, he made a telephone call to me saying that they would leave the building only as corpses. I told him not to be overdramatic and just recognize the futility of his stand and to surrender. End of call. Not much later, Berisha's then young lieutenant, Genc Pollo – who had struck me earlier as basically sensible, albeit not always straightforward, and who, I was sure, could not possibly agree with the destructive politics at play – called Ismije and asked to see me at the OSCE office. There he pleaded for our intervention with the military, which had surrounded the TV building and had given the militants an ultimatum to leave within an hour. He was afraid that there would be fatal shootings and asked whether I would come along with him to guide the occupants out to safety. I quickly consulted the Ministry and received the assurance that the militants could leave the building without risk of being shot provided they carried a white flag and held their hands over their heads. This was in turn communicated to Pollo and to the rebel head who had told me earlier so emphatically that he would lay down his life. Fortunately, reason prevailed at that point and, indeed, the occupation of the TV building was ended without violence. It signalled the end of the coup attempt.

New dynamics

Remarkably, and speaking well for Albanian politics, there was no vicious, vindictive aftermath. It was as if most people wanted to get over the nasty episode like a bad dream. There seemed to be considerable embarrassment about this relapse as not befitting the new Albania that wanted to become a normal European nation. Of course, there was also strong pressure from abroad, especially United States and the EU, to de-escalate the situation. In the end there were no trials for treason or for endangering the state. Although the Prosecutor-General did prepare for legal action and the Parliament did lift Berisha's parliamentary immunity, there was no effective follow-up. The government was reshuffled, though, with Nano having lost credibility. There was international pressure on him to resign. I remember a rather uneasy conversation in his office, during which I tried to convey a message on behalf of the local Friends of Albania, a group of resident ambassadors from friendly countries. The message was that stepping down would be an honourable thing to do and that the role of senior statesman would be most befitting and respectable. He looked at me in blank puzzlement and did not bother to reply. Resign he did, however, and some new, younger players stepped to the plate. From among them Pandeli Majko emerged as the new prime minister – quite a contrast to Nano by age and demeanour: a family man and ideal son-in-law rather than a shrewd, narcissistic politician. Another new face was Ilir Meta who became the vice prime minister. I had known him as a young promising euro-socialist. He would later start his own party (still called socialist: the Socialist Movement for Integration) and through clever political dealings with both SP and DP become prime minister, foreign minister, speaker of parliament and president in successive years, becoming more wealthy and less socialist over time ...

The whole nasty episode did not spell the end, however, of either Berisha or Nano. Political dinosaurs, they both survived their self-inflicted political damage and in due course returned to positions of prominence. Nano reinvented himself, adopted a new, modern look and cleverly orchestrated his political comeback to SP leadership and the prime minister's post in 2002. Berisha never loosened, let alone give up, the grip on his party, eliminating any challenges to his leadership. When, again during an exasperating period of parliamentary boycott, Genc Pollo finally mustered the courage to break ranks, he and his newly founded New Democratic Party did not last long. After the DP won the elections of 2005 and Berisha returned to the helm of government as prime minister, Pollo – born opportunist – ate humble pie, returned to the fold and was rewarded with a minister's post. (To the internationals who had dared to be critical of him, Berisha proved to be less magnanimous. He never forgave me personally for our critical reporting on his political scheming. When in 2009 the OSCE proposed me as head of an election observation mission in Albania, he strongly and – being the prime minister – successfully objected to the proposal).

The popular perception of our role in helping to abort the coup attempt reinforced the OSCE's good standing among the wider public. The organization was considered a vital link to the outside world of the 'international community'. It was therefore a natural move for me, after the September events, to suggest that the OSCE help convene an international conference of donor countries and international organizations. The idea was to impress on the population the international commitment to assist Albania on its rocky path towards democracy and European values. Under the banner of 'Friends of Albania' the Conference was held in Tirana on 30 October. It forcefully called for restoration of law and order, resumption of political dialogue, support for the work on a new Constitution, and reform of administration together with concerted efforts to fight corruption and smuggling. It was the first major intergovernmental gathering in Albania and, as such, a matter of national interest and pride. Flags, delegations, limousines, speeches, interviews crowded the TV screens and newspapers. To the Albanian population it was definite proof that Albania was firmly and positively on the international map. Donor conferences in this format were repeated at later dates, co-chaired by the EU which by its scope and capacities was obviously a more logical lead agency than the OSCE.

A new Constitution

An additional reason for the timing of the Friends of Albania conference was to give a final boost to a major endeavour that was nearing completion, the drafting of a new Constitution. The work had been started a year earlier by the new SP-dominated Parliament, following the June elections in 1997. It had created a Constitutional Commission consisting of members from major political parties, chaired by Arben Imami of the SP and Sabri Godo of the Republican Party, assisted by technical staff. Imami had been one of the student protest leaders of 1990 that led to the demise of communist rule. Godo, as the widely respected centre-right politician with an unblemished past, was to compensate for the absence of the DP at the time because of its boycott of the new parliament. The OSCE Presence, on its part, had created a special unit to provide technical assistance. In a stroke of bureaucratic mockery it was named the Administrative Centre for the Coordination of Assistance and Public Participation (ACCAPP). The unit was made up, with support from the American Bar Association, of a small group of highly dedicated, very professional, young lawyers. Propelled by Scot Carlson and Rob Pulver, the unit worked incessantly and in remarkably good cooperation with the Albanian drafters. It also received backup from the Council of Europe and its Venice Commission, the latter well known for its constitutional expertise. President Meidani had thrown his weight behind the project declaring 1998 'the Year of the Constitution'.

The drafting of the Constitution had proceeded well, in a transparent fashion, with numerous public consultations in the form of seminars, conferences and hearings. Even the DP had been, on and off, part of the process. The final draft of the Constitution was to be approved or rejected by a national referendum. The twenty-second of November 1998 was picked as the day of judgement. Unfortunately, the DP again chose not to cooperate, despite the encouragement from 'the Friends of Albania'. Sali Berisha, far from humbled by his failed coup attempt two months earlier, declared his opposition by insisting – as he had done in the past – that a new Constitution should be approved by a specially elected Constitutional Assembly rather than a national referendum. The obstinacy of his stand might well be explained by the fact that exactly four years earlier, in November 1994, he himself had failed to provide the country with a new Constitution. His draft was – much to his surprise and chagrin – firmly rejected by 54 per cent of the voters in a referendum. That outcome was at the time interpreted more as a condemnation of the authoritarian tendencies of his presidency than as a verdict on the text itself. Also this time, his message did not seem to resonate convincingly. He called an anti-referendum rally at the Skanderbeg square that was supposed to draw tens of thousands of people. Instead, only a few hundred demonstrators turned up ...

The Constitutional referendum of 22 November was organized with the help of OSCE's Office for Democratic Institutions and Human Rights (ODIHR). No small challenge, if only because the voters' registration had to be completely redone and updated, on the basis of a very flawed civil registry. We went all over the country to encourage participation. Media were used to the maximum. Given the boycott call from the DP – at least, they did not advocate a NO vote – it was key to ensure a decent turnout. With less than 50 per cent of voter participation, the text would not stand and all efforts had been in vain. On polling day, 50.4 per cent of voters did cast their vote, with 93.6 per cent in favour of the Constitutional referendum. Both percentages were, of course, influenced by the abstention campaign of the Democratic Party. The outcome, however, was never in doubt and the Constitution was duly approved in Parliament. It became the cornerstone of Albania's new legal identity. The weight of the momentous event was obvious to all. In celebration we organized a concert by my favourite Albanian National Music Ensemble. It was followed by a huge party during which the Ensemble volunteered – against their protocol but persuaded by Ismije – to display more of their incredible skills. The event was the talk of the town for several days thereafter. Prime Minister Majko brought his full cabinet of ministers along. Even former prime minister Nano showed up, as did most of the diplomatic community. I felt bad, though, that the DP was not in a position to join the rejoicing.

The students' strike

As the fight over the referendum showed, Nano's resignation from the Government had not really affected the testy relationship between DP and SP at the official level. Berisha, unperturbed by his political setbacks, stuck to his confrontational approach. He spoke dismissively of the new, youngish Prime Minister Majko ('psychologically unfit'). But then a typical Albanian phenomenon occurred in December 1998 that brought about a remarkable change: a students' hunger strike. I had become acquainted with this form of protest from the recent past. It was first used, famously, by students early in February 1991 when their protest against the eating facilities turned political with the demand that the Enver Hoxha name be removed from the university. The strike ended with their demands met ... and the towering statue of Hoxha on Skanderbeg square being unceremoniously toppled and hacked to pieces. It symbolized another step towards the end of communist rule. Another well-remembered hunger strike had been undertaken in August 1997 by Pjeter Arbnori, the iconic political prisoner from Hoxha's time and former DP speaker of parliament. He called for fairer political coverage by the State TV after the SP had won the 1997 elections and taken control over state institutions. Although a far less lofty cause and event, his twenty-day strike did achieve the redress he sought.

The December 1998 student strike was of a different category, resembling somewhat the 1991 strike in terms of publicity and impact. The strike had begun in Shkodra over mainly academic and economic demands, but had moved to Tirana and developed into a major political confrontation. Not satisfied with the government response, the students entered into an indefinite hunger strike. With strong support from the DP, political demands were added to the wish list, such as a better handling of the Hajdari murder investigation and a united Albanian stand on the Kosovo issue. One key demand was that Prime Minister Majko should personally come and sit down with them to discuss their grievances. Although government officials, including a minister and a deputy minister, had gone to see them, they remained adamant that Majko himself should pay them a visit. The stalemate lasted long enough for doctors to warn the authorities about the deteriorating physical condition of some of the strikers. When the two ministers failed to convince the students to come to the PM's office, the government decided to break the strike. At 4 am on 18 December, the police entered the building and forcibly brought those striking students who were in poor health to the hospital, and dropped the others halfway between Tirana and Shkodra. That very same day, however, with encouragement and support from the DP, the students re-entered the building and resumed their hunger strike. A new demand was added: the resignation of Prime Minister Majko.

One day later, late in the evening, I was approached by DP member Ylli Vejsiu – a soft-spoken moderate – with the request to help find an acceptable way out of the impasse. He also spoke on behalf of the concerned parents. After contacting the government, I went to the scene with Vejsiu and spent nearly two hours with the students. Two thin-faced, unhealthy-looking boys did most of the talking, with the others sitting or lying around. I noted the poor health situation but also a willingness to engage in a dialogue with the government and drop outrageous political demands. I assured them that the government was prepared to discuss their grievances seriously and advised them to seize this late, if not last, opportunity. They asked for time. The next day, again late in the evening, they called me to say that they were ready to discuss the terms of the talks. The following morning I revisited them with Vejsiu, spoke to the doctors (who confirmed my impression that some students were in a very serious condition) and had another emotional session of about an hour. After several mood changes and considerable infighting among themselves, I left with an agreement to arrange a confidence-restoring meeting with the Prime Minister, to be followed by a serious round of talks with a government team.

The follow-up on the next day was nothing less than spectacular, in the form of a DP-proposed meeting between Government and Opposition at the highest level, ahead of the talks with the students. Why did Berisha choose this moment to propose such an unprecedented meeting? He probably saw an opportunity here to burnish his image – so tarnished after the September revolt and boycott of the constitution referendum – and salvage his leadership role. He had been under considerable international pressure to mend fences with the new SP leadership and the government. Also, moderate forces within the DP, including Genc Pollo and long-term DP prominent Tritan Shehu, had become more vocal and gained strength. In fact, in a meeting of the leading DP steering committee, several party members had argued in favour of a more conciliatory attitude, not only towards the students' issues but also towards the Majko government in general. I remember how in that period I was approached by these same members with candid suggestions that our office help improve the political climate and repair the strained relations.

The meeting between Berisha and Pollo and, on the other side, PM Majko and Vice PM Meta was set for Monday at 4 pm on the neutral ground of my favourite

Rogner hotel. I remember the tantalizing waiting game of who would come first and wait for the other. Berisha and Pollo were the first to arrive, with the prime minister and Meta following shortly thereafter. The handshake that followed caused great excitement among the assembled press. It was splashed over the front page of all newspapers the following day. With the students' deputation waiting outside the meeting room, the four leaders first spoke for more than an hour. After the meeting Majko left quickly, Berisha made a brief, but very positive, statement to the assembled press, while the other two met with the students and worked on a common statement. During a packed press conference Pollo and Meta announced that full agreement had been reached by both sides.

The agreement referred not only to the students' issues but also to a more effective handling of the Hajdari murder case and, politically important, to a common position with respect to the Kosovo conflict. The non-political student demands were dealt with the next day, in my presence, during a meeting competently chaired by Minister of Education Ethem Ruka. A Memorandum of Understanding was signed, the strike discontinued and the press informed. There was great relief all around, not least among the parents, some of whom later came to our office to express their thanks.

A new beginning?

The outcome brought considerable excitement both at home and abroad. Many expressed the hope that it would mark the beginning of a new era of normalization of political relations, in which cooperation would replace rigid confrontation. Yet, on both sides there were still party members who felt bypassed or were squarely opposed to the dialogue. Especially, SP members of the old signature voiced strong reservations about the new thaw in SP–DP relations. Nonetheless, the moderate forces in both parties were in the ascendancy – at least for the time being. When I called on Berisha to convey the international appreciation for his initiative to engage in the dialogue, he mentioned the stormy opposition from party militants he had to cope with. He added that the litmus test for better relations would be the way the government pursued the Hajdari case, which until then had been handled poorly. It helped that I could tell him that the Norwegian Chairmanship of the OSCE had made available an experienced Norwegian prosecutor who would assist in giving this matter special, bipartisan attention. (It was not before 2002, though, that the murder case was finally settled with the conviction of three men from Tropoja – Hajdari and Berisha's native village in the north – ruling out political motivation).

In order to boost the new mood of dialogue and civility between the SP and the DP, we launched the idea of a soccer match between the two parties. The suggestion was welcomed all around and widely covered by the media. On the day of the match the stadium was filled with thousands of spectators and the two sides had fielded teams that listed many of their party prominents. I had the honour of acting as referee – in an official FIFA outfit, no less. Of course, our preconceived notion was to ensure a politically correct outcome. It took some creative whistling on my part to achieve the desired result, including cancelling an early goal by the DP team because of a questionable offside. The match ended with a satisfactory 1-1 and both teams, all the spectators and the press left the stadium in a festive spirit. Much later, in post-war Kosovo, I was approached by some Kosovo Albanians who suggested that we should repeat such a political reconciliation match in Pristina, this time between the Kosovo Albanian and Serb sides. Alas, interethnic strife is much harder to overcome with playful ploys than mere political rivalry. No wonder that the suggestion never materialized.

Unfortunately, the clearing of Albania's political skies did not last long. Soon enough, the old rivalry played up again, somewhat symbolized, if not triggered, by Nano's return to power in 2002. The problem of Albanian politics as in so many 'new democracies' was (and is) that the political fight is not about ideologies and visions for a future society but about personalities and power. The parties are almost interchangeable were it not for their regional roots and clannish linkages. With political power come spoils in the form of economic and financial benefits. Politics pays, and can pay handsomely, through favouritism, nepotism or outright corruption. Throughout the post-communist decades the Albanian political and governing elite – whether of Socialist or Democratic signature – has taken good care of itself, more so than of its lesser brethren. Another 'New Class', to use Milovan Djilas's famous term, but this time – compared to the communist ancestors – more materialistic and blatant.

In such a political climate the electorate is left with little programmatic choice, resulting in cynicism, resignation or apathy. This resembles the authoritarian communist past except that the competition within the political establishment is real and publicly displayed. The rivalry between the parties, especially the main contenders, the SP and the DP, is fierce and highly personal, with accusations and innuendos freely flying around, pots accusing kettles and cats fighting dogs. As in other 'new democracies', in the Balkan and elsewhere, during election time rumours of vote buying, abuse of administrative resources and ballot manipulation, whether real or perceived, are constantly recycled. Such elections, in the end, are to most people little more than an elitist game of musical chairs. Meanwhile, foreign election observers keep noting, dutifully but predictably, that 'progress has been observed, although serious shortcomings remain'. Even if the quality of elections improves, the problem of the self-serving governing class will not disappear unless transparency in government and rule of law are more firmly established. This may well be the most compelling argument for integration in the European Union.

There are, of course, Albanian politicians who have maintained high standards of integrity. I have met and admired many of them, more than I can list, but they are often outsmarted by those who put private over public interests, or, in more euphemistic terms, who pursue self-interest at least as vigorously as public goals. How else could one explain the display of wealth in real estate, conspicuous consumption, foreign travel, private education and other pursuits of the privileged class? Or the thriving of illegal drug production and trade, condoned under both Democrat and Socialist governments? I have heard Albanians refer to their country as 'Benzy land' (for the ubiquitous presence of expensive German cars). They question the origin of the private investments in hotels, apartment buildings and luxury villas that have turned not only Tirana but also Durres and Sarande into booming construction sites – with Vlore and smaller coastal villages soon to follow. The respectable economic growth, slightly over 4 per cent annually between 2000 and 2018, has brought limited benefit to the common people. Income distribution has become very skewed. More than half of the respondents in a 2018 Gallup poll expressed the desire to go abroad. Not surprising then that both old taxi drivers and young students told me at the time of writing that they did not consider Enver Hoxha's time all that bad. After all, had he not maintained law and order and imposed socioeconomic equality (exempting, of course, the privileged party cadres as they would ruefully admit)? How telling also that the walls of official buildings are adorned with pictures of Ismael Qemali, the undisputed founding father of Albania in 1912, instead of the sitting head of state as is common in most countries!

Kosovo calling

With party political strife somewhat deflated, Albania seemed to be heading for calmer waters in 1999. So was our OSCE Presence. The escalation of the Kosovo conflict next door, however, changed everything. As ethnic violence spread and Kosovo Albanians kept fleeing across the border into Albania in steadily growing numbers, Kosovo became the predominant issue of concern. By March refugees already numbered several tens of thousands, in the Kukes border area alone. With the onset of the war on 24 March, the influx dramatically increased to hundreds of thousands. The Presence became involved practically full-time in the absorption and management of the refugee flows. As all of this was a spillover effect of the Kosovo war, it shall be dealt with in the next chapter. Suffice it to state here that the refugees challenge was unprecedented in scale and scope in post-WW II Europe. The same can be said about the hospitality with which Albania and the Albanians responded. When the war came to an end in early June and the refugees streamed back massively, I went the same way. The Norwegian Chairmanship had asked me to head a new OSCE in Kosovo that was to assist in rebuilding that devastated society. My many Albanian interlocutors gave me a warm send-off. President Meidani graciously commented that Albania's loss was compensated by Kosovo's gain.

Notes

1   Joep Zonne, *Lodewijk Thomson – De mediamajoor*, (chronology of his life, 1969–1914), Skanderbeg books, 2019.
2   OSCE, Special Report, OSCE Presence in Albania, May 1998.

3   The Kanun is often simplistically associated with the blood revenge practice. Although a significant feature and the cause of recurrent violence, the Kanun is much broader in scope. In the absence of state authority it did provide for the much needed rule of law in the isolated, mountainous regions of modern-day North Albania, Montenegro and Kosovo. Some authors have explained the Kosovo Albanian rebellion against Serb rule, and even the 1999 Kosovo war, in Kanun terms of revenge. I find this highly dubious and mainly stemming from fascination and unfamiliarity with 'exotic' custom. The Kanun pertains to a limited ethnic setting of small communities with family traditions and personal interaction, not a general uprising against a totalitarian government.

2

The unstoppable war

Escalation of violence; end of autonomy

While Albania struggled forward towards democratic maturity, the situation in next-door Kosovo had steadily grown from bad to worse. It had been a contested area with ethnic strife, competing national ambitions and territorial fights for well over a century (about which there will be more in the following chapter). When the Ottoman territories were definitively carved up after the Balkan Wars of 1912–13, the annexation of Kosovo by Serbia was blessed by the major European powers at the time but much resented by the majority population of Kosovo Albanians who were vying for self-rule. After the First World War it was incorporated as part of Serbia in the new Kingdom of Serbs, Croats and Slovenes, later renamed Yugoslavia (South Slavs). It was not until 1974, with the adoption of a new decentralizing Constitution, that Kosovo obtained a considerable degree of autonomy in Tito's Socialist Federal Republic of Yugoslavia. It acquired the status of an Autonomous Province, which put it almost on par with the constituent republics of the Federation – Serbia, Croatia, Slovenia, Bosnia and Herzegovina, Montenegro and Macedonia – except for the right to secede. Tito's death in 1980 signalled the end of the vision of a stable, united and multi-ethnic Yugoslavia. Separatist sentiments along ethnic lines, stirred up by nationalist leaders, became ever more intense and vocal. Also in Kosovo the mood became more radical and tensions over its provincial status escalated, with massive strikes, demonstrations and severe countermeasures. The two main ethnic communities, Albanians and Serbs, grew ever further apart. Moderate communist, Kosovo Albanian leaders were purged from party and government. Matters became worse with Slobodan Milosevic's rise to power. He was riding a nationalist wave that he himself had stoked up in 1987 in Pristina. Until then a rather bland, albeit competent, communist party apparatchik, he shot to fame when he publicly pledged his solidarity with the minority Serb population in Kosovo that felt demographically threatened by the ever-increasing Albanian majority. Confronted with a complaint about a physical altercation he infamously declared, in front of television cameras, that 'no one shall beat a Serb'. After successfully scheming to replace his former mentor, Ivan Stambolic, as president of Serbia in 1988, he further inflamed nationalist passion with a fiery speech in Gazimesta, just north of Pristina, on 28 June 1989. The occasion was the 600th anniversary of the legendary Battle of Kosovo Polje against the Ottomans, an event of mythical proportions to Serb nationhood. Well over one million Serbs attended from all over Yugoslavia. In true totalitarian fashion more mass demonstrations and political propaganda followed. One year later Kosovo was downgraded to a mere province of the Serbian Republic, under direct rule from Belgrade. The existing Kosovo parliament was abolished and the autonomous government disbanded, its moderate leader Azem Vlasi arrested. A stringent policy of Serbianization followed. The use of Albanian as an official language was banned, Albanian language education and newspapers restricted. Introduction of Serbian school curricula resulted in a massive boycott of education facilities. Over time many tens of thousands of Kosovo Albanians were thrown out of work and positions of responsibility to be replaced by Serbs, many of whom were brought in from outside Kosovo. Besides government officials, they included doctors, teachers, judges, journalists and policemen, among many others.

Non-violent resistance; emergence of KLA

The situation deteriorated into a state of quasi-apartheid with the 75 per cent Albanian majority bitterly resenting their second-class status – 'the forbidden nation', in the words of Rexhep Qosja, Kosovo's prominent writer and intellectual whom I would get to know and respect in later days. In defiance of Serbian rule and dominance, Kosovo parliamentarians declared Kosovo a 'Republic' early in 1990, still within a Yugoslav Federation. Inspired by the Slovenian and Croatian declarations of independence, the Kosovo Albanians organized a referendum of sorts on full independence (99 per cent in favour), followed by the declaration of an independent 'Republic of Kosovo' in October 1991. An underground 'parallel state' emerged, with separate education and health services, financed largely from abroad where a government-in-exile, under 'Prime Minister' Bujar Bukoshi, had been formed. Following self-styled elections in May 1992, Ibrahim Rugova's Democratic League of Kosovo (LDK), a party founded in 1989, became the lead political force and he himself the 'shadow' president. He advocated a strategy of strict non-violence so as not to provoke Serbia. This earned him international acclaim but failed to bring about any positive change. In fact, this strategy enabled Milosevic to maintain the status quo by 'repressive tolerance' – to use the famous term coined by my old Brandeis professor, Herbert Marcuse – while it gave the international community a convenient excuse to let the Kosovo question remain unresolved.

The Dayton Peace Accords of 1995 that ended the Bosnian war and to some extent restored Milosevic' international standing, were facilitated by Kosovo's passivity. The agreement made only oblique reference to the Kosovo problem. As such Dayton became a political turning point. It ended the illusion of the many Kosovo Albanians who had been led to vest their hopes for change on the 'international community'. LDK's vice-president and foremost intellectual, Fehmi Agani, acknowledged that Dayton had proven the ineffectiveness of the non-violence strategy. With the passive resistance discredited, prominent personalities like Adem Demaci, Rexhep Qosja and the journalist/publisher Veton Surroi reinforced their calls for a more active opposition. As mentioned earlier, Demaci was considered 'Kosovo's Nelson Mandela', having spent twenty-eight years in prison but with his spirit of tolerance and inclusion unbroken. Since his release from prison in 1990 – only to enter what he called 'the largest prison in the world', meaning Kosovo – he had been heading the Council for the Defense of Human Rights and Freedoms of the People of Kosovo. The European Parliament awarded him, in 1991, the prestigious Sacharov Prize for Freedom of Thought (Mandela had been an earlier recipient, Rugova a later one in 1997). In 1996 he turned to more active politics by becoming the president of the Parliamentary Party of Kosovo (PPK), the only opposition party – founded by Surroi – that challenged the LDK supremacy in the early years of the shadow 'Republic of Kosova'. Rexhep Qosja, on his part, created the 'Democratic Forum of Albanian Intellectuals' as another counterweight movement to Rugova's LDK. He, too, soon turned to party politics by forging, in 1998, a broad coalition of political groups under the name United Democratic Movement (LBD by its Albanian acronym).

More momentous, in retrospect, was the armed resistance that had started to surface. Ex-students in exile in Switzerland, who had fled the Serbian repression in the 1980s, had founded the Popular Movement of the Republic of Kosova (LPRK) in 1982, transformed and renamed Popular Movement of Kosova (LPK) in 1987. More or less simultaneously, armed rebellion had begun to spread on the ground in Kosovo which, although widely scattered, was soon grouped together under the name Kosovo Liberation Army, KLA (or UCK by its Albanian acronym, Ushtria Clirimtare e Kosove). As an underground resistance movement it attained first notoriety with an attack on a Serbian police post in September 1992. Despite its growing popular support, the official response to the emergence of the KLA was negative, not only on the outside as predictable but also from Kosovo Albanian politicians. As late as 1997 Rugova suggested, for example, that the Serbian secret service might be behind the KLA to discredit his own legitimate, non-violent movement. And, even in 1998, his 'shadow' prime minister Bujar Bukoshi spoke to me, in Tirana, about the KLA in dismissive terms. In Albania Sali Berisha, then in power, sided with Rugova and even had Hashim Thaci – then a little-known KLA foreman – momentarily arrested in Tirana on some flimsy ground. It did not stop the KLA from gaining popular support, both inside Kosovo and among the Albanian diaspora. Its first public appearance was at a funeral in the Drenica area, Kosovo's heartland, in late November 1997. Some 20.000 people had gathered to mourn the death of a teacher at the hands of the Serbian police. The image of three KLA soldiers in black uniforms with the KLA insignia drawing huge cheers from the crowd, sent shock waves in and outside Kosovo. Who were these guys? What were they up to? Whom did they represent? As we shall see later, this same Drenica region was at the centre of the Kacak rebellion immediately after the First World War. And it was also in

Drenica that after the Second World War another Albanian, pro-independence uprising had been crushed, this time by Tito's forces. The symbolic significance did not escape those with long memories or a good knowledge of history.

International pressure and military action

By 1998 Kosovo began to witness violent clashes and assassinations with increasing frequency. The massacre of Adem Jashari and his extended family by Serbian security forces in March in Prekaz, again in Drenica, became a tragic turning point. No less than fifty-eight people perished, among whom were eighteen women and ten children. Ever since, Jashari has been revered as the primordial patriot and founder of the KLA. Instead of defeat, Prekaz brought the KLA more reputation and popular support, both at home and abroad. Thousands of people demonstrated in Pristina in its support. Surroi's Koha Ditore newspaper published shocking pictures causing outrage among the diaspora and alarm in foreign capitals. The UN Security Council adopted a Resolution (1160) on 31 March that condemned the 'excessive use of force by the Serbian forces' and called on Belgrade to offer a 'genuine political process' to the Kosovo Albanian community, a 'greater degree of autonomy' and 'meaningful self-administration'. It imposed an arms embargo, but also denounced the 'acts of terrorism by the KLA' while emphasizing the 'territorial integrity of Yugoslavia'. Far from chastised, the Serbian government responded with a referendum in April, in which 95 per cent of the respondents rejected foreign mediation as a means to solve the Kosovo conflict.

In order to counter misinformation and reassure the international audience, the KLA-command issued a 9-point programme in April that spelled out its aims and principles. These included adherence to international conventions of war and rejection of terrorist acts and violence against civilians. It appealed for international support for the 'just cause of the Albanian people of Yugoslavia'. The US was first and foremost in turning a willing ear. Although US special envoy, Robert Gelbard, had still labelled the KLA a 'terrorist' organization in February after consultations with Rugova in Pristina and Milosevic in Belgrade, the US State Department had started to develop a positive interest. In June secretive contacts were made in Tirana and Geneva, while Dayton architect Richard Holbrooke openly met with KLA military inside Kosovo, in the village of Junik, between Gjakova/Djakovica and Peja/Pec. Both CIA and the State Department began to consider the KLA as a viable party in the conflict and established lines of communication. The KLA spokesmen had met their preconditions by pledging not to engage in any activity outside Kosovo (meaning Serbia and Macedonia), to limit offensive action to military and police targets only and to disavow any linkage to Marxist or Islamist ideology. The public image of the KLA, and credibility, was further boosted when Adem Demaci, with his international standing as a human rights defender, accepted to be its political (figure) head and spokesperson.

In the meantime, at the prodding of the US, Rugova had gone to Belgrade in mid-May to have the first-ever meeting with Milosevic. It produced no results, but as a reward for his effort he was invited to Washington later that month to meet with President Clinton and Congressional leaders. He used the occasion to plead for an 'international protectorate' as a transitory phase towards independence, but was countered by the US priorities of 'autonomy' and 'security'. He went on to the UN in New York to ask for UN and NATO involvement in resolving the conflict. Shortly thereafter, NATO, spurred on by, especially, the US and the UK, gave off a warning signal by issuing a mobilization order that initiated first preparations for a potential intervention.

Unperturbed by the foreign concerns and threats, Serbia started a massive summer offensive to eradicate the KLA. Vast areas were razed by systematic and total eviction of people and destruction of villages and neighbourhoods, including bazaars and mosques. Reliable sources, including the UNHCR (the UN refugee agency), estimated that over 200,000 Kosovo Albanians fled their homes to seek refuge elsewhere in Kosovo and across the border. They brought disturbing tales of intimidation and brutality, including killing, rape and torture, often committed by paramilitary militias moving ahead of the regular troops. For all intents and purposes, this was nothing less than ethnic cleansing. New international appeals and warnings to stop the violence and de-escalate the conflict failed. Another UN Security Council Resolution was adopted (nr. of 23 September 1199), which demanded a cease-fire, withdrawal of Serbian forces and the return of displaced persons and refugees. It warned of 'additional measures' in case of non-compliance. A day later, NATO took the formal step to prepare a plan for air strikes, thus building up further pressure on Belgrade.

The Holbrooke–Milosevic agreement

With violence raging on the ground, massive displacement of people and winter approaching, a humanitarian disaster was looming. In an ultimate attempt to prevent the outbreak of a full-fledged civil war, a cease-fire was agreed upon, on 13 October, by the US negotiator Richard Holbrooke and Slobodan Milosovic. Both had, of course, been key players in reaching the Dayton Accord that had ended the Bosnia war in 1995 (but had left the Kosovo time-bomb ticking). The October agreement was to end the violence and restore the status that Kosovo had enjoyed before 1990. It called for compliance with UN Resolution 1199, withdrawal of troops and 'substantial autonomy' for Kosovo. As Milosevic categorically refused to have foreign troops on Serbian soil, a novel way was found to check compliance with the agreement. It provided for the stationing by OSCE of some 2,000 international monitors, through the establishment of a Kosovo Verification Mission (KVM). It also allowed for aerial verification by NATO which in return suspended its preparation for air strikes.

In retrospect, the October 1998 agreement was probably the last opportunity to avert war. At that point in time the KLA, although no longer treated as a terrorist organization, still had an ambivalent reputation. Most of the Europeans players were still favouring the non-violent approach of Rugova who was seen as the more reliable long-term political option, with more domestic support. The KLA had incurred heavy losses over the summer and had lost most of their terrain. They had pre-agreed with Holbrooke to a unilateral cease-fire in order to facilitate the agreement. With strong international resolve they might well have been compelled to join in a lasting peace agreement. As the then political director of the KLA, Hashim Thaci, told me many years later, agreement on a path to independence within a definite time frame would have forestalled further escalation towards war: 'Why would we kill and be killed, if our goal was achieved – even with a time lag'. Then again, the US itself seemed not overly convinced that the agreement could, or even should, permanently end the conflict. Secretary of State Madeleine Albright qualified it as a 'Band Aid' measure, obviously seeking a more radical solution for the longer run.

A lasting solution of the conflict would have required foresight and preparedness for concessions on the part of the Belgrade regime – including a road map towards Kosovo's independence – as well as unequivocal support for the same by the European Union members. Such conditions were totally absent at the time. The Europeans, as usual, were hopelessly divided, while the mood in Belgrade was anything but conciliatory. There were also sinister forces at work to sabotage any kind of rapprochement. In mid-December six young Kosovo Serbs were killed, and about a dozen wounded, in the Panda bar in Peja/Pec. The murder caused outrage all around, with the KLA getting all the blame. Many years later, the Serbian government officially acknowledged that the murder had been perpetrated by agents of the Serbian Secret Service.[1] The motivation was, of course, to sow discord and prevent compromise – which is exactly what they achieved.

As it happened, the October agreement was more in evidence by violation than compliance. It was already flawed because of the absence of any official Kosovo Albanian representation and input. The FRY/Serbian side did withdraw army troops, which at least halted the large-scale eviction of people. The Ministry of Interior police, however, and even more so the paramilitary militias, continued their intimidation and brutality against civilians. On the opposite side, the KLA was quick to take advantage of the agreement to reorganize and regain areas under their control – as one of their commanders (and the future prime minister) Ramush Haradinaj later acknowledged. In this poisoned environment the KVM could hardly be effective, restricted as it was to reporting on incidents and occasionally trying to defuse local tensions. Also, it never reached the target of 2,000 monitors; at its peak it counted around 1,100. The overall outcome, therefore, was that tension on the ground did not diminish.

Watching from Albania

In Tirana I had been following the deteriorating situation in Kosovo both from the OSCE office and my home base in Hotel Rogner where Kosovo was a ready topic for Albanian politicians who frequented the place for coffee and rakija. They shared solidarity with the Albanian Kosovars although their allegiance differed. The Democrat Party had historically been siding with Rugova's LDK. The Socialist Party had more affinity to KLA with which it shared old socialist roots. In order not to jeopardize Western support for Albania and their own political pursuits, both parties officially echoed the international line that advocated a self-governing status for Kosovo while 'respecting the inviolability of the international borders'. In other words, a separate, autonomous entity within the confines of the current Federal Republic of Yugoslavia. The SP prime minister Nano had even gone as far as meeting Milosevic one to one during a meeting in Cyprus of Balkan leaders in late 1997, using the occasion to plead for a dialogue with Rugova. The gesture was not much appreciated back home, but did earn him international credit.

From the informal setting of the Rogner hotel all this tactical positioning looked to me little more than 'politically correct' posturing. Both parties were clearly favouring Kosovo's independence as an ultimate objective – sooner or later. Nonetheless, they did consistently speak out in favour of negotiations and peaceful resolution of the conflict. Contrary to anti-Kosovo/Albania propaganda at the time, I also did not hear, even informally, any serious advocacy of the idea of a Greater Albania, even though Albanians, especially the Ghegs in the north, could be expected to be in favour of this, given their proximity to and kinship with the Kosovo Albanians. It was only when violence inside Kosovo seemed to become unstoppable that the conviction took hold that an armed intervention from the West was needed to bring an end to the fighting and impose a political solution. It was also then, over coffee in the Rogner, that the gentle grand old man of Albanian politics, Sabri Godo, kept asking me routinely, rhetorically and wistfully, 'When is NATO coming to the rescue?' He did not have long to wait.

In the course of time I had become acquainted with some of the prominent Kosovo Albanian politicians as well as KLA foremen in Tirana where they often passed through and could count on sympathy from the Albanians and their politicians. Thus I met Mahmut Bakalli, a respected politician from earlier Yugoslav days. Part of the communist nomenclature in Kosovo before 1989, he assured me that he and his peers had been 'neither Stalins nor Hoxhas'.

He struck me as not only a jovial but also a reasonable man who had not given up hope for a political settlement of the conflict. He would re-emerge as a political icon in later Kosovo party politics. More inscrutable was Bujar Bukoshi who also claimed a prominent role in the Kosovo saga as the LDK 'prime minister in exile'. He seemed to pursue his own ambitions from his base in Germany with little regard to – and backing from – other prominent Kosovo Albanians. Like Rugova he was closely linked to Sali Berisha and also not in sync with the KLA which he had tried to undercut by attempting to launch, not very successfully, a competing armed force, the FARK (Armed Forces of the Republic of Kosovo). As late as January 1999, in my meeting with him, he made light of the KLA because of its 'lack of prominent military and political commanders'. His political clout was based on his position among the diaspora and the funds his government had collected through voluntary 3 per cent self-taxation. At the invitation of President Meidani I also sat in at a meeting with Veton Surroi, the editor of Kosovo's daily Koha Ditore. Raised abroad, English-speaking and sophisticated, he was already then a favourite of the internationals and would become even more so in Pristina in later days, as I would find out. He had been a protagonist of democratic change rather than playing the ethnic card in earlier times. By now he had become convinced that only forceful international intervention could free the Kosovo Albanians from the 'Serbian yoke'.

Also, the KLA could be seen and heard in Tirana and in the Rogner. Several times I encountered Xhavit Haliti, the official KLA representative in Tirana who played an important role in mobilizing Albanian and international support, both political and material. He obviously maintained excellent relations with the Albanian institutions that mattered most to the KLA such as the defence and intelligence departments. An easy-going, boisterous and talkative man, he did not quite look the effective arms trafficker that Fred Abrahams depicts in his 'Modern Albania' – a role Haliti himself denied to me many years hence. Someone who struck me as most reasonable and likeable was the soft-spoken Bajram Kosumi. Courteous and intellectual, he seemed to me almost too gentle for the hardball politics of his peers in latter-day Kosovo. This notwithstanding his role as an early student leader in the riotous year of 1981 and his subsequent ten-year imprisonment in Serbia. He had been at the cradle of the Parliamentary Party, the only opposition party to the LDK in the 'underground' Kosovo of the early 1990s. He had respectfully handed his presidency of the party to Adem Demaci, only to see the latter move on and become the political frontman of the KLA in 1998. Kosumi himself and the PPK joined forces with Qosja to form the United Democratic Movement coalition (LBD) in that same year. A decade later he did make it, briefly, to the position of prime minister before retiring from politics to pursue a more fitting, academic career.

And then there was Hashim Thaci, foremost among the KLA political frontmen. Smartly playing his cards and cultivating international contacts, he was eventually to replace Demaci as KLA's leading politician. I had met him and a few co-leaders earlier, very informally, on the occasion of a trip to the EU headquarters, at the suggestion of a Belgian parliamentarian who was favourably disposed towards the movement. She was from Luik (Liege) where many a Kosovo Albanian expatriate had made his residence. We met in Brussels over a simple meal in the basement of an inconspicuous restaurant. He struck me as a rather shy, not overly sophisticated, youngish man – anything but a Che Guevara and not yet the strong-minded political leader he would become. He mentioned the plight of the Albanian population in Kosovo and the necessity to end Serbian rule. According to him, failing peaceful means, only armed resistance was left as an option to obtain independence. Together, this group of young Kosovo Albanians left me with the impression of a dedicated, determined lot who were remarkably 'Western' and secular in their outlook and aspirations. Although they were leftist by origin, I could find no trace of communist sympathies, while radical Islam seemed to be completely outside their mindset.

From Racak to Rambouillet

The beginning of 1999 saw a sharp deterioration in the situation. On 15 January a massacre in the village of Racak, with forty-five Albanian Kosovars found dead, caused a massive public outcry and, basically, paved the way for the international intervention that was soon to follow. Despite its momentous impact the true nature of this mass killing was never unanimously agreed upon. Did it constitute an act of 'genocide' as the American head of the KVM, William Walker, had declared and Western countries readily accepted? Or, as the Serbs alleged, were the victims KLA fighters who had not survived a combat with Serbian forces and who had been re-dressed in civilian clothes in order to mobilize public opinion against Serbia? Reconstruction of the event remained disputed, also because the Chief Prosecutor of the International Crimes Tribunal for former Yugoslavia (the ICTY, based in The Hague) and her staff were denied entry to the scene. There had definitely been an active KLA presence in the area, with recent lethal attacks on Serbian police posts. On the other hand, the human rights monitors of the KVM reported in their crime scene documentation that among the dead there were elderly men, an eighteen-year-old woman and an eleven-year-old child. They had no doubt that the victims were not combatants, but civilians. Having worked with the same mission members later on and knowing their meticulous reporting procedures, I have no doubts myself about the veracity of their conclusions. A team from Human Rights Watch also testified later that the matching bullet holes in the clothes and bodies proved that the victims were civilians and not re-dressed militants.

Enraged by what they considered a premature judgement, the Serbian authorities declared Walker persona non grata (later revoked). They brought in a Serbian–Belorussian team of pathologists who quickly reached the conclusion that the dead bodies were not shot at close range and should be considered combatants. A Finnish investigative team, sponsored by the EU, did not reach a joint conclusion. Its head came out with a personal statement that no evidence had been found that the dead were other than village civilians. In other words, they could not be proven to be KLA fighters. A full report was never published. The same head repeated her finding at the later trial of Milosovic before the ICTY in The Hague. In a still later interview she mentioned that she had been under pressure from the KVM head and the Americans in wording her initial statement – something that the Serbian side used to refute her version of the event. The ICTY, in the end, concluded that there was no compelling evidence either way. This inconclusive outcome, however unsatisfactory, does not alter the fact that the initial Western perception of what had happened, contributed to tipping the scale. It led to stepped-up international involvement, ultimately leading to war. Within a day of the Racak massacre, the hawkish US Secretary of State Madeleine Albright had already seized the moment to reiterate her call for a military ultimatum (as she had done, unsuccessfully, on earlier occasions).

Racak was symptomatic of the dire situation on the ground. Violence kept flaring up, with Kosovo Albanian villagers caught in the middle and the KVM effectively incapacitated. Apart from being concerned about the ongoing humanitarian crisis, Western capitals had also become increasingly impatient with the Serbian government's uncompromising policy and non-compliance with the October Agreement.[2] NATO, which had already established a ground presence in neighbouring Macedonia, was instructed to continue its preparations for an eventual military intervention. Official warnings were repeated from many sides, but to no avail. In a final attempt to turn the tide, and at the urging of, especially, the European nations, a Contact Group (consisting of France, Germany, Italy, Russia, the United Kingdom and the United States) issued an ultimatum to both the Kosovo Albanians and the FRY/Serbia to start peace negotiations. On the 6 February the two sides entered into their first-ever talks in Rambouillet, near Paris. To the surprise of outsiders, it was not Rugova but Thaci who was chosen to head the Kosovo Albanian delegation. He had de facto replaced Demaci as the political leader of the KLA, because the latter had opposed the conference and refused to attend. To a majority of the sixteen Albanian delegation members – fairly distributed over the three main political factions (KLA, LDK, LBD) plus four independents[3] – this choice was logical since Rambouillet would not have occurred without KLA's activism. It catapulted Thaci into the role of main player and strengthened the American intent to further invest in him as a future political leader and ally.

Much has been written about the Rambouillet meeting and the asymmetry between the heavyweight Kosovo Albanian delegation and the relatively lighter representation on the Serbian side. To neutral observers it appeared as if the Serbs, also in their daily behaviour, were the less serious party, with little intent to seek compromise. After protracted talks the Contact Group, quite exasperated, tabled a final take-it-or-leave-it text. It provided for an international military presence in Kosovo and disarmament of the KLA but also a continued, be it reduced, presence of Serbian military and police. It did not give a promise of an early referendum on independence, but referred to consideration of 'the will of the people' after an interim period of three years. It did confirm the sovereignty of the Yugoslav Federation and its territorial integrity.

While the rest of the Kosovo Albanian delegation was prepared to accept the text, the KLA representatives showed great reluctance, partly because of the disarmament clause and partly because of the absence of an explicit reference to a referendum (on independence). Throughout the negotiations Thaci had been stubbornly pursuing text improvements, to the annoyance of even other Kosovars such as Surroi. His tactics had paid off but now he had reached the point where the Western mediators' patience had run out. Under immense pressure to sign, including from Madeleine Albright personally, he asked for time to consult his rear guard, meaning the KLA field commanders. In Pristina, Adem Demaci had been quick to declare his opposition to the draft agreement, which he saw as a formula for continued 'slavery' under Serbia. A specially arranged meeting with Thaci in Slovenia did not make him change his mind. Out of tune with his younger colleagues, Demaci resigned from the KLA. By opting out of Rambouillet he missed a historic turning point in Kosovo's history, with the loss of his political relevance as a consequence.[4]

The whole Kosovo delegation flew home via Skopje, with a stopover in Tirana. At the Rinas airport President Meidani came over 'for coffee', no doubt with his advice that the draft agreement be accepted. The stakes were obviously high for Albania, too. It had been actively advising the Kosovo delegation in Rambouillet through envoys, including Foreign Minister Pascal Milo and the *eminence grise* Sabri Godo. Curiously, after landing Rugova opted to stay in the airplane, probably because he was uncomfortable with the idea of being in the midst of a KLA-friendly gathering. Thaci, together with KLA co-delegates Agim Ceku and Ram Buja, secretly went on to see KLA field commanders in Kosovo via a circuitous, hazardous route, partly on foot so as to avoid capture. Their message was simple: the 'international community' – whose support, as everyone knew, was crucial for success – would not take NO for an answer. When later the delegates had to return to Paris to sign the agreement, there was another brief stay in Tirana. It was on this occasion that I first met with

Rexhip Qosha, at an OSCE gathering. Already then he struck me as singularly self-effacing and dignified. With his stern, bearded look and moral fortitude he looked, indeed, like a Kosovar Abraham Lincoln. Back in Paris the Kosovo delegation declared their acceptance and, on 18 March, signed the agreement. In contrast, the Serbian side refused to yield, remaining adamantly opposed to foreign troops on Yugoslav soil, thus causing the talks to collapse.

From Rambouillet to war

The Serbian rejection could not really have come as a surprise given the humiliating terms of the draft agreement. The earlier Holbrooke–Milosevic text of October 1998, for instance, had still respected the Serbian 'red line' against foreign military boots on their ground. Since then, some Serbian politicians like Vuk Draskovic had evolved to the point that they were prepared to accept a UN-led military presence. To the United Kingdom and the United States, especially, this was not a viable option. The recent record of UN peacekeeping had been abysmal. In Ruanda they had stood by passively when almost a million Tutsis were killed by their ethnic rivals, the Hutus. And in Bosnia and Herzegovina, UN peacekeeping had failed miserably in providing safe havens for ethnic minority groups, reaching a nadir with the massacre of 8,000 Muslim men and boys in Srebrenica in 1995. Hence the insistence on NATO-led forces in Kosovo. For the Serbs, the requirement of NATO to have unrestricted access to all of Yugoslavia's territory as well as blanket immunity from prosecution added insult to injury. On the other hand, the draft agreement did respect Yugoslav sovereignty and territorial integrity while allowing for a significant presence of Serbian military (2,500) and police (2,500) in Kosovo. And it did deny the Kosovo Albanians a ready prospect of independence while requiring a complete demilitarization of the KLA. But these pluses did not weigh up to the much-loathed NATO deployment.

With the situation on the ground in Kosovo being as calamitous as it was in terms of human suffering, the collapse of the negotiations in France could only spell military consequences. There was no tolerance for further procrastination. The case for a humanitarian intervention seemed evident. Holbrooke still went to Belgrade for a last attempt to arm-twist Milosevic to concede but, predictably, without success. On 22 March the OSCE Chairmanship, citing security concerns, decided to withdraw the KVM. The next day the Serbian Parliament made a last, frantic attempt to find a way out by proposing wide-ranging autonomy for Kosovo and agreeing to an international presence on the territory of Kosovo. It even protested against the withdrawal of the KVM, which until then had been much maligned.

The last-ditch efforts in Belgrade to avert an all-out war obviously came too late. On 24 March, NATO started its aerial bombing campaign and Serbia declared war. A Russian Federation proposal in the UN Security Council to condemn the intervention was rejected by a 17 to 3 vote. By implication, an endorsement by the Security Council, requiring unanimity, was also out of reach. In an underhanded move, Milosevic forced Rugova to come to Belgrade in early April to strike a pre-emptive deal. A statement was issued that appeared to imply agreement on 'the establishment of a provisional administration in Kosovo' and a shared view that 'the presence of foreign troops was not required for resolving the Kosovo conflict'. It made Milosevic's spokesman – Ivica Dacic, who would much later reincarnate as a Serbian foreign minister – triumphantly proclaim, barely a week into the war (!), that the FRY had already won 'this imposed and unjust war'. Milosevic himself declared that '(this) agreement is the first joint victory of Serbs and Albanians for peace'. Rugova later exculpated himself by explaining that it was all a Serbian propaganda ploy to which he had been subjected by force. The event, however, caused a definite break between the KLA and the LDK. As a consequence the LDK refused to join the new Provisional Government of Kosovo that had been agreed to by the full Kosovo Albanian delegation in Rambouillet and that was being formed by Thaci around this time.

Tragically, for the Serbs the war meant a repeat of history. They, again, had held out too long for the politically unattainable and shown willingness to make significant concessions only when it was too late. As they had done before, in 1995, when they refused to agree to a special status for the Serb-populated Krajina region within an independent Croatia – with the complete loss of that region and an exodus of over 200,000 Croatian Serbs as the tragic outcome. In Kosovo, too, they reaped the result of a stubborn, self-destructive intransigence, linked to poor statesmanship, that had been at play since 1990 – and had even hardened in the last months before Rambouillet when the writing was clearly on the wall. Again they did not miss the opportunity to miss an opportunity ... only to shoot themselves in the foot.

The inevitability of war

In later assessments many political analysts questioned whether the negotiations had ever had a chance to succeed as they also doubted the international resolve to reach a peace-making compromise. By the time of Rambouillet, NATO was well prepared to launch attacks. Milosevic had lost whatever credit he had regained after Dayton in Western capitals. In the public eye the humanitarian crisis in Kosovo spilling over in Albania and Macedonia demanded resolute intervention. The United States, the dominant Western party to the conflict, was clearly after a regime change in Belgrade. The CIA had already established good connections with the KLA, both its political and military wings. Through direct contacts and its surreptitious presence in the KVM it was well acquainted with the situation on the ground. It had become convinced that the KLA posed neither a Marxist nor a jihadist threat and could be useful in the wider strategic context – not unlike the anti-communist revolt in neighbouring Albania earlier in the decade. It also happened to be the time that American bases were closing in Western Europe and the United States was actively pursuing a policy of military relocation closer to the new, post-Soviet Russian border.[5]

By insisting on NATO deployment, the United States, strongly backed by the United Kingdom, knew that the chances for a Serbian acceptance of the Rambouillet text would be nil. James Rubin, Assistant Secretary of State under Albright, said so in as many words in the excellent BBC documentary 'Behind the Kosovo Crisis' of March 2000. By reaching an outcome that the Serbs would reject and the Albanians accept, the collapse of the peace talks could be blamed squarely on the Serbian side and an intervention in support of the Kosovo Albanians politically justified. Apart from politics and strategic considerations, there were probably other, non-germane factors also at play in favour of a military venture. NATO at the time was in a post-Cold War identity crisis and in search of a new mission to justify its existence. And military planners and technicians would, no doubt, welcome the opportunity to actually test NATO capabilities in what would be a first, real, yet low-risk, military confrontation. Anyone who has witnessed from the inside the surrealistic dynamics of war rooms – as I did much later in Kabul, Afghanistan, in my capacity as civilian head of the NATO-led International Security Assistance Force (ISAF) – cannot but be disturbed about the 'bubble' mentality and fascination with military options and technologies.

However, whatever warmongering factors might have been at play in the Western camp, they by themselves do not suffice to account for the outbreak of the war. The Serbs on their part did nothing to avert the oncoming disaster. Quite to the contrary. In the given circumstances – after wasting the opportunity of the Holbrooke – Milosevic agreement – the Rambouillet package was the best possible deal they could get. It was total hubris to think that the Kosovo crisis could be resolved on Serbian terms. Not after a decade of ignoring every moderate Kosovo Albanian demand and then replacing self-government in Pristina by direct, repressive rule from Belgrade. And not after years of ignoring and defying diplomatic mediation efforts, entreaties and warnings. This uncompromising arrogance of power is the original sin that lies at the root of the conflict and, ultimately, the war.

The withdrawal of the KVM immediately after Rambouillet was a subject of emotional debate and disagreement. From my admittedly safe position in Tirana, and ignorant of the deeper motives at work, I felt that withdrawing international monitors was untimely. It would expose the Kosovo Albanians to even more violence and ethnic cleansing by Serbian police and militias, who would no longer be restrained by foreign eyes and ears on the ground. It was a devilish dilemma for the Norwegian OSCE Chairmanship. Keeping the monitors in place might forestall escalation of violence and international military intervention, leaving a window, however small, for continued peace efforts. If, however, military intervention was known to be imminent, then there was every reason to take the monitors out to safety. They might otherwise be taken hostage, as had happened before in the Bosnian war.

Many countries that had provided monitors to the KVM did not want to see their countrymen in harm's way and pressed the Norwegians to abort the mission. It is also probable that the Americans put pressure on the Chairmanship to withdraw the KVM so that the anticipated military intervention would not be hindered by the taking of hostages. For a continuation of its role it did not help that the KVM was perceived by the Serbs as an American-inspired, CIA-infiltrated and unfriendly presence biased in favour of the Kosovo Albanians. The American Head of Mission, William Walker, had been associated earlier with murky CIA operations in Central America in the 1980s, in support of right-wing dictators. The allegation of bias was not wholly without ground, as the French Deputy Head of the Mission, Gabriel Keller, has publicly acknowledged since then. Later in Pristina I would find out that among the many KVM members who were enlisted in the new OSCE Mission in Kosovo, there was a group of 'intelligent' American monitors who surreptitiously reported to Washington directly, bypassing me as the new Head of Mission. I made short shrift of this anomaly and they disappeared through the back door.

During the war that followed the Rambouillet/Paris failure, the situation on the ground in Kosovo only turned grimmer and more vicious in terms of human suffering. The combination of NATO air strikes and KLA attacks on the ground unleashed a retaliatory reign of terror over the civilian population. With the horrors of war came greatly stepped-up displacements of people, both inside Kosovo and across its borders to neighbouring states. Including refugees from earlier months, a total of well over half a million people were pushed into Albania and about a quarter million to Macedonia. Whether there was a sinister strategic plan underpinning this ethnic policy, named 'Horse Shoe' as German intelligence alleged, never became clear. It was highly suspicious, however, that one day after the outbreak of war, a systematic deportation of Kosovo Albanians was started over railways and roads. There was no doubt that the new expulsions accelerated and expanded the 'ethnic cleansing' – in clear violation of international law and the customs of war. It provided further justification for the humanitarian intervention – conveniently ignoring the fact that the bombing campaign itself triggered more ethnic violence and displacement. The allegation by Noam Chomsky, well-known American scientist and political activist, and other critics of Western power politics that the NATO bombing was the main or sole cause of the ethnic cleansing is, however, demonstrably incorrect. As I had observed with my own eyes at the border, large-scale expulsion of Kosovo Albanians out of Kosovo was underway well before the war began. Not to speak of the many more who had been displaced inside Kosovo during the summer offensive of 1998.

An unequal war

The asymmetric war – overwhelming aircraft superiority versus ground troops – lasted much longer than anticipated. The initial sense, and hope, of the NATO allies was that it would take only a few days of bombing to bring the Serbs 'to their senses' – as had happened before with the Bosnian Serbs in the Bosnian war in 1995. This time, however, the situation was different. Milosevic knew that there was extreme reluctance on the part of the NATO partners, including the United States, to commit ground troops, so he only had to expect and endure air attacks. He also knew that he had Russia's diplomatic backing and that prolonging the war might work in his favour in world opinion. Meanwhile it gave him the licence to step up and complete the ethnic cleansing. When this combination of factors changed, notably with the growing impatience of Russia, the end came quickly. With active German diplomacy (Germany being rotating president of the EU), the ad hoc Contact Group was replaced by the higher-status 'Group of 8' nations (United States, Russia, Canada, Germany, United Kingdom, France, Italy and Japan) as a forum for negotiations. A new Russian special envoy, Chernomyrdin, proved Russia's – or rather President Yeltsin's – greater readiness to find solutions of compromise. Neutral Finland's former president Athisaari was brought in as a credible mediator. Also, the odds against Milosevic worsened when President Clinton – freed from his Monica Lewinsky scandal and impeachment threat – indicated serious consideration of deployment of ground troops in order to bring the war to a rapid end.

Ultimately, the war lasted two months. As later critical NATO self-assessments have shown, the NATO campaign was tarnished by coordination and targeting errors. The 'smart bombing' of bridges, railroad tracks, military convoys and defence-related infrastructure, including in Belgrade, was not all that smart. Many civilians were among the victims, an estimated 500. They included children, as a monument in Belgrade's central Tashmaidan park still testifies. Even so, Serbian people tried to cope and in Belgrade they even managed to display their typical sense of humour. When an American Stealth Bomber was shot down, they apologized: 'Sorry, we did not know it was invisible.' There were Serbs also who strongly disagreed with Milosevic's bellicose attitude and condemned his repressive regime and war crimes, past and present. Prominent among these critics were courageous journalists such as Dejan Anastasijevic and Slavko Curuvija, and the weekly 'Vreme' under chief editor Stojan Cerovic. Curuvija was murdered by Serbian Security Service agents on 11 April. It took sixteen years to finally get them indicted and another four years for their conviction.[6]

Among serious NATO bombing errors was a strike against a bus carrying civilians near Pristina; the bombing of a column of Kosovo refugees (killing at least sixty); strikes on a market in Nish (killing fifteen), a mistaken KLA position near Koshare (killing sixty-seven), a residential neighbourhood in Surdulica (at least twenty victims), and misfired missiles that landed in Bulgaria and Albania. In Belgrade the Chinese embassy was erroneously hit although conspiracy theories suggest otherwise. The villa of Milosevic was spared, reportedly for a good reason: the suspected presence in it of a Rembrandt painting (it was later found out to be a copy). One hurtful, late-night strike was carried out on 23 April against the TV tower of the State Broadcaster RTS. Sixteen employees were killed, to the dismay of the Belgrade population and evoking fierce protests of government and media representatives. In later years this calamity became the source of sharp controversy. Surviving spouses and relatives sued the authorities for not having evacuated the tower although they had been warned about the strike in advance. Ostensibly, they had kept the remaining occupants in the building unaware of the imminent bombing for the cynical reason of war propaganda. In the end, the director in charge was sentenced to ten years in jail.

Albanian response

In Tirana we had witnessed the war in Kosovo looming larger and larger. The Albanian politicians were understandably preoccupied with the ominous developments, certainly when ever-increasing numbers of Kosovo Albanians were pushed across their border. I witnessed the result of this ethnic cleansing first-hand in early March, weeks before the war. In the company of Ismije, my political adviser, I saw the harrowing entry of thousands of Albanian Kosovars at the Morine border crossing between Kukes and Prizren – on foot, and in horse carts, tractors and semblances of cars and vans. They had been stripped of their passports and licence plates by Serbian police before the border so as to discourage their return. Poor Ismije, she cried her eyes out seeing the misery of those she considered her kin leaving everything behind. 'All is lost now,' she lamented, no doubt remembering from her PhD studies how in the 1870s and in the 1912–13 wars the Albanian population had suffered similar losses of life, goods and territories. I had little to offer by way of consolation, but fortunately there was a strong woman whose commiseration helped somewhat. Christiane Amanpour of CNN fame had been standing next to us watching and reporting on the unfolding drama.

The enormity of the influx was for me a reason to call on the spot my old colleague from the Foreign Ministry, Niek Biegman, who was Dutch ambassador to NATO at the time. I told him that the stream of refugees was way beyond the capacity of the UN, meaning the UN High Commission for Refugees, to handle. Greater capacity to move and accommodate such numbers was needed and I suggested NATO logistical support. By then, NATO had already established a ground presence in next-door Macedonia. Shortly after NATO had embarked on its bombing campaign, the Albanian parliament made a formal request to the same effect, which met with a positive response. With the war raging, the influx of refugees kept swelling, reaching well over half a million. That they were all accommodated inside Albania without major problems, is much to the credit of the Albanian people, their solidarity and hospitality. It certainly enhanced Albania's image in the West.

The initial scepticism I had voiced about the UN's handling capacity of this refugee 'caseload' was not shared by the UNHCR representative, although it was borne out by the reality on the ground. My comment in a Dutch newspaper that UNHCR in Albania could not make a dent in a pack of butter, was not much appreciated by their headquarters in Geneva. For the sake of good 'interorganizational relations' I had to make the apologetic trip to Canossa to assure the High Commissioner, Ms Ogatha, that I had been somewhat misread. I did get my way in Tirana, though. I convinced Prime Minister Majko that the coordinating body which was to handle the refugees and their future return should be headed by an Albanian official rather than an international refugees 'expert', and that international organizations should have a formally subordinate, however decisive role. It was so decided. Kastriot Islami was appointed head with two internationals as adjuncts. The format turned out to be quite successful and was later described, and monographed, as a model for international–local cooperation in crisis management.

In addressing the refugee problem we were also supported by the Kosovo Verification Mission that had been relocated to Skopje, Macedonia. One team of their monitors was deployed in Albania to assist in registering refugees and to continue their important documentation of human rights violations. As they were also OSCE staff, I had to work out their working relationship with our own Presence. This brought me in first contact with William Walker, of Racak fame, who was still heading the relocated KVM in Skopje, Macedonia. I remember being somewhat taken aback on one occasion when he declined to join us on a flight up to Kukes – the first entry point for refugees in Albania – because he was not provided with a dedicated KVM plane in Skopje. I could not quite square such concern about status with humanitarian engagement.

In a later phase, towards the end of the war, another challenging issue came up: refugee return. It was the international experts' view that we had to prepare for the task of convincing and organizing the refugees to go home, once conditions in Kosovo allowed it. Various international organizations were eager to prepare for that presumably Herculean job. No doubt that many of their staff also had an extension of lucrative contracts in mind. It all turned out to be a non-problem. Almost as quick as they had entered, the refugees returned spontaneously after the end of the war in early June 1999 – not only those in Albania but also the several hundreds of thousands in Macedonia and Montenegro. Seldom has history seen such an enormous flow of refugees reversed so quickly on a voluntary basis.

End of the war; new OSCE mission

The war came to a halt when Serbia yielded to diplomatic pressure and accepted the outlines of a peace deal, elaborated in the G-8 context. On the

9 June 1999, a Military Technical Agreement was concluded covering the withdrawal of Serbian forces. Formally, the war ended with the UN Security Council Resolution 1244 of 10 June. It gave the territory an as yet uncertain status under interim international governance, civilian in the form of UNMIK (the United Nations Mission for Kosovo) and military by way of the NATO-led KFOR (Kosovo Forces). The UNMIK structure brought together the UN, the EU, UNHCR and the OSCE as constituent partners. Of these four pillars, the UN was to have the overall lead and to organize the civil administration, the EU to be responsible for economic reconstruction, the OSCE to take charge of democratic institution building, elections, media and human rights, and the UNHCR to cover the refugees' return and resettlement. As KFOR moved in and established its headquarters in Pristina, the civilian international agencies followed in its wake. The KVM was formally dissolved on 9 June and replaced by the OSCE Mission in Kosovo (OMIK) as of 1 July.

The entry of international forces into Kosovo had some likeness to a comic Italian opera – were it not so serious. In a surprise move immediately after the signing of the military accord, a Russian battalion blitzed from Sarajevo, where it had been stationed as part of the international peacekeeping force, to Pristina. They were welcomed by cheering, Serbian flag-waving Kosovo Serbs, and took control of the airport. At the same time the NATO-led KFOR force had moved from Macedonia to Pristina, cheered on by thankful Kosovo Albanians along the route, with children clapping and chanting 'UCK, UCK, UCK' (the Albanian acronym for KLA). An uneasy military stalemate ensued. The NATO Supreme Commander, Wesley Clark, issued an order to the KFOR Commander, Michael Jackson, to undo the Russian occupation of the airport. Famously, General Jackson refused to engage in a military confrontation by saying 'I am not going to start the Third World War'. Instead, he opted – brilliantly – for deprivation tactics. While international diplomacy was trying to defuse the situation politically and air space was denied to Russian planes, he simply kept the Russians in isolation at the airport. Deprived of fresh support by air and on the ground, the Russians soon gave in. In fact, they became a regular part of the international military presence. I personally benefited from their integration in KFOR when I had an acute ear problem treated in the small Russian military clinic by a good-humoured Russian doctor, with prehistoric tools but very effectively.

It was the Norwegian Chairmanship of the OSCE, through its dynamic ambassador in Vienna, Kai Eide, who asked me to head the new OSCE mission in Pristina, to build on what was left of the former KVM. In retrospect, probably the most lasting, graphic legacy of the KVM is the elaborate, detailed report 'Kosovo: As Seen, As Told, Part I', published in July 1999. It covers human rights violations in Kosovo from the start of its mission, in November 1998, until the end of the war in June 1999. It documents numerous acts of ethnic violence and, in often gruesome detail, the atrocities committed. It shows the indiscriminate way in which civilians of all ages, men and women, were subjected to inhuman treatment, including torture, rape and killing – purely on account of their ethnicity. As we shall see later, a companion sequence of this report, published in December 1999 by the OSCE Mission in Kosovo, on my watch, produced a similar catalogue of human rights violations, this time committed by Kosovo Albanians against Serb citizens in the period between June and December 1999 ('Kosovo: As Seen, As Told, Part II'). While it is no less depressing, the second report differs too starkly in terms of the quantity and seriousness of the crimes to speak of moral equivalence. Together, however, they do show how virulent, vengeful and traumatic the ethnic violence has been. And how difficult it was, still is and will be, to try and achieve lasting reconciliation and good neighbourly relations between the Serbs and the Albanians.

Tellingly, only the first report was widely acclaimed and quoted by the Albanian side, while only the second report received favourable Serbian comments.

Notes

1. Later evidence showed that they belonged to the same circle of conspirators found guilty of the murders of Milosevic's moderate predecessor, President Ivan Stambolic, in 2000, the anti-Milosevic journalist Slavko Curuvija in April 1999 during the war, and the then prime minister Zoran Djindjic in 2003 when he was known to be willing to reach out to the Kosovo Albanians.

2. The non-compliance was, in the Serbian view, provoked by the KLA's taking advantage of the Agreement to recoup lost terrain.

3. All four happened to be (well-known) journalists: Veton Surroi, Baton Haxhiu, Blerim Shala and Dukagin Gorani.

4   When I last talked to him in late 2018, shortly before his death, he expressed sympathy for the new Vetevendosje political party – led by his former collaborator Albin Kurti.

5   The speed with which a huge American military base, Bondsteel, was built in Kosovo after the war points to a pre-existing military interest in a pro-Western post-Yugoslav Kosovo. The size of this base had nothing to do with peacekeeping tasks in Kosovo. I had a chance to meet President (George W) Bush in this Bondsteel base – jovially, of course, over a beer – but could not have felt further removed from Kosovo reality.

6   See also footnote 1.

3

Ethnic revenge

Kosovo Serbs under threat

Those entering Pristina after the war, in June 1999, found an eerie town. Like most places, it had been depopulated by the war and ethnic cleansing. The streets were empty but for the KFOR and international vehicles. Stray dogs roamed around left behind by their owners and there was the nightly, Hitchcock-like spectacle of thousands of black crows descending on the trees for the night. Water and electricity supply was very erratic at best. Bottled water, torch lights and candles were dire necessities. Failing street lights made it risky to navigate the cracked sidewalks at night. Only a few shops were open to provide bare necessities. Their supplies had to be trucked in from Macedonia. In some outer areas like Podujevo near the north-eastern border with Serbia even airdrops were needed for several weeks after the cease-fire.

I found decent accommodation in an apartment complex that had been constructed by the Yugoslav Airport Authority for its staff. The ownership was claimed by an absentee, former Serbian employee but disputed by the new, Kosovo Albanian airport management. Ownership disputes between displaced persons and newcomers would soon plague municipal administrations all over Kosovo, and for a long time to come. In my case it took over a year to settle the issue and enable the retroactive payment of rent. The apartment was conveniently located in the centre of town near a former bank building that used to house the old Kosovo Verification

Mission and since 1 July had become the headquarters of its successor, OMIK, our OSCE Mission in Kosovo. The office building had not survived unscathed: there were shattered windows, broken doors and a defunct elevator. A bullet hole in one of the windows of my office room served as a permanent reminder of past violence – and a ready conversation piece for visitors.

A roundabout balcony on the top floor of the OMIK office offered a panoramic view of Pristina and the surrounding hills. It later became a favourite hang-out for international and local staff during Friday's Happy Hour, but in those early days it offered anything but happy views. For weeks on end, day and night, smoke could be seen going up all around where houses had been set on fire – houses of Serbs who had left on their own initiative, fearful of reprisal, or who had been forced out under threat. As Kosovo Albanians were returning in massive numbers (650,000 within one month!), a wave of ethnic revenge followed the withdrawal of the Serbian security forces. Kosovo Serbs, Roma, Muslim Slavs and others suspected to have collaborated with the oppressive regime before and during the war fell victim to harassment, expulsion, abduction and murder. In contrast to the earlier, systematic ethnic cleansing of Kosovo Albanians by the Serbian forces, however, the ethnic violence this time was not part of a centrally directed strategy but individually motivated and enacted. As mentioned before, it would be false to speak of equivalence, given, also, the difference in scale and intensity.

The first UN SRSG, Sergio de Melo, and the KFOR Commander, Michael Jackson, issued a joint appeal within a week of their arrival in mid-June, urging the Serb population and other minorities under threat to stay, and pledging KFOR's protection – a rather gratuitous gesture since they did not have the capacities in place to actually ensure a safe environment. While the Serbian police and military were fast withdrawing, KFOR took over local control only gradually. The resulting security void in most towns and rural areas was filled by the KLA and its self-styled police units (Policia Ushtarake), much feared by the Serbs and other minorities. No wonder then that neither fear nor exodus came to an end. Among the first to flee were, predictably, the Serbian latecomers who had replaced the Kosovo Albanians after 1990 when Milosevic imposed direct rule from Belgrade. Others, however, had been Kosovo Serbs for generations, like the three elderly ladies who shared an apartment across the street from mine. When I had not seen them for a while on their regular walk to and from the sole nearby corner store, I went over and knocked on their door. An intimidating, burly man appeared who answered my query with a curt 'there are no Serbs living here' before slamming the door in my face.

Well over 100,000 Serbs are estimated to have fled Kosovo in the first six post-war months, close to half the then Kosovo Serb population. Many others became Internally Displaced Persons (IDPs). Towns with sizable Serb communities saw their presence reduced to small numbers: Pristina, for example, had a pre-war Serb population of over 50,000; after the war it rapidly dwindled to no more than about 500 by the end of 1999. In Prizren only 300 remained of the original 8,000, while in Gjilane half of the 12,000 Serbs left in the post-war months. The Serb exodus was joined by tens of thousands of Roma, who were seen by the ethnic Albanians as 'enemy collaborators'. In Pristina the pre-war Roma population of over 5,000 diminished to around 100. I recall how, on a first visit to Mitrovica in the north, I was shocked to see a whole Roma settlement south of the Ibar river completely razed. All inhabitants had been forced to flee to the northern part of the town, mainly inhabited by Kosovo Serbs. This part, together with its hinterland, had been sealed off from the Kosovo heartland by Serb militants – known as the 'bridge watchers'. In the process most of the Kosovo Albanians in North Mitrovica, some 8,000, had been expelled southward. This Mitrovica segregation was a precursor of the problem, as persistent as pernicious, that would preoccupy the international rule for years to come: how to create peaceful, multiethnic coexistence between two communities that harbour deep-seated antipathy, mistrust and enmity towards each other.

In the first post-war months ethnic harassment and violence were rampant. Inside OMIK, the Department for Human Rights was inundated with calls, visits and reports about such incidents. Under the driven leadership of Sandra Mitchell the human rights group did a tremendous job of trying to record any and all incidents that came to our notice. Most of the seventy-five team members had done the same job with the Kosovo Verification Mission before, and demonstrated great professional skill and integrity. They followed rigorous, objective procedures of interviewing, verifying and reporting. The OSCE report 'Kosovo: As Seen As Told, part II' which covers the period from June to November 1999, documents the violations of human rights in disturbing detail. My own role in this was to play the devil's advocate, challenging the findings until we were sure that they could stand up to future scrutiny. I have no doubt about the veracity of the contents. It was with a heavy heart, I remember, that we wrote the introductory pages together. The report was submitted to the first Human Rights Conference that we organized, early in December 1999, in Pristina. We did make the point, though, that there was no moral equivalence to the ethnic cleansing campaign against the Kosovo Albanian population by Serb forces and paramilitary from December 1998 to June 1999, as covered in the companion report, 'Kosovo: As Seen As Told, part I'. Many years later, the Prosecutor of the Kosovo Special Chamber on War Crimes in the period between 1998 and 2000 (more about this later on), in The Hague, told me that this introduction to Volume II was obligatory reading for his team. Interestingly, around that same time Hashim Thaci – by then president of Kosovo – made the same, respectful reference to the report to me.

While most of the violent incidents seemed to involve individual acts of revenge, there were also disturbing reports of more organized forms of intimidation. As the Report points out, there was an underlying motive to expel. It was for that reason that orthodox churches and monasteries, being symbols of Serbian nationhood, were targeted. A thorough review[1] of the damage inflicted on cultural heritage concluded that close to 100 orthodox buildings had been destroyed or badly damaged in the first year or so after the end of the war (to which should be added another thirty burned during the much later riots of 2004). This compares with 200 mosques, out of more than 600, that were demolished by the Serbian forces before and during the war. In either case the destruction was obviously deliberate as is typically the case in the event of ethnic cleansing and violence. In the process great cultural damage was inflicted. Some ten orthodox churches from medieval times or otherwise listed monuments were lost, while the earlier attacks had destroyed several centuries-old mosques and tekkés (religious centres of the Bektashi

Sunnis) as well as most of the typical Albanian kulas (fortified tower houses) in the western part of Kosovo. Along with them some historical bazaars and the unique library of Gjakova/Djakovica, with irreplaceable manuscripts, were burned to the ground.

Whom to blame

The general post-war climate of lawlessness and impunity also permitted greed and criminal intent to come into play. Houses and lands were seized by sheer intimidation or brutal force. The crimes, retaliatory or otherwise, often involved armed men in black uniforms claiming to be KLA fighters or, more 'officially', representatives of the self-declared Provisional Government of Kosovo (PGoK). The senior leadership of the KLA/PGoK categorically denied any involvement in these unlawful acts, blaming 'rogue elements' or misguided, independently operating loyalists. As later court cases would show, however, there were several KLA commanders holding positions of influence and exercising local control who had records of past violence, including war crimes. Some of them were linked to the KLA detention camps that had been set up in the run-up to, and during, the war in KLA-controlled areas and across the border in the rugged terrain of North Albania. It is hard to believe that they were not aware of the criminal activity if not actually condoning it or even colluding in it. The violence was directed not only against non-Albanians such as Serbs, Roma and Muslim Slavs but also against ethnic Albanians who were, justly or unjustly, accused of collaboration or who simply belonged to a rival political side. A particularly nasty aspect of the ethnic violence in the first post-war months was the participation of juveniles, as reported by our human rights officers. Enjoying de facto immunity in the absence of any juvenile detention system, they were frequently seen harassing and threatening defenseless, elderly victims.

The constant exhortations by representatives of the international community – echoed by leading Kosovo Albanians – to refrain from violence and start 'building a multiethnic society' rang hollow in the ears of the non-Albanian Kosovars. This did not change when the ambition was scaled down to 'peaceful coexistence'. The enclaves where they had taken refuge, and the orthodox churches, required protection around the clock by KFOR troops, road blocks and barbed-wire fences. Ethnic attacks kept recurring on an almost daily basis. They took many an innocent life, some 500 over the first half a year –among them the fourteen Serb farmers who were found dead in the village of Gracko, a small village south of Pristina, on 23 July. The perpetrators were never found but the execution-style killing seemed to point to more than just village-level violence. The murder sent shock waves through the nascent international presence. I joined with others to represent UNMIK at the funeral to commiserate, offering condolences and appealing publicly for the cycle of violence to end – amid a crowd of distressed, distrustful and disbelieving mourners.

In the leading newspaper, Koha Ditore, Veton Surroi – quite courageously, given the mood of revenge and retaliation – wrote an editorial on 18 August condemning as 'fascist' the indiscriminate ethnic attacks by his fellow Kosovo Albanians. As late as 3 November, I myself felt compelled to issue an official OSCE statement to appeal to the Kosovo Albanian population and its leaders to stop this violence. I warned that the goodwill was wearing thin: the international community had intervened in Kosovo to stop ethnic killing and cleansing, not to pave the way for another wave of ethnically motivated violence. As he happened to be in town, I persuaded Ismael Kadare – the Albanian author laureate – to make a similar appeal to the public on television. And the same message was voiced by all visiting dignitaries and at international forums such as the OSCE, UN and Council of Europe – alas, to little avail.

Among the worst ethnic crimes, one – as alleged – gained particular notoriety later on. It was Carla del Ponte, the Special Prosecutor for the International Criminal Tribunal for the former Yugoslavia (ICTY) in The Hague, who came out with a most serious accusation in 2009 – after her departure from the Court. Based on a still earlier journalist report, she alleged that the KLA had been involved not only in detaining Serbs and Albanian collaborators in prison camps but, far worse, also in torture and trafficking of prisoners' organs. The allegation was picked up by a compatriot of hers, Dick Marty, a right-wing Swiss senator who also happened to be a member of the

Council of Europe (CoE) – Europe's oldest, intergovernmental human rights organization. On behalf of the CoE he went out to verify the story. His report in 2011 claimed to validate the accusation and suggested high-level KLA connivance. It did not provide any hard proof, however, and contained mainly rumours and innuendos. Nevertheless, the report led to a CoE resolution that set up a Special Investigation Task Force. This SIFT issued a report in 2014 stating that evidence had been found of war crimes by senior KLA staff as well as 'compelling' indications of organ trafficking by 'a few individuals' – without clearly linking the two. It provided reason for establishing in 2016, under strong pressure from the international community, a special Kosovo Court Chamber on War Crimes (but only those committed by Kosovo Albanians), located in The Hague.

There is no doubt, that during the war and its aftermath, war crimes were committed, also by, or under the guise of, KLA militants. There are no wars without war crimes. The harvesting and trafficking of organs of prisoners, however, seems far-fetched. First, there is the improbability of having the sophistication and clinical conditions in place for such complicated operations and handling in remote locations. Second, it seems unlikely that such abhorrent practices would have gone completely unnoticed by the international monitors and NGOs active in the region. Moreover, there seems to be no credible motive for the KLA leadership to encourage such practices. Money could not be a driving force, as the KLA had ample resources available through its diaspora network. Also, KLA leaders were far too conscious of their dependence on international support to squander their credit with such heinous crimes. Top-level directives and responsibility seem therefore most implausible, which leaves only the possibility of criminal behaviour by rogue elements. But that again begs the question of how they could have possibly created the conditions necessary for such complicated operations. In short, unless the special War Crimes Chamber comes up with irrefutable evidence, I would ascribe the whole story to conspiracy theories and anti-Albanian, anti-KLA propaganda.

All self-serving propaganda aside, the fact remains that the Serb exodus and the precarious fate of those who remained inside Kosovo were shameful aftermaths of the war. In retrospect, one wonders why this 'ethnic revenge' could not have been prevented or at least brought to an early halt. Two main contributing factors are to blame: on the one hand, a combination of callousness and limited leverage on the part of the Kosovo Albanians leaders and, on the other hand, the impotence of the international community to enforce the rule of law it was responsible for. For a proper understanding of both, some background information is needed – not to give in any way a justification of the wanton violence but to provide a context to the happenings that elicited so many later recriminations and allegations in books and articles on the subject.

Kosovo Albanian liability

First, the Kosovo Albanians. There is no doubt that they had not only lived through a decade of abject apartheid rule in the 1990s, but had also faced many prior times of official neglect, discrimination and, at times, outright persecution. Ismael Kadare laments in his literary 'Three Elegies for Kosovo' that everlasting Serbian–Albanian enmity is at the centre of the war-plagued Balkans. Tim Judah, of *The Economist* reputation, provides a useful insight into Kosovo's volatile history, and the dominant ethnic factor, in his 'Kosovo – What Everyone Needs to Know'. Borrowing from him and various other sources, listed in the annex, I will highlight some salient details below for a better understanding.

The 'ethnic cleansing' of 1998–99 – whether part of a 'Horse Shoe' strategy by Belgrade or not – had not come out of the blue. For the root causes of the Serb–Albanian hostility one should go far back in time. A critical historical event that sowed the seeds of perennial ethnic conflict and future war was the redrafting of the Balkan map after the Russian–Turkish war of 1876-78. The dominant powers at the time basically served the territorial interests of Bulgaria, Serbia and Greece and ignored the aspirations of the Albanian people although the latter inhabited a comparable size of Balkan territory. Being a predominantly Muslim presence in the region, deliberately and erroneously identified with Ottoman Turks and without a national state-predecessor, the Albanians lacked a resolute European sponsor nation. An initial, tentative

British suggestion for an equitable distribution of Ottoman lands among all the four main inheriting populations never gained traction. The inequitable land distribution benefiting the Serbs, Bulgarians and Greeks brought uprooting and displacement of masses of people, including Albanians. It left behind deep scars and ethnic hostility that was easily rekindled into violence in later years.

During the Balkan Wars, in 1912–13, when chasing the Ottomans from Kosovo, Serbian and Montenegrin forces engaged in a murderous campaign against the resident Albanians. The latter already then constituted a sizable majority of the population. They had themselves, in the course of 1912, started a revolt against the Ottoman Young Turks, claiming the formation of what would basically be an Albanian quasi-state. Their rebellion, in fact, helped to pave the way for Serbia, Montenegro, Bulgaria and Greece to embark, in October, on the war that expelled the Turks from almost all of their European territory. In the process, the Kosovo Albanians, however, were trampled and their aspirations quashed. At the same time, more southwards and largely outside the reach of the conquering armies, a group of Albanian leaders led by Ishmael Qemali did proclaim a new, independent Albanian state in the southern town of Vlora, on 28 November 1912. This was the nascent Albania that the Netherlands' 'peace mission' of 1913 –14 was supposed to bolster (as described in chapter 1).

Witnesses ranging from foreign war reporters – among whom was Leon Trotsky – to local Franciscan priests wrote extensively about the carnage perpetrated by Serbian and Montenegrin troops throughout the Kosovo region, causing an estimated 20,000 deaths and forcing many more to flee. There were also Serbian voices at that time condemning this onslaught such as the anti-war Social-Democrat Dimitrije Tucovic. And the celebrated British Balkans specialist Edith Durham – of *High Albania* fame – was so appalled by the cruelties that she returned an honorary medal she had received from King Nikola of Montenegro. The commemorative medals awarded to the Serbian military who had participated in the campaign were quite different. They spelled 'Osvetjeno Kosovo' ('Kosovo Avenged'), a reference to the lost Battle of Kosovo Polje of 1389. The wording suggested a justifiable act of revenge – conveniently forgetting that in that legendary battle the Albanians had sided with the Serbs against the Ottoman Turks ... The 1912–13 events led the Carnegie Endowment for International Peace to issue, in 1914, a 'Report of the International Commission to Inquire into the Causes and Conduct of the Balkan Wars'. It concluded that the aim of the armed conquest was the 'entire transformation of the ethnic character of regions inhabited exclusively by Albanians'. In other words, ethnic cleansing avant la lettre.

During the First World War, Austro–Hungarian forces took possession of most of Kosovo in 1915. The Serbian army, rather than surrendering, chose to evacuate from the region in what turned out to be a hugely traumatic escape to the Adriatic coast over the high, forbidding mountains of northern Albania and Montenegro in winter time. The Austrians, for self-serving reasons always inclined to pursue an Albanian-friendly foreign policy in the Balkans, allowed the Kosovo Albanians to participate in the local government and use their language in work and school. This respite was not to last long. In the fall of 1918 the withdrawal of the Austrian and German forces, pushed by the Allied Powers, enabled the Serbian army to bring Kosovo back under Serbian control. A new Kingdom of Serbs, Croats and Slovenes, also incorporating Montenegro, was established on 1 December 1918 (renamed Yugoslavia in 1929). The new government in Belgrade undid whatever nationalist advances the Kosovo Albanians had made under the Austrians, notably the use of the Albanian language. It actively resumed a policy of Serb colonization and Albanian depopulation in order to alter the ethnic makeup of the region.

The colonization program brought some 70,000 colonists, raising the share of the Serbs from 24 per cent to 38 per cent of the Kosovo population between 1919 and 1925 – this despite the active resistance to Serbian rule by Albanian rebel groups called *kacaks*. The Kacak movement is also interesting in the context of latter-day Kosovo. It offers a rather striking similarity, in message and methods, to the Kosovo Liberation Army of the 1990s. Its rules of engagement – only armed targets, no wanton destruction of property and churches – resemble the stated code of the KLA. Operations were highly decentralized, with local initiative and command. Also, the movement was vitally dependent on support from outside, which in the Kacak case meant, exclusively, from Albania. The movement lost its impetus when that crucial support fell away because of the enmity between the then Albanian Minister of Interior Zogolli (the later King Zog) and his Kacak-supporting political rivals such as Hassan Pristhina. As related earlier, Zog conspired with the Yugoslavs (and General Wrangel's White Russians!) to finish off the movement and main leaders such as Bajram Curri, and Azem Bejta – who together with his warrior-wife Shota is still revered in Albania and Kosovo.

The Yugoslav–Serbian expulsion policy was also much resented, even if tens of thousands of Kosovo Albanian families were induced or pressured to migrate to Turkey. In 1937 an infamous publication, 'Expulsion of the Albanians' by a prominent Serbian ultranationalist, Vasa Cubrilovic, called on the government to evict 'the Albanian colonists before it is too late', by all means possible – which he went on to describe in shameless detail.[2] As he cynically suggests: 'At a time when Germany can expel tens of thousands of Jews and Russia can shift millions of people from one part of the continent to another, the shifting of a few hundred thousand Albanians will not lead to the outbreak of a world war.' Even Nobel Prize winner Ivo Andric spoke out in favour of an ethnic realignment and supported the idea of large-scale deportation of Kosovo Albanians. Again, in fairness, it should be recognized that not all Serbs agreed with such bigotry. A student strike in 1938 at the Belgrade University, for example, was also directed against government plans to expel 150,000 Kosovo Albanians to Turkey.

In World War II, the Yugoslav Partisans – Serbs and Montenegrins by a vast majority – fought their heroic battles against the German occupation army largely on Bosnian soil. A collaborator regime in Belgrade, under General Nedic, faithfully copied its Berlin masters. It adopted similar ethno-centric, nationalist views in policies and language, to the detriment of non-Serb communities. Particularly appalling in this regard was the pride it took in declaring Belgrade the first 'Judenfreie' (free of Jews) capital city in Europe in 1942. It had assisted in the deportation of the whole Jewish population of some 35,000 to the death camps. In the meantime, Germany's axis partner, Italy, had taken control over most of Kosovo, together with parts of Montenegro and Macedonia with a majority of Albanian population. Ruling from Albania proper, which it had invaded already in 1939, the Italians held out the promise of a Greater Albania by eliminating the former borders. In Kosovo they allowed the Albanian community to retake control over their region and use the Albanian language (and flag) in the administration and in schools and media. Lands lost under the Yugoslav colonization program were reclaimed. Again, reverse violence flared up. In addition to indiscriminate revenge killings, some 20,000 Serbs and Montenegrins were expelled with the help of the Italian army. They were replaced by poor Albanian settlers from North Albania and Montenegro. Thus the paradoxical situation evolved that the Albanians in Albania organized active, communist-led resistance against the Italian occupiers, while many of their ethnic kin in Kosovo opted for cooperation – an obvious case of 'the enemy of my enemy is my friend'. In Yugoslav eyes, of course, such cooperation was simply collaboration with the fascist invaders.

After the Italian capitulation in September 1943 the Germans took full control in Kosovo. Feeding on the Serb–Albanian strife, they tried to enlist Albanians in their fight against the Yugoslav Partisans. This was easier in Kosovo than in Albania itself for the obvious reason that the Kosovo Albanians had axes to grind with the Serbs. Thus an Albanian SS division was formed in April 1944, named 'Skanderbeg' and garrisoned in Prizren. About 6000 men-strong, it became less known for military exploits than for engaging in indiscriminate terror against Serbs and Montenegrins.[3] The ethnic crimes were so appalling that some of the Skanderbeg officers were even arrested by their German superiors. The division was formally disbanded in November 1944, as the German army started to withdraw from the region. By that time some 40,000 Serbs had been driven from the territory.

When the victorious communists under Tito re-incorporated Kosovo in the newly founded Socialist Federal Republic of Yugoslavia, the option of unification of Kosovo with Albania – as it had de facto existed under Italian–German occupation – was ruled out. This was met with fierce armed resistance by Kosovo Albanians, notably in the central Drenica region, also the key area of the Kacak movement after WWI and the place of origin of the Kosovo Liberation Army in the 1990s. It took a ruthless show of force and several thousands of victims to quell this rebellion. Instead of ceding Kosovo to Albania, the idea was fancied to incorporate Albania – now under friendly communist rule – as an additional Republic in a new Federation. There was even serious talk about bringing Albania into a wider Federation comprising

Yugoslavia, Bulgaria and Albania. Tito's right-hand man, and later nemesis, Milovan Djilas recalls in his *'Conversations with Stalin'* that the Soviet leader, over a characteristically lavish, six-hour dinner, rudely suggested that Yugoslavia just 'swallow' Albania. This to the apparent consternation of Djilas who felt that the problematic presence of a compact Albanian region inside Yugoslavia (Kosovo!) could only be resolved by creating a Yugoslav–Albanian Federation of equals that would also do justice to the distinct 'Albanian identity'. Nothing came of this, of course, as Tito and Hoxha were soon to pursue their separate socialist paths following Yugoslavia's break with the Soviet Union and withdrawal from the Warsaw Pact in 1948. Djilas remained concerned about the problem of Kosovo: 'a millstone around the neck of Serbia'. He considered its resolution a prerequisite for achieving the democracy in Serbia that he had championed since his *New Class* denunciation of the communist regime.

With the stress on 'unity and brotherhood' in the new, socialist Yugoslavia, there was the implicit recognition of the need for improved ethnic relations. There was official acknowledgement of the rights of Albanians, albeit as a 'minority' in the strongly centralist, Serb-dominated Federation. On the ground in Kosovo the situation did not change, however, at least not in the first twenty post-war years. Kosovo policies in Belgrade were then largely run by the notorious Minister of Interior and Chief of the Military and Secret Police, Alexandar Rankovic, a Stalinist *pur sang* whose ideological outlook left little room for Kosovo Albanian aspirations. The push to Turkey, for example, through active persuasion or more forcefully, continued on his watch to the tune of, reportedly, well over 100,000. Ethnic Albanians in Kosovo generally felt like second-class citizens and were regular targets of police investigations and harassment. Among the many who were arrested on charges of anti-State activities was Adem Demaci, then a young writer with Marxist–Leninist ideas. He would end up spending, altogether, twenty-eight years in prison – without losing his basically humanistic outlook and conciliatory approach, which earned him the honorific reputation of Kosovo's Nelson Mandela.[4]

After Rankovic was finally sacked in 1966, things brightened somewhat in Kosovo. Tito – himself half Croat, half Slovenian, and wary of Great Serbianism – had already embarked on a policy of greater devolution of powers to the constituent parts of the Federation. A revision of the constitution in 1974 upgraded Kosovo to a Socialist Autonomous Region (together with the similarly new, autonomous region of the Vojvodina). The new status implied virtual equivalence to other constituent republics of Yugoslavia except for the right to secede. Despite this upgrading, anti-Albanian feelings never really waned. Neither did anti-Serbian feelings among the Kosovo Albanians. Tito's death in 1980 spelled the end of the multiethnic 'unity and brotherhood' ideal. Nationalist tendencies became stronger and more vocal throughout the Federation, with unscrupulous leaders such as Franjo Tudjman in Croatia whipping up separatist sentiments. In Kosovo, huge demonstrations took place in 1981, by workers and students clamouring for full Republic status (and the release of political prisoners, including Adem Demaci). There was a ruthless clampdown by the Serbian police, followed by excessively severe jail terms for the organizers. It was a turning point in so far as it led to more radicalization on the Kosovo Albanian side and an increase in the harassment of Kosovo Serbs, which, in turn, brought on harsher rule with constant (threats of) arrests and detentions. It is estimated that, roughly, every fourth Kosovo Albanian was at one time or another taken in by the police for questioning and/or detention.

A critical event was the appearance of the Memorandum of the Serbian Academy of Sciences and Arts, in late 1986. A highly nationalistic document,[5] it lamented the disadvantaged position of large numbers of Serbs living in various republics of Yugoslavia. It deplored the fact that the 'Serb nation' was the only one in Yugoslavia that did not have 'its own state'. This curious observation had to do with the fact that large clusters of Serbs lived outside Serbia in other republics, notably Croatia, Bosnia and Herzegovina and Montenegro. It even referred to the 'genocide' of Serbs in Kosovo where their share of the population had steadily declined to 15 per cent (against a steady rise of the Kosovo Albanian population, from 67 per cent in 1961 to 78 per cent in 1981). This SANU Memorandum was widely endorsed in Serbia. It provided fuel for the nationalist wave that Slobodan Milosevic rode on his way to power. As mentioned earlier, he ended Kosovo's political and cultural autonomy in 1990, which led to years of apartheid, resistance, armed rebellion and, ultimately, the horrors of ethnic cleansing and war.

Given this background of mutual enmity and violence and the more recent history of humiliation and crimes against humanity, one cannot be surprised about the feelings of resentment and revenge. The horrendous ethnic cleansing that preceded, and accelerated during, the 1999 war could not but have left a deeply traumatic impact on the Kosovo Albanians. Practically every one of them had been affected. Responding with violence was seen by many as a matter of retributive justice. Understanding human nature, however, does not mean condoning indiscriminate, retaliatory acts of violence against innocent victims. Even less so under an international, UN-sponsored administration that was established and justified on humanitarian grounds, to protect human rights and dignity. International law simply does not sanction the biblical 'tooth for a tooth, eye for an eye'. For the international civil servants in Kosovo it was not always comfortable to square empathy with past suffering and injustices, with outrage over the incessant acts of revenge.

Reactions by the Kosovo Albanian leadership to the vengeful, ethnic violence were always 'politically correct'. I have heard not only Rugova, Thaci, Qosja and Demaci but also former KLA commanders such as Agim Ceku and Ramush Haradinaj repeatedly expressing concern, making public statements of condemnation and appealing for reconciliation and peaceful coexistence. As such, they dutifully responded to the admonitions of prominent international visitors such as UN Secretary General Kofi Annan, the EU High Representative Javier Solana and a host of foreign ministers and other dignitaries who made their obligatory stop in Pristina. Nevertheless, the question remains whether these Kosovo Albanian leaders could not have been more forceful and compelling in reining in the feelings of hate, vengeance and greed.[6]

This seems to be especially true for the leaders of the KLA/ Provisional Government of Kosovo (PGoK), given their clout with the militant following that was so often implicated in the ethnic and other crimes. Were they themselves involved in some of these criminal acts? Or did they simply lack the prior knowledge – or moral courage – to prevent them? My own take is that the leaders at the top echelons found themselves in a very ambivalent position. On the one hand, they needed to maintain credibility with their followers and cater to their militancy. They could not be seen to be hapless puppets on international strings. On the other hand, to be credible to the internationals they had to act responsibly and openly condemn the human rights violations. In other words, they were caught between a rock and a hard place. And so they acted like the mythological, two-faced Janus of ancient Rome, showing a conciliatory side to the internationals and a militant one to their constituents. Their uncomfortable predicament was not made easier by the fact that the KLA had never been a tightly controlled, top-down movement, but, rather, a loosely structured association of locally operating, armed groups. This limited their ability to control events on the ground. To which should be added the prevailing climate of impunity that contributed to the lawlessness. All these factors combined give me reason to reject accusations that ethnic crimes committed in this period are directly attributable to the top PGoK/KLA leaders. Nonetheless, even if innocent in action, they could still be guilty of inaction, as the International Crisis Group put it. In retrospect, I do wonder whether a more determined stand on the part of these leaders could have helped to reduce the ethnic violence and the resulting exodus. But then again, I ask, how many Nelson Mandelas are there in this world? And who is he, in Western Europe or elsewhere, to cast the first stone? As I shall argue later on, a different political premise underlying the international intervention – notably a clearly marked path to independence – might well have motivated the Kosovo Albanian leaders to discourage the ethnic violence more resolutely and effectively.

International shortcomings

Of course, the lack of effective, official law enforcement was a crucial factor in the widespread lawlessness. In the absence of justice, revenge goes unpunished – which brings up the other contributing factor of the 'ethnic revenge': the international shortcomings. To be fair, the basic parameters of the international administration of Kosovo should be recognized. Restoring stability and normalcy in a war-torn society is a formidable task under any circumstances but in Kosovo the UN had a singularly difficult situation to cope with. It had to literally start from scratch. The Serbian provincial government had collapsed and disappeared, with no trained Kosovo Albanian replacement available. Over a million refugees and internally displaced persons were returning en masse in a matter of weeks and months to often abandoned and destroyed locations. The whole rule of law system – police, prosecution, courts – had imploded. In this institutional–administrative desert the UN had to embark on the task of actually governing, something it had never done before. In other words, the conditions for bringing about effective law enforcement and governance could not have been worse. Unless the international community was prepared to overwhelm the place with an army of civilian administrators, police and judges, as well as massive funds, no early return to law and order was realistically possible. As it turned out, Kosovo was already to receive more per capita international assistance than any UN intervention had provided before and after. And yet, when I arrived to build up the OSCE Presence, there were only a handful of UN staff on the ground, with Sergio Viera de Melo as first SRSG. When Bernard Kouchner took over from him by mid-July, the whole UN contingent could barely fill a modest-size auditorium.

The recruitment and deployment of UN administrators took many months to reach the minimum required levels. This was also true for the crucial area of law enforcement where the absence of an adequately sized and equipped police corps was, of course, critical. While the OSCE made a much lauded effort to begin rebuilding a domestic police corps, also from scratch, this was going to take years. In the meantime, law and order was supposed to be maintained by a UN international police force, with initial help from KFOR although the latter was, of course, a military force not prepared for police tasks. This international police force took painstakingly long in forming and then often with international officers who were ill-prepared for the local circumstances. Their time of duty was also limited, as they were subject to frequent rotations. I remember well-intentioned Sven Frederiksen, the international police chief, complaining more than once that he had received a batch of policemen from faraway countries whose knowledge of English and of the use of firearms was very limited at best. The force never reached the required level. I often made the telling comparison between the UNMIK police force of 2000 and the 20,000 that the British deployed in Northern Ireland to contain ethnic strife. The same sorry tale applied to the judiciary. Grooming new judges was going to take time, while bringing in judges from donor countries was cumbersome, slow and often controversial. It is hard to see how the international community could impose the rule of law under such shabby conditions. The fact that over a six-month period the numbers of ethnic murders declined from fifty per week to about three had certainly also to do with the reduction of targets following the steady exodus of Kosovo Serbs and other non-Albanians to Serbia or protected enclaves.

To conclude, in the first six months after the war the prospect of peaceful, multiethnic coexistence was severely compromised by the fact that the Kosovo Albanians lacked a resolute moral leadership while the international community could not rise to the occasion because of political, financial and human resource constraints. The continuing ethnic violence illustrates the difficulty if not near-impossibility of creating inclusive self-government – as per UN Resolution 1244 – in an ethnically divided, war-torn society. With the wisdom of hindsight it seems to me that the ethnic violence in the early phase of Kosovo's reconstruction could have been avoided only if the enforcement of law and order had been the *absolutely overriding first priority of both the domestic leadership and the international presence, civilian and military*. It is obvious that this was not the case. While such a total, single-issue commitment was not even realistically possible given all the other tasks at hand, I nonetheless would argue that law enforcement could have been given far higher priority all around – with considerable mitigating impact. Unfortunately, the Kosovo case is not unique in this regard. In fact, when we indulge in an admittedly dubious exercise of comparing international interventions in situations of civil strife and ethnic rivalry worldwide (Ruanda, Afghanistan, Iraq, Libya, South Sudan, Syria and the list goes on), post-war Kosovo compares favourably in terms of (far less) human and material losses.

Natural hatred?

Habitual comments suggest a 'born enmity' between Serbs and Albanians as an explanation for the mutual violence. They point to the virtual absence of intermarriage between the two communities, unlike in the relations between Serbs and Croats or Bosniaks (Muslim Slavs). It is also true that both Serbs and Albanians, certainly in their interrelationship, are very identity focused, stressing their distinctive traditions, language and religion. Serb nationhood is intricately linked with the orthodox church, while a proverbial saying holds that 'the only religion of Albanians is Albanianism'. Serbs display their national motto SSSS wherever they can ('Samo Sloga Serbina Spasava = Solely Unity Saves the Serb). All Albanians identify with the double-eagled national flag of Albania (going back all the way to Skanderbeg, a born and later reconverted Christian). They refer to each other in pejorative terms: Shiptare for Albanians, Shka for Serbs. I recall the story that mild-natured Bajram Kosumi, the later-prominent politician, told me. As a student leader he was arrested in the wave of protests in 1981 and given a jail term of fifteen years. Imprisoned in Nish he befriended a former Serbian partisan, after talking him out of suicide. The old patriot told Kosumi that during the long partisan struggle for freedom and dignity, it had never occurred to him and his comrades that these ideals should also apply to the Kosovo Albanians. He then mentioned how from his early childhood he had always been told – by his mother and by his teachers – that Albanians were 'the bad people'. The negative perception is common, reciprocal and deep-rooted. According to Ismail Kadare, 'it will be hard to find in world history two peoples (nations) who harbor as deep-rooted and ineradicable a hatred as the one between the Serbs and the Albanians'[7].

While passed-on stories and a long history of strife may seem to lend credence to the theory of 'born enemies', it is, of course, fundamentally incorrect. As President Obama used to paraphrase the famous sentence of his icon, Nelson Mandela: 'No one is born to hate anyone on the basis of his racial, ethnic or economic background.' History has proven, over and over again, that atavistic, antagonistic feelings are evoked when people are made to think and speak in terms of 'us ' and 'them', of communities and minorities as single entities, of collective wrongdoings – and deal with 'them' accordingly, indiscriminately – no matter whether 'they' are Jews, Blacks, Muslims, Albanians or Serbs. It takes an enlightened leadership to defuse such mass bias, resentment and, at its worst, hysteria. The Balkans saw little of this in the past and, unfortunately, in recent times. In fact, the opposite is true. The earlier disintegration of Yugoslavia had much to do with leaders – civic and religious

– in Croatia, in Bosnia and in Serbia stirring up rather than containing ethnic bigotry. Warren Zimmerman, US ambassador in Belgrade during Milosevic's presidency, refers in this connection to the 'criminal inculcation of children and young adults in racial hostility'. Media and public education did – and still do – very little to correct the perceptions and prejudices. To the present day, Belgrade tabloids peddle in hate-mongering vis-à-vis Kosovo Albanians on an almost daily basis. Much more so, I should note impartially, than what one may find in the kiosks of Pristina – or Tirana, for that matter. I remember how stunned I was during a football match in Belgrade's Partizan stadium – twenty years after the war – to watch a large crowd of young fans jumping up from their seats while yelling 'Ko ne sak, je Siptar' (who does not jump, is a Shiptar). They acted probably more in ignorance than hatred but still it was quite telling and demeaning.

Competition for space and jobs may well have been real in certain locations, but that by itself cannot explain the intensity of the ethnic friction. There had, in fact, been a longtime trend of Serbs migrating out of Kosovo – the poorest region of Yugoslavia. It had led to the official but not very successful policy before and after World War II to repopulate Kosovo with Serbs and encourage or force Kosovo Albanians to migrate, with ethnic cleansing as the ultimate, tragic option. The theory of 'born hatred' is also refuted by enough instances of good neighbourly relations between individual Serbs and Albanians in Kosovo. As a personification of such a truly multiethnic spirit I could mention Bekim Fehmiu, the internationally famous actor of Kosovo Albanian extraction but a true 'supranational' whose fame throughout the region and wider Europe reached iconic proportions. Tellingly, he abruptly walked off the stage in Belgrade in 1987 in protest over the hate-mongering and poor treatment of the Albanians by the Yugoslav government. He never went back to stage or film and remained silent for fifteen years until the publication of his perceptive autobiography, *Blistavo I Strasno* (Brilliant and Awful).

Clearly, what was quite possible at the individual level – peaceful coexistence if not friendship – was not raised to the collective level. I recall telling many a Kosovo Albanian leader after the war that the remaining Serb population – hardly exceeding 5 per cent of the population – could not possibly pose a threat politically, economically or otherwise. Hence, I suggested, there was a unique, risk-free opportunity to act like true statesmen and earn the respect of the whole world by forcefully insisting on reconciliation and peaceful co-citizenship. The meek response was usually that they were powerless and had very little control over the pent-up feelings of retaliation after so many years of discrimination and humiliation. Yet, the Kosovo Albanian and Kosovo Serb leaders immediately after the war had started off well with a joint declaration stating that 'there is no such thing as born hatred among the people of Kosovo' and that 'peace cannot be built on revenge'. Like on the proverbial road to hell, there were the best of intentions initially ...

International callousness

The tragedy of the expulsion of Kosovo Serbs, and Roma, did not end with their displacement. Many of them continued to face real hardship after arrival in Serbia. They joined the well over 200,000 Internally Displaced Persons (IDPs) from the earlier wars in Croatia and Bosnia. Together, they could not count on much international sympathy although the vast majority of them were innocent by-standers deprived of property and livelihood. The 'international community' was distinctly less concerned with their plight than it had been before with the Kosovo Albanians displaced by the war. Considering the overall picture, the displaced Serbs may well have been the least acknowledged casualties of the Yugoslavian wars. Serbia conveniently blames the foreign powers – EU/US/NATO – for their plight. The inconvenient truth is, of course, that they are victims of misguided policies – first and foremost of Milosevic, but also of his chauvinist counterparts inside Yugoslavia and of an incoherent, hesitant European Union on the outside. Whatever the blame game, the international callousness and systemic neglect of this displaced population are discriminatory and shameful. They have undoubtedly contributed to a deep-seated, collective sense of victimization in Serbia, and to anti-Western and revanchist sentiments. This probably also accounts for the unhelpful if not obstructionist policies of Serbian governments towards Kosovo ever since.

Notes

1 Andrew Herscher and Andreas Riedmayer, *The Destruction of Cultural Heritage in Kosovo, 1998-1999: a Post-War Survey*. Cambridge: Kosovo Cultural Heritage Survey, 2001.

2 Cubrilovic had been part of the group of young, nationalist conspirators of which Gabriel Principe became the most (in)famous member: his assassination of Archduke Franz of Austria triggered World War I. Cubrilovic himself returned to prominence after World War II as minister of agriculture under Tito.

3 And rounding up 281 Jews in Pristina for deportation to the death camps: 'the most shameful episode of Kosovo's wartime history' according to Noel Malcolm in his classic 'Kosovo, A Short History'.

4 Interestingly, Demaci had at one point adopted a notion similar to Djilas' concept of a Yugoslav–Albanian Federation. Finally freed in 1990, he initially advocated the idea of 'Balkania', a federation of three equal states Serbia, Kosovo and Montenegro. In his view this offered the only way to avoid war. How equal such states were to be could be questioned given their differences in size and levels of development. The idea was soon overtaken by reality when in the course of the political strife of the 1990s the dispute over Kosovo's status grew ever-more-polarized and ethnically charged.

5 Not surprising, judging from its membership that included the infamous Cubrilovic as well as Dobritsa Cosic, the ultranationalist ally of Rankovic and the writer who coined the saying that 'Serbs are victors in war and losers in peace'. Cosic would later have a stint as president of the FRY in 1993.

6 In this connection it is pertinent to note that Ramush Haradinaj had two brothers – Luan and Shkelzen – killed in the war, while Hashim Thaci lost some forty in-law family members and related kin in the Izbica massacre (of March 1999) and had his native village (Buroje in Drenica region) erased.

7 In the introduction to Rexhep Qosja's 'Death and the Naked Eye'.

4

International protectorate I
Starting from scratch

Organizing the government

Immediately after the end of the war that came with the adoption of UN Resolution 1244 of 12 June 1999, the most involved international agencies started to send down people to make a beginning with the setting up of organizational structures. The general system of governance had already been agreed upon by all the main players. The international government was to be under the supervision of the UN with four agencies (called 'Pillars') responsible for the operations: the UN itself for civil administration, the EU for reconstruction and the economy, the OSCE for institution building, elections, human rights and media, and the UNHCR for the return of refugees and internally displaced. Under the overall guidance of the special representative of the Secretary General of the UN (SRSG) – who was supported by a principal deputy SRSG – each of these four pillars of government was headed by a deputy SRSG. Together they formed the Executive Council, which was to meet almost daily. As such this was a more effective set-up than seen before in Bosnia and Herzegovina where agencies had been notoriously operating in isolation and on their own terms. There still was considerable room for each Pillar to pursue its own policies and priorities, but in areas of overlap the formal structure provided for useful feedback and impulse. For example, the OSCE Pillar – the third Pillar, known as the OSCE Mission in Kosovo (OMIK) – worked closely together with the UNHCR (fourth Pillar) in producing periodic 'minority reports' calling attention to the harsh circumstances of the ethnic minorities. Similarly, OMIK was to work closely with the second UN pillar for civil administration when compiling voters' lists for elections.

As the incoming Head of OMIK (and DSRSG) I had already arrived for a first exploratory visit on 17 June. I had flown to Skopje from Vienna, where I had attended the OSCE Permanent Council meeting establishing the new Mission. In Skopje I met up with Ismije Beshiri, my political adviser, who had come in by jeep from Tirana. She was to join me in my new assignment, again as the indispensable right hand. At the border with Kosovo we had to negotiate our entry with the Serbian border guards who were still in place. We stayed only briefly in Pristina in a very gloomy Grand Hotel – speaking of misnomers! – where not so long ago the likes of Arkan, the notorious militia leader, had conspired over coffee. After a quick reconnaissance and inventory of what could be inherited from the dissolved Kosovo Verification Mission I returned to Albania, to officially take charge of the Mission in Kosovo as of 1 July.

In the first weeks and months after the end of the war, internationals from many different countries descended upon Pristina to give shape to the international rule. What they found was a place in shambles. Kosovo had basically imploded. There were no working institutions to build on. The administrative capacity at the centre and in provincial towns was gone with the departure of the Serbian governing class. The economy had ground to a halt, with production capacities idled and jobs few and far between. Many communal buildings such as schools, clinics, but also mosques and cultural sites had been destroyed. The housing stock had been severely damaged, with some villages and neighbourhoods completely razed. In rural areas livestock had been killed and wells contaminated. Added to this came the chaos of hundreds of thousands of returning refugees and displaced persons, with tens of thousands Kosovo Serbs fleeing to Serbia or mainly Serb-inhabited areas and enclaves inside Kosovo. An atmosphere of lawlessness and impunity prevailed, since the police and judiciary system had collapsed. Ethnic violence was a daily occurrence. Moving around had to be in the protective company of bodyguards. As a simple Dutchman I could not quite demand, as head of

Mission, the security detail of my American KVM predecessor – an armoured vehicle, armed bodyguards and four drivers – but this was more than compensated by the incredible dedication and skills of the two drivers (Burim and Ardian, driving an ordinary but reliable Pajero) and two bodyguards (Leci and Dugi, without side arms) who would stay with me throughout my tenure – and remain friends ever after.

The Kosovo social and political landscape was also very much in disarray. There was, of course, the perilous position of the minorities – first and foremost the Kosovo Serbs – who feared for their future without Belgrade's protective presence. There were also sharp divisions between the political forces. In fact, no less than four domestic 'government structures' claimed legitimacy and vied for a prominent role in the post-war governance: the old Serbian provincial government of Kosovo, the 'shadow' presidency of the LDK-leader Ibrahim Rugova, the LDK-related government-in-exile under Bujar Bukoshi and the KLA's provisional government of Kosovo (PGoK) headed by Hashim Thaci. Of these only the PGoK actually exercised local control through its KLA units that had filled the security vacuum. UN Resolution 1244 Kosovo stipulated, however, that Kosovo was to be ruled by one *international* interim administration. So, while we internationals were setting up new government structures, we made it clear that there was no room for competing domestic governments but that key politicians and personalities would, of course, be amply consulted.

The Serbian provincial government, headed by 'Governor' Zoran Andjelkovic, was little more than a phantom institution since it was without practical authority and effective powers. When the Norwegian OSCE Chairman, Knut Vollebaeck, made a visit to Pristina in early July and had Andjelkovic included in his schedule of meetings, I could convince him to drop the idea. Rightly so because within days the governor was recalled to Belgrade and unceremoniously gone, never to return. In contrast, the Rugova presidency was certainly a factor to be reckoned with. Tragically, his prominent and widely respected deputy, Fehmi Agami, also a Rambouillet veteran, had been cowardly murdered in the war after being taken off a deportation train to Macedonia. The 'shadow' president himself was still in exile in Rome. There was, however, a large and faithful LDK-following in Kosovo itself. Rugova had been 're-elected', as the only presidential candidate, in unofficial elections in March 1998 that were boycotted by the KLA and other parties because of the warlike conditions after the Jashari murders. The third 'government' demanding to be taken into account, was the LDK-linked government-in-exile, led by Bukoshi from Germany. It led a quite separate existence, as its relationship to Rugova was tenuous at best (during all of my subsequent time with Rugova, I have never heard him refer to the Bukoshi government once). It did have clout, though, because of its strong links with the diaspora from which it had been collecting considerable funds over the years through a voluntary 3 per cent self-tax. It was a dispute over the allocation of these funds that had led, in 1995, to a rift between Rugova and Bukoshi. Still, Bukoshi was among the five LDK-linked delegates in Rambouillet.

And then there was government number four: the KLA-led provisional government of Kosovo (PGoK), which claimed precedence over all others because of its successful armed resistance and leadership role in the Rambouillet talks. The PGoK had originally been envisaged as a united government by an agreement with Rugova, Qosja, Thaci and Surroi in Paris at the time of Rambouillet. After outbreak of the war Thaci went ahead to formally create the PGoK in early April 1999, much at the prodding of Madeleine Albright. She had told him – over a satellite phone while he was up on the Pastrik mountain in the southern war zone – that the outside world needed 'an address' to communicate with. It was around the time that Rugova was coerced to visit Belgrade and signed an anti-war 'agreement' (2 April). Although seats were reserved for the LDK in the new PGoK, Rugova refused to join because he 'did not agree with the military methods of the KLA'. Since Bukoshi also did not agree with this 'rival' government, the seats of the LDK in the cabinet remained vacant. The PGoK did include non-KLA cabinet members, mainly from its junior but influential partner, the LBD. As mentioned earlier, this LBD was a multiparty coalition, created in November 1998 and headed by Rexhep Qosja, the author who had gained prominence as one of Kosovo's foremost intellectuals. The main constituent party of this coalition was the Parliamentary Party of Kosovo (PPK). Its lead man Bajram Kosumi became the minister for information. Among other LBD cabinet members were Mehmet Hajrizi (deputy prime minister) and Hydajet Hyseni (deputy foreign minister), who had left the LDK a year earlier with other dissidents. Like Kosumi they were both ex-political prisoners who had served ten-year terms after arrest during the student protests in 1981.

The Parliamentary Party had been an interesting 'third party' in between LDK and KLA. It had been founded in 1990 by Veton Surroi (who left in 1992) as a democratic but more activist alternative to Rugova's passive, pacifist approach. Among its early, leading personalities were other prominent figures such as the aforementioned Kosumi (who became its president in 1993), Bajram Kelmendi (respected human rights lawyer, brutally murdered with his two sons during the 1999 war) and Vjosa Dobruna (paediatrician and human rights activist). The venerated human rights champion Adem Demaci was handed the PPK presidency in 1996. Like the KLA, the PPK did not recognize the parallel elections of March 1998 that re-elected Rugova as president (and an LDK-dominated parliament that was never to meet in session). Demaci moved on to become KLA's political frontman in mid-1998. With Kosumi back in the Chair, the PPK joined Qosja's new LBD coalition later that year.

All of these main Kosovo Albanian political forces – LDK presidency, LDK government-in-exile, KLA and LBD – had been partners in Rambouillet. By the end of the war there was, however, little mutual trust and respect. Rugova had lost his credibility because of his visit to Belgrade – and handshake with Milosevic. He had not yet returned from his self-exile in Rome. As regards Bukoshi, he had been quite inimical to the KLA before the war, while trying to organize a competing resistance force, the FARK. He had publicly spoken dismissively of the KLA and had criticized Thaci for setting up the 'rival' PGoK (and Albania's President Meidani for recognizing it). Here, too, there was little love lost the other way around. I remember Thaci complaining bitterly about Bukoshi withholding the considerable funds collected from the diaspora. When in the aftermath of the war, hundreds of Serb houses in the Prizren area were plundered and burned, Thaci at one point tried to put the blame on FARK members, mostly expatriate volunteers, who had been based in northern Albania. (By an agreement with the Albanian government, FARK fighters, several hundred-strong, had to leave that country after 18 June 1999.) The interparty divisions also showed in the links to Albanian politics. Rugova and Bukoshi were supported by Berisha's Democrats, Thaci and Qosha by the then ruling Socialists.

There had been early attempts to bridge the divide between the main Kosovo Albanian actors. In late May 1999, with the end of the war in sight, President Meidani and Prime Minister Majko of Albania had tried to organize an all-Kosovo Albanian political platform in Tirana – with backing from the US and opposition leader Berisha. Thaci and Qosja had agreed with the idea of a National Security Council, representing all Kosovo Albanians. Rugova, however, refused to join. He also declined a later invitation to come to Tirana. It was clear that in his perception the Albanian government was biased in favour of the KLA/PGoK. The mighty US took over the initiative and Madeleine Albright herself brought together Rugova, Thaci and Qosja in Bonn in Germany on 8 June. At Qosja's request, my political adviser Ismije joined to provide a helping hand with interpretation. The occasion was a crucial G-8 meeting in neighbouring Cologne where the upcoming UN Resolution 1244 was being negotiated. The Kosovo Albanians would have an opportunity to respond to the draft. In reality, the main result of their get-together was that the three key political personalities were back on speaking terms. On 1244 they had no substantive comments, probably in the knowledge that anyway higher powers than them would decide on Kosovo's near future ...

KLA dominance

There was no doubt that on the ground the KLA/PGoK was by far the dominant factor. They had also taken pre-emptive control in areas outside their traditional base while the international rule was still in its formative stage. Local commanders and others acting on behalf of the KLA/PGoK (or claiming to do so) filled the administrative and security void by installing their own people. These could be former municipal employees (from before 1990 when they had been purged), but just as well self-appointed newcomers from their own ranks. KLA policing units acted to enforce their interpretation of law and order. And behind the scenes a KLA secret service (Sherbimi Informativ I Kosova, SHIK) conducted its non-transparent business in consolidating local political and economic control. The international response to this power grab was one of reluctant acquiescence. On the one hand, we had to acknowledge that the KLA/PGoK did provide a semblance of the needed local order and administration. On the other hand, there was reason for concern about the abuse of power and heavy-handed tactics by some of the self-styled, local bosses and policing units. The human rights officers of OMIK, familiar with the areas from their KVM times, reported with disturbing frequency instances of thuggish behaviour and intimidation – always involving men, never women! – directed against not only Serbs and other minorities but also Kosovo Albanians of different (political) inclinations.

There were instances when the abuse transgressed into serious human rights violations, including abductions and murder. They were covered in our periodic human rights reports, with the most serious ones documented in Volume II of *Kosovo As Seen, As Told*. While many of these early crimes remained outside the reach of the law, some notorious cases were prosecuted, albeit with great delay and often with great difficulty. A few of them led to convictions, others ended in acquittals because the judges deemed individual culpability not proven. Some dramatic assassinations in the early post-war months were later revealed – but also disputed – to have been the work of SHIK. A notorious case in point is the murder of Rexhep Luci, a municipal architect who tried to block illegal construction in the Germije park, Pristina's favourite 'green lung'. What this murder also made clear was that much abuse of power was driven by sheer greed. As so often in post-war unsettled situations, the climate of impunity was seen by some as a licence for plunder and theft. It also facilitated self-enrichment through the monopolization of scarce resources such as fuel, cigarettes and drugs. It was only from January 2000 onwards, when irregular governing structures were formally disbanded, that the UN pillar for civil administration began to gain control at the municipal level. Unofficial policing by self-styled PGoK units, and no doubt SHIK machinations, continued well into 2000, however, while the informal power networks and illegal economic activities became too entrenched to be effectively countered for many years to come – if at all.

Starting international governance

Given the general post-war disarray, it was obvious that setting up international governance would be a truly Herculean task. The first one tasked with making a start and one of the first international arrivals – in early June 1999 at the heels of KFOR troops – was Sergio Viera de Melo, a Brazilian national who had been appointed special representative of the UN Secretary General (SRSG). I had come to know him in earlier years in Cambodia – after the fall of the infamous Pol Pot regime – as a very competent UNICEF official. Over improvised dinners at his apartment in Pristina, a stone's throw from Rugova's still uninhabited residence, we discussed with a handful of new colleagues the challenges to organizing the huge tasks at hand. He was, however, to leave Kosovo within a month because the UN needed his considerable skills in East Timor when that former Portuguese colony was recoiling from Indonesian occupation. It faced a similar situation as Kosovo in that it required an interim international administration. Tragically, Sergio was one of the victims of a horrific blast in 2004 that destroyed the UN headquarters in Baghdad, where again he was serving as a UN SRSG in post-war reconstruction: another indirect casualty of disastrous American warmongering. His successor in Pristina was Bernard Kouchner, clearly more the well-known politician and human rights activist than an administrator but whose dedication to the cause was never in doubt. With him I built up a good and cordial working relationship. (So much so that, at the end of his term in January 2001, he stopped his departing plane on the runway in order to step out and give me a farewell hug after he had spotted me arriving late to say goodbye.) Unknown to either of us at the time, we had shared a rebellious episode in 1968 during the Paris student revolt. When that tumult broke out, I had been quick to jump into my old Citroen 2CV to drive to Paris – at a frustratingly slow maximum speed – and join the youthful, anti-establishment crowd.

Among Sergio's first acts, within days of his arrival and jointly with the idiosyncratic KFOR Commander, Michael Jackson, was an emergency meeting with Kosovo leaders, Serb and Albanian, to address the deteriorating security situation. The participation was reflective of the political landscape at the time: on the Kosovo Albanian side, it had the LDK (Kole Berisha in the absence of Rugova), the LBD (Rexhep Qosja), the KLA/PGoK (Hashim Thaci) and journalist Blerim Shala as an 'independent'; on the Kosovo Serb side, it had Bishop Artemije (Radosavijevic) and Father Sava (Janjic) representing the Orthodox Church, and Dushan Ristic and Momcilo Trajkovic as civic leaders. The meeting lasted no less than seven hours, including breaks, and concluded with a signed document that stated that 'peace can only be built on justice, not on revenge' and that 'the road to reconciliation will be long and difficult, (but) there is no such thing as a natural hatred among the people of Kosovo'. It 'condemned the crimes of the Milosevic regime' and asked for the Kosovo Albanian prisoners who had been transferred to prisons in Serbia just before the end of the war (an estimated 1,800) to be handed over to UNMIK. Presenting the statement in a joint press conference, Trajkovic expressed 'deep and sincere regrets' about what had happened to Kosovo Albanians – a remarkable, first acknowledgement of wrongdoing from an (semi-) official Kosovo Serb side. Thaci, in turn, said that he was 'disturbed by so many Serbs leaving the province' and that he was 'not interested in a militarized society'. The joint statement was later read by Thaci and Father Sava and broadcasted over the radio several times in the next few days. Not surprisingly, it was not appreciated in Milosevic's Belgrade. Unfortunately, also inside Kosovo this encouraging, positive statement was not to have the effect that was intended and hoped for.

A key question of discussion in those early days was how to ensure adequate, representative input in governance from the Kosovar side as a first step on the long path towards 'provisional institutions for self-government'. Sergio de Melo made a first beginning by suggesting the Kosovo Transitional Council (KTC). It was to be an advisory body consisting of political, civic and religious leaders. Initially, the Serbs indicated their unwillingness to participate as long as 'the terror against Serbs is not visibly reduced'. By the time of its creation in mid-July, roughly a month after the peace agreement, almost 60,000 Kosovo Serbs had already moved out and registered for assistance in Serbia, according to the Yugoslav Red Cross. In comparison, by that same time, ten times that number of Kosovo Albanian refugees (some

600,000) had made their spontaneous return to Kosovo. The LDK also showed hesitation to take up its seat, as it did not agree with the formula. It had argued, in vain, for reinforcement of its representation in the KTC by the small, allied parties in the LDK-dominated, but basically defunct 'shadow' parliament of 1998. These included the Christian Democratic Party, the Liberal Party and the Social Democrat Party. When the KTC formally met for the first time – on 16 July, under the chairmanship of the newly arrived Bernard Kouchner – the LDK abstained but the Serbs did attend. The LDK was, of course, still without Rugova, who, returning from exile, had made quite a triumphant entry into Pristina the day before, but had departed again that very same day, to everyone's surprise. Many years later I was told that he had been receiving death threats, which might explain his unexpected, quick departure. Rugova did not return permanently before the 3 August.

Meant to be a sounding board, the KTC was little more than a talk show. It did enhance the profile of its more vocal members, though. It also gave a much needed wider audience to the Serb representatives. Their interventions were impeccably translated into English by Lazar Stojanovic – a much lauded Serbian filmmaker fiercely critical of the Milosevic regime and, in later days in Serbia, a much-maligned defender of the international intervention, and NATO, in Kosovo. The Kosovo Serb participation was not a certainty, however, as at times they felt compelled to withdraw when ethnic violence against them had flared up unacceptably. They had started to boycott the KTC already in late July after the Gracko massacre, mentioned before. The KTC meeting of 25 August was, in fact, the first time that all political factions, and all key leaders, were present. The Kosovo Serb side (Bishop Artemije and Momcilo Trajkovic) used that occasion to present their cantonization concept – local autonomy for Serb-majority areas – that they would persistently push throughout the following years. I recall from that meeting that Veton Surroi voiced strong objections while Hashim Thaci refused to even discuss the idea. The KTC was later expanded to include more parties and more women; it remained in place until the first Kosovo-wide elections, in November 2001, when it had to yield to a more representative body: the first democratically elected parliament.

To provide a sense of the early days. I reproduce the entries in my diary from 28 July to 4 August*:

Diary Pristina: 28 July–4 August 1999

In the first formative weeks of the international presence, many newcomers were settling in and trying to find their way around Pristina. A host of international organizations, governmental and non-governmental, were moving in, keen to be part of the reshaping of a whole society. A massive search (and competition) was on for interpreters, translators and local assistants in general. Drivers and security staff were in urgent demand. Procurement of even the simplest of supplies was a common challenge. The frontier mentality was tangible and, in fact, quite enjoyed by many of the self-proclaimed pioneers, especially in the evenings over a beer – the commodity that somehow never seemed to be scarce.

Wednesday (July 28)

Today was a day that could have filled a week. With a deep sigh at the end why a man does this to himself – and his family. It did start off well, though: there was water and electricity in Pristina. The morning ritual at the office, with latest news and announcements, remains a good beginning of the working day. More important was the next meeting, of the Interim Administrative Council (the Executive Committee of the United Nations Mission in Kosovo), consisting of the UN Special Representative Kouchner and his five Deputies including myself. A Latin-Anglosaxon quintet that has grown quite comfortable with each other, after initial uneasiness.

There is concern about the aftermath of the Gracko massacre and about the lack of manpower and means to effectively work with the UCK and political parties. In the follow-up meeting with OSCE staff it starts to dawn on me that we are becoming a strong team, with a good mix of nationalities and a decent male-female ratio.

The good news of the day is that Mirjana – our soft-spoken, vegetarian, homeopathic (if not homeopathetic) Francaise – has succeeded in getting a new Radio Pristina in the air – in keeping with my commitment to Kouchner – in spite of all scepticism. That she annoyed some male egos in UNMIK and KFOR in the process, we would take in stride.

---

*Translated from Dutch, as it appeared in the newspaper NRC, 10 August 1999.

After dealing with various visitors, I departed for Gracko to attend the funeral of the 14 slain Serbian peasants. Just in time I realised that the Albanian driver should be replaced by his Serb colleague. At the cemetery emotional scenes. A lot of wailing, a lot of bitterness, and a plethora of accusations against KFOR and UNMIK. My appeal to break the cycle of violence rings hollow. I drink and sprinkle some raki, take a cube of sugar, press hands, mutter condolences. The crowd of journalists, with cameras and satellite discs, is relentless.

Back in the office, UCK leader Thaci makes an unexpected appearance for a one-on-one conversation in less than perfect German. He has to get something off his chest. After him more visitors, among whom old acquaintances from Albania who want to invest in Kosovo. They offer me half an estate for my past services in Albania and, I may safely presume, for giving them preferential treatment in Kosovo. I don't understand them, of course, and give high praise to the virtues of competition and enlightened entrepreneurship.

During cocktails at my French political advisor's I encounter well-known Kosovars, among whom the jovial, former government leader Bakalli ('I was a communist but no Stalin or Hoxha'). It remains a miracle that we are all together in this composition in Pristina. Two months ago this would have been unimaginable.

Thursday

Pristina is in a mess. Medlin Olbrajt (they spell phonetically here) is coming to visit. The three newspapers that are available for free thanks to support from abroad, carry the news big time. In one of them, Kosovo Sot, I also happen to come across the news that (football trainer) Louis van Gaal had signed a lucrative contract with Barcelona. Here they have other priorities, although a friendly soccer match might do a lot of good. Maybe I should organize a match between Thaci's UCK and Rugova's LDK. In Albania such a match between political rivals – in which I was officiating as referee – had been a great success and the beginning of a political dialogue.

The meeting with Albright is short and forceful. Rugova is conspicuously absent, something not appreciated even within his own circles.

With the courageous journalist and legal scholar, Blerim Reka, I discuss plans for a School of Journalism as well as a Legal Centre. In the evening dinner with two 'Ministers' of Thaci's 'Provisional Government'. One had served ten years in prison, the other – one of the early UCK leaders – had been convicted to 20 years imprisonment but had managed to remain at large. A young man but marked by his trials. They protested the international distrust of their movement. We have always fought against the (Milosevic') regime, we have always been anti-

communist, we have fought alongside NATO, we participate constructively in the Kosovo Council (advisory to UNMIK), why do we receive less credit than those who, at best, stood by the wayside, they lament. I try to explain.

A late evening interview with two Reuters reporters completes the day. The candle has again burned at both ends. We have to slow down, I tell myself.

Friday

Early rise in order to explore a new jogging route. We run to a largely deserted Serbian town, protected by British KFOR paratroops. Sadly isolated. Destroyed or burned houses of Albanians on the way offer an equally depressing testimony to what has been happening before. It reminds me of the macabre ghost villages in the Croatian Kraijna region and the razed areas in Bosnia. It is incomprehensible how for the third time Serbian leaders have triggered ethnic violence. Hopefully, today's Sarajevo summit will be an historic turning point and, through the Stabilisation Pact, create so much mutual dependence and common good that primitive ethnic strife will be a thing of the past once and for all.

The rest of the day is spent on meetings, visitors from here and there and another surprise visit by a UCK leader in search of understanding and advice. The LDK calls to announce that Rugova is about to arrive for a meeting.

In the evening dinner with a colleague from my UN days who brings latest news and gossip from New York. Stories about professional jealousy and self-promotion that are not particularly uplifting. From the OSCE restaurant on the top, ninth floor we look down over Pristina, a provincial copy of Sarajevo, with red-tiled roofs and no high-rises. The picturesque sight is spoiled by the smoke from new house burnings.

Saturday

A sleepless night, for the first time since long. Best remedy is to go for a healthy long run. The number of joggers is growing steadily. We run through a large, green area outside the town up to a hotel that had been the headquarters of Serbian paramilitary and police, but now lies in ruins because of a Nato raid. A target of precision bombing just like the telecommunication center in the middle of the town.

Later in the morning a frank discussion with Sven, the chief of the UN police. His good news is that a new contingent of policemen has joined his force. The bad news is that they do not know English nor how to handle weapons. Not exactly what he needs to enforce law and order.

In the afternoon consultations with KFOR about current affairs. In passing I ask them to please remove the wreck of a burnt out car in front of the house of Rexhep Qosja, the 'Abraham Lincoln' of Kosovo, as he had been described by the US State department. With his beard and stern looks, but also his towering moral authority, a striking likeness indeed.

At four o'clock fatigue strikes and I steal an hour from work to rest at home listening to Paganini's duets for violin and guitar. Already three years without a real vacation and now a seven days working week, this job is no joke.

The evening brings all of Pristina's youth to life. In the car-free main street hundreds of youth are strolling up and down. Cafés and terraces are crowded as if there had never been a war. But minority groups are sitting at home, anxiously waiting if the night will bring new tragedy. Complaints about anonymous threats and intimidation keep coming in. Feelings of revenge, whether or not accompanied by motives of greed, are not easily contained. What happened to the promise of a 'robust' international police force?

Sunday

I mount my mountain bike and ride out of Pristine, followed by my chauffeured car. A rather redundant security requirement, I think. I ride past an industrial complex in ruins. I avoid a few craters in the road, result of bombing. Somewhat further a red ribbon indicates danger of mines, but on the hard surface I ride without risks. In the fields people are working. A group of peasants is encouraging a clumsy bull to provide a cow with new life. Surely proof of new confidence in the future!

Somewhere along the route I see 22 freshly dug graves in rows. Probably reburied corpses from a mass grave. New evidence of mass murder is still being found. This does not help our appeals for reconciliation. After an hour I stop for Ruski Caj, Russian tea, and return to Pristina.

In the afternoon a conversation with Rugova at his home. He seems relaxed since his return from his self-sought exile in Rome. So is our talk. He promises the best of cooperation and shows me his collection of stones.

A subsequent discussion on the terrace of the Grand Hotel, that has become anything but 'grand'. A political meeting place. The manager joins. Two months ago he was a refugee in Macedonia, deeply troubled. Now full of plans for the future. He is going to restore two other decrepit hotels.

The nearby stadium hosts a benefit concert. Patriotic songs fill the air. Like so many other places, the stadium used to be taboo for the Albanians. To them the war means the end of discriminatory 'apartheid'.

Monday

I woke up early because of the rotating power of two helicopters that for some unclear reason keep circling above my roof. The evening before had seen an attack on the orthodox church that is still under construction. Opposite my place live three elderly Montenegrin women who have not dared to go outside for weeks and only open the door to special knocking signals.

I find time to call home in the Netherlands. I exhort son Gilles in Amsterdam to try to finish his studies before the end of the century. It is about time that he frees himself from the paralyzing hold of Amsterdam's inner-city. The misguided self-satisfaction of Amsterdam is not helpful to rolling up one's sleeves. I also call Foreign Affairs in The Hague, but everyone is on leave, travelling or attending seminars.

Tuesday

There are problems in the town of Gjilane. The Roma quarters have been reduced to rubble. They, the Roma, are accused of collaboration with SerbIa and most of them have fled the town. It is more likely that they had had been forced to aid and abet, for instance with the digging of mass graves. We listen to stories of fires, abductions and murders. The UCK denies to have had a hand in this; nevertheless they seem to condone such acts of revenge.

On the other hand, we also hear of Serbian raids from across the nearby border, and of hundreds of Albanians being pushed from there into Kosovo. Ethnic cleansing on both sides. We drive by a Russian KFOR checkpoint and are treated professionally. On the way back we stop at a 14th century monastery in Gracanica. I had been looking forward to visiting this place for years, but find the exterior disfigured by large glass panels. The orthodox monasteries of Pec and Decani are more beautifully situated, in better original state and richer in frescoes.

Again a working dinner to end the day, in mixed company. The South Europeans drink wine, the Northerners beer and a Kosovar mixes wine and cola.

Wednesday, August 4

Today we assemble all Non-Governmental Organisations, both real and phony. The electricity fails us again, but a new generator keeps the computers running. And again there is some good news. Foreign Affairs in The Hague

> has agreed to my request for more staff. Three new members. Not quite the package that my American predecessor availed of, eight bodyguards, two armored cars with drivers and a team of personal assistants, but that was rather excessive.
>
> The electricity does not come back and we are going to have a very dark Pristina at night. Candles are needed for dinner, also in the street. Helicopters skim over town like flying torches. I stumble home and need matches to find my door, the keyhole and my way inside the house. The screen of my laptop – on battery – is the only other source of light. I end this diary in the dark.

OMIK and law enforcement

Within our OMIK Pillar the prime tasks were clearly defined: building democratic institutions, monitoring human rights, promoting a pluralistic media climate and preparing for elections. But first we had to build up our organization and develop the field office structure. Fortunately, we could recruit many of the former KVM staff – minus the 'intelligent' ones who were directly reporting to their own capitals. This gave us a head start in the provincial towns. Because of their early deployment the OSCE field officers were quite a help to the UN pillar in identifying local individuals who could serve in municipal government and other public functions. It took many months, though, before the UN effectively replaced the self-styled power structures that had taken charge of the local situations.

One of the first priorities we in OMIK tried to address concerned the general climate of lawlessness that was causing so much agony among the non-Albanian Kosovars as well as dismay among the internationals and well-meaning Kosovo Albanians. With the old order gone and the new one still to be established, law and order was sorely lacking. The old police force, largely Serb and Serbian-led, had, of course, lost its credibility and disappeared. A new Kosovo Police Service (KPS) needed to be created alongside the UNMIK police force that was supposed to meet the initial policing needs. The urgency was pressing as donor countries were slow in contributing officers to the international force. To their credit the Americans, among all donors, were pushing the hardest for us to start building up this new domestic police. They also put their money where their mouth was and so we could move with unusual speed to find a location (a former Serbian police school in Vushtrri/Vucitrn, some 20 kilometres north of Pristina), renovate the premises, buy equipment and other necessities and recruit instructors. Already by mid-July we had sent out forms for application, to which no less than 18,000 responded. By early September the school was up and running.

Much credit is due to the first director of the school, Steve Bennet, who combined great professionalism with a true missionary spirit. Thanks to him, it was possible to implement an enrolment policy that was almost revolutionary. We had decided that the force should be multiethnic, so from the very beginning we made it a point to recruit Kosovo Serbs and other minorities along with a majority of Albanian Kosovars. Also, we felt that the future corps would benefit from a substantial proportion of female recruits: we aimed at 20 per cent as an initial target. It was not easy to convince the Kosovo Albanian leaders about this objective. I remember Rugova expressing serious doubts to me about enlisting women in the force. In his mild-mannered way he was usually agreeable to international initiatives, but this time he objected that 'it is not in accordance with our culture'. I convinced him to give it a try. History proved us right. In later years, the policewomen were generally regarded as among the best of officers. They greatly contributed to the good reputation of KPS that was built up over the years.

At the first graduation ceremony in mid-October Kouchner and I proudly presented certificates to the first 173 students, among whom sixteen were of non-Albanian ethnicity (eight Serbs, three Turks, three Roma, three Goranis). Quite unprecedented, almost 20 per cent of them were female. There was an awkward moment when the class leader – a likeable ex-KLA commander with obvious natural authority, known by his *nomme de guerre* Leka – invited Thaci, who had made an unexpected appearance, to say a few words as 'the prime minister of Kosovo'. Fortunately, it did not detract from the joyous atmosphere, as he sensed our uneasiness and kept it short and politically correct. The school continued to become a veritable success story. It became a preferred destination for visiting dignitaries. I remember how I had my first flight in a Black Hawk helicopter in the presence of NATO's Supreme Commander for

Europe, Wesley Clark, and three US senators. Among them was John Turner, best known as the ex-husband of film diva Elizabeth Taylor, and Nighthorse Campbell, mainly remembered for his American Indian name. They had come to inspect the school and left duly impressed.

One telling early story recounts how a group of police school cadets were confronted in the street by Kosovo Albanians. They were, ominously, asked to identify the Serbs among them. The answer was powerful: 'there are no Serbs or Albanians among us, we are all Kosovars'. End of confrontation. Over time the Kosovo Police Force succeeded in effectively replacing the international police. Many years hence, when speaking to Kosovars in and outside Kosovo, I was always reminded of the great job the OSCE had done in building this new police force. It has scored consistently high in opinion polls about trust in government institutions. No wonder then, that the KPS served as a model for similar attempts elsewhere to develop a multiethnic police force in an ethnically sensitive environment, for example in the southern Serbian area of Preshevo where Serbs and Albanians lived in tenuous coexistence. International law enforcement experts seem to agree that the Kosovo Police Force developed into probably the best of its kind in the Balkan region, in terms of discipline, incorruptibility and popular respect. It has been justly considered a 'jewel in the crown' – if we can speak of a crown – of the international legacy in Kosovo.

While the police-building efforts were underway, other law enforcement challenges required attention. The judiciary system had fallen into total disrepute. Serbian legislation was challenged but could, of course, not be overhauled or adapted quickly. The question of what constituted 'applicable law' (the pre-war legislation of 1999 or the pre-apartheid legislation of 1989) became a very problematic issue, It set off fiery discussions, inconsistent rulings and protests as well as boycotts and resignations by judges from earlier times. There were very few judges of non-Albanian ethnicity left who were willing to serve in the unclear judicial circumstances. Making an unfavourable ruling, especially in an ethnically loaded case, was likely to lead to threats to life and property. The UN, having the responsibility in this field, tried to cope with this challenge by bringing in legislative advice from abroad and judges from donor countries to assist the courts. In OMIK we did what we could to assist in selecting and (sort of) vetting judges, both new and old, and helping mobile courts to function outside the capital. In due course we helped to set up a Kosovo Law Centre for judicial advice and support as well as a Judicial Institute for research and training.

It took many months to clarify the legal premises, but the whole system remained flawed and widely distrusted. Differing from OMIK's approach in building the domestic police corps, the UN chose to rely on a pool of judges and prosecutors from pre-1990 times, many of whom had very little credibility with the public. Gaining popular respect and support turned out to be an arduous process. Even fifteen years after the war there was still widespread doubt among the population about the objectivity and fairness of the courts. Unlike in the case of the Kosovo Police, allegations of arbitrariness, nepotism, corruption and political interference remained rampant.

The bad reputation of the justice system was among the reasons, besides witness protection, to establish, in 2016, the special Court Chamber for War Crimes in The Hague rather than in Kosovo. An unfortunate decision, in my view, as it would be much more persuasive – and educational – to have war crimes prosecuted and judged – with international involvement – in all transparency and objectivity in Kosovo itself. Placing the Court outside Kosovo and only targeting Kosovo Albanian suspects added fuel to the popular perception that this was a court of foreigners going after their war heroes (and helping leftovers from the earlier Yugoslav Tribunal, the ICTY, also in The Hague, to a cosy job). With adequate resources and prominent backing it should have been possible to convince the population of the necessity and possibility of dealing with all war crimes fairly, whatever the ethnicity of the perpetrators. As I mentioned earlier (page 67) this Court Chamber was established on rather dubious grounds. I suspect that it was at least partly established in order to compensate for the anti-Serb bias of the ICTY – as perceived not only in Serbia but also by many impartial observers, including me.[1] In Dutch this would be called, very appropriately, an act of '*vervangende schaamte*' ('shame substitution').

With regard to an Ombudsman institution, the task was, of course, infinitely easier. This was an OSCE initiative, supported by the Council of Europe, which found ready approval all around. No one objected to an institutional check against administrative neglect or abuse. Nevertheless, the incubation time took longer than anticipated because of a legal tussle with the UN in New York. In November 2000 the Institution took off to a flying start once it was properly staffed. Finding the right ombudsman was an initial problem, as the person had to be widely acceptable. I argued for the appointment of Vjosa Dobruna, the outspoken paediatrician-cum-human rights activist, also for gender reasons. At the time it was one bridge too far, however, although she was to serve in other high government capacities and in due course ended up as Kosovo's ambassador in The Hague. Instead, a Polish legal expert, Marek Novicki, was appointed, partly for the reason that he, being of Slavic background, would be in a better position to address ethnically motivated abuse of power. Although completely new to Kosovo society, the Ombudsman institution developed well over time. Some fifteen years later I could personally assist in the celebration of its viability and decent record of public service.

Demilitarization

A special security issue that required early attention was the demilitarization of the KLA, as had been agreed in Rambouillet. There were up to 15,000 KLA fighters that had to be re-integrated in society. The dismantling of the KLA was to take place in three months. A huge challenge because there were strong feelings and expectations that the KLA could be transformed into some sort of a Kosovo national defence force. Given the extreme post-war sensitivities and uncertainty about Kosovo's future status, this was, of course, out of question. Only KFOR was entrusted with the mandate to defend the borders and maintain overall security. A Kosovo army would be interpreted as a major step towards independence, was internationally unacceptable and hence not negotiable. The KLA leadership nevertheless tried hard to push for an army-like structure. They were under strong pressure from their militant following who felt they had the right to continue their military role in an official capacity. Both Thaci and Ceku had always hinted in meetings with them that they would constitute the core of a future Kosovo army. When they came up with a detailed plan to that effect, it was resolutely dismissed by SRSG Kouchner and KFOR commander Jackson in a highly charged, emotional meeting. The positions were so far apart that afterwards Kouchner intimated in an offhand comment: 'We are no friends anymore.' Any reference to 'army', 'defence' or 'military' was rejected. What was offered, instead of a national defence force, was a much less ambitious 'emergency corps', to respond to natural disasters, to assist in crowd control, etc. This Kosovo Protection Corps – KPC or TMK in the Albanian abbreviation – was to consist of no more than 3,000 active members, with 2,000 on standby. It was to be only lightly armed and not to be deployed at the border.

It was a bitter pill to swallow for both the political leaders and the military commanders of the KLA. Their position was truly awkward. On the one hand, they had to deliver to the international rulers (UNMIK and KFOR) in order to remain relevant and stay on workable terms, while on the other hand they had to maintain their credibility with their former soldiers. The predicament was obvious from the different tone they struck when addressing their following – militantly – and when they talked to us internationals – reasonably. It did not help, of course, that there were hardly any employment opportunities to offer by way of compensation. Much to their credit, Thaci and Ceku did yield and 'sold' the formula without causing any serious rebellion. I felt – then and now – that they deserved a lot more credit for this major achievement than they received. After all, they succeeded in a demobilization process that in many other post-war situations around the world had resulted in serious strife if not new armed conflict. We in OMIK felt the urgency of the matter when we were pressured to accept a large quota of former KLA fighters into the Police School for absorption in the Kosovo Police. We could, however, keep this inflow down to manageable numbers and as much as possible in line with the entry requirements.

The scaling down of the self-proclaimed Liberation Army to a small, semi-military force was hurtful and disheartening to many former KLA fighters. This probably was another factor that contributed to the wave of rancorous acts in the post-war months. As mentioned earlier, the OSCE monitors reported many human rights violations by men in KLA uniform and/or with KLA insignia. KLA leaders denied any personal responsibility and blamed 'rogue elements'. Several of these 'rogue elements' were pretty high-ranked, though. I remember that I was asked to mediate after an altercation between the British military and the KLA/PGoK 'Minister of Public Order', Rexhep Selimi. During the reconciliation meeting with General Jackson and Thaci, the latter forced Selimi to come and apologize for his thuggish behaviour. On the other hand, it also happened on several occasions that local KLA commanders assisted in undoing criminal activity such as abduction of an alleged 'collaborator' or threats against Serbs. This by itself proved that the lines between perpetrators and higher level commanders could be short. Which comes as no surprise, of course, given the size of Kosovo's territory and the closely knit ties between clans and families. So, while the crimes may have been 'rogue', there certainly was occasional awareness if not collusion at higher levels. In other words, there were options to intervene. This is why, after a spate of house burnings in Prizren, I called in Sylejman Selimi – another prominent commander substituting for Agim Ceku – to strongly object to the lax attitude towards presumed KLA-involvement. His response was remarkably subdued as if, indeed, they were guilty of inaction. Whether or not by coincidence, a then ongoing abduction case in Rahovec/Orahovac was suddenly resolved ...

By the middle of September the KLA came to its formal termination when agreement was reached on mandate and size of the KPC. Agim Ceku became the KPC commander, and Ramush Haradinaj, an early and popular KLA commander from the Gjakova region, became one of his deputies. Both would later take turns as prime minister of Kosovo. The transformation did not yet spell the end of all 'rogue elements' as some KPC members were subsequently linked to delinquent acts, both past and current. For example, the regional commander of the Llap region, Rrustem Mustafa, known as 'commander Remi', was sentenced in 2007 to four years in prison for human rights violations committed in a KLA detention camp during the war. He was also rumoured to have used his position, after the war, to acquire a dominant share in petrol distribution. Similarly, Sami Lustaku, a KLA commander from the first hour and subsequent KPC regional commander in the Drenica region, was known for his roguish and defiant behaviour. He was later, in 2008, convicted for assault but with little consequence because soon thereafter he was re-elected as mayor. Most intriguing is maybe the case of Sylejman Selimi. An original member of the KLA Drenica group (to which Thaci had also belonged), he volunteered to be KLA's chief commander for a few months before Ceku took over in the beginning of the war. He became one of the three ceputy Commanders of the KPC. In 2011 he was appointed Kosovo's Ambassador in Tirana. In 2015, however, he was found guilty of war crimes committed in 1998–1999 in a KLA detention centre in Drenica and sentenced to eight years' imprisonment. After a review by the Supreme Court in June 2018 he was released on probation in January 2019 … to be appointed adviser to the then prime minister Ramush Haradinaj (only to be released soon thereafter, under international pressure).

Against the disquieting reports about individual misconduct of ex-KLA fighters, real and alleged, two major incidents stick out where former commanders-turned-KPC frontmen played a critical, constructive role. The first one concerned a convoy of buses transporting 160 Kosovo Serbs to Montenegro, towards the end of October. Half of the convoy made a wrong turn in Peja/Pec and ended up in the centre of the town. They were soon surrounded and attacked by a hostile crowd of Kosovo Albanians. The Dutch KFOR escort managed to extract the buses from the crowd and guide them to a nearby Italian KFOR compound. The crowd followed and laid siege. It was then that two former commanders, Ethen Ceku and Daut Haradinaj (brother of Ramush), showed up and convinced the crowd to disperse. The convoy continued its way in the middle of the night and reached Montenegro in safety.

The other event was the 'March on Mitrovica', in December, organized with the support of all Kosovo Albanian parties and soon swelling into a huge nationalistic demonstration (nearly 100,000 participants) with strong anti-Serbian and sometimes even anti-KFOR/UNMIK overtones. The purpose of the march was to tell the world that Kosovo's territory included the area north of the river Ibar, mainly inhabited and controlled by the Serbs, with UNMIK having very little say. Their notorious 'bridge watchers' were blocking entry at the northern side, while French KFOR troops remained stationed at the southern end. The mood of the demonstrators was militant and the atmosphere grew very tense as they were nearing the bridge. Teargas was being used to stop them in their tracks, while armed bridge watchers were readying themselves to meet the oncoming crowd with fire power. At the height of the tension, KPC commander Ceku stepped to the plate at the urgent request of Kouchner and addressed the crowd. Together they convinced the demonstrators to end the march before the bridge and go home with a 'moral' victory rather than losing all credit and international support by engaging in violent confrontation.

Media development

With the country in a post-war shambles, it was, of course, crucial that the population had access to reasonably dependable information about current happenings, developments, challenges and policies. Hence, there was a sense of urgency to get the media back in shape. While the printed press resurfaced rapidly thanks to private initiative, with or without support from abroad, the electronic media required a great deal more of governmental attention. Not only were relatively large investments needed, but the use of the airwaves also needed official regulation. It quickly turned out that there were competing interests and ideologies at play. We in OMIK – responsible for media development – felt strongly that Kosovo would benefit from an independent, public broadcaster, not beholden to commercial and/or political interests and serving all Kosovars, including minorities. Radio Television Pristina, fully Serbianized after 1990, had, of course, been abandoned by the end of the war, so there was an opportunity to build a new broadcasting entity, a 'Kosovo BBC' as I used to suggest wishfully.

With the financial, technical and managerial help of the European Broadcasting Union – a union of European public broadcasting companies, headquartered in Geneva, Switzerland – we made a beginning to revamp the RTP on a new footing and under the name of RTK (Radio Television Kosovo). We found a temporary new location (the old premises were in disrepair) and I successfully appealed to an old diplomat friend in Norway, Kim Traavik, to raise the necessary extra funds for the new venture. The Norwegian government made an early, generous monetary donation ($1 million), local journalists were recruited and on 19 September 1999 the first transmission of an initial two hours-a-day programme took place. When financial restraints threatened its continuation a few months later, I found the Dutch willing to support the venture with an additional $ 2.5 million, while still later my fundraising trip to Tokyo landed a massive Japanese gift of (Japanese) equipment.

We had made sure that there was also a Serbian-language component in order to make clear that the RTK would cater to all Kosovars. It was not easy to find Serbs to act as news presenters. Our first Serbian speaker on the program happened to be a half-African Serb, which did not go well with the Serb viewers. Generally, things went well, though, with RTK. By the end of the year it moved into the former RTV Pristina studios, after their complete refurbishment. *Tout le monde* was there to nod approvingly when I welcomed them with an emphatic plea to keep RTK free from political interference and become a truly independent public broadcaster, a 'Kosovo BBC'. Within a year it had expanded its TV programme to four hours a day and also included broadcasts in Turkish. As we shall see later on, by fall 2001 RTK was standing on its own feet, formally established by an UNMIK broadcasting regulation as a public broadcaster, with an independent board of directors, and almost fully 'Kosovarized'. 'Kosovarization' was a useful catch-all concept that I had used from the very beginning to define the process of handing over ownership and management to Kosovars rather than holding on to international management.

I took great personal interest in the fortunes of RTK. A key issue turned out to be, predictably, the financing of this new public venture. At the advice of the EBU a modest licence fee was introduced, to be included in the electricity bills. This funding modality remained a moot issue, with many people objecting to what had been a free service in the past. Collection remained difficult and in later years had to be abandoned when it was declared to be unconstitutional in court. Funding of the RTK was then made part of the Kosovo Government budget. This made the financing more reliable but also exposed RTK to governmental control. Under government funding, the board of directors became more politicized with its members now chosen by parliament and representing major political parties. As a result, the RTK developed into a state broadcaster rather than a 'Kosovo BBC' as originally envisaged. It did steadily expand its transmissions, though, both in time and geographical reach and remained widely watched. Its more politicized character became unhappily clear, however, in its covering of a serious ethnic incident in Mitrovica when it whipped up nationalist, anti-Serb sentiments and contributed to the ugly riots of 2004.

While trying to build the public broadcaster, we met with stiff opposition from two sides. Firstly, and surprisingly, there was the United Nations. It thought it should start a UN Radio, called Blue Sky, to provide the public with news and information – and, in the process, explain and promote the international rule. I had a basic problem with this. We had seen how after the Bosnia conflict a UN-run radio in Sarajevo had not been a success. I felt that here also a UN radio station would be seen as a government mouthpiece rather than an authentic Kosovo broadcaster. It did not meet the test of 'Kosovarization'. Granted, the management of the RTK was also foreign, but it was a Kosovar institution with the explicit intent that management would be handed over as soon as technically and financially possible and politically feasible. I recall some heated exchanges on our different approaches with Kouchner and his public information chief, Nadia Younes, who was in all other respects a marvellous professional. She also fell victim to that horrifying bomb attack on the UN building in Baghdad, along with Sergio de Melo and others who had served in the Kosovo Mission. Among them was also Fiona Watson who had been a superb staff member of the OMIK. They were among the finest of the '*guerriers de la paix*', peace soldiers, as Kouchner appropriately called them later.

Blue Sky started radio broadcasting in October, as a separate UN media outlet. Redundant in my view, as we had already a functioning public broadcaster with RTK Radio. The internal rivalry – and duplication of money and energy – did not last very long. In 2000 Blue Sky was fully absorbed by RTK. More lasting and fundamental was the ideological divide we had with the Americans who as a matter of principle did not believe in public broadcasting. We were under strong pressure from them to give way to the private sector. In line with their ideological preference, the Americans lavishly sponsored private media enterprise and poured money in Koha Vision and TV21. The first one was created by the owner and chief editor of the newspaper Koha Ditore, Veton Surroi. He already had a proud record as an independent journalist, in Serbian times. As mentioned earlier, it was he who showed great courage when writing, two months after the war, a scathing piece condemning revenge acts against Kosovo Serbs. With his fluent English and sophistication, he remained a favourite among the internationals, both resident and visiting. More so, in fact, than among his countrymen, as evidenced later when he started a political party and unsuccessfully ran for president. On media policy I had some differences with Veton. He demanded, for instance, access to the old RTP premises while I basically held that this part of the public realm should not be appropriated by private ventures. Similarly, we disagreed with him – and, of course, the Americans – over our policy to let RTK supplement its uncertain and meagre public income with commercials, albeit on a very limited scale. And there was the sensitive issue of 'hate speech' and what to do or not to do about it. Here we internationals – arguing for some (self-)constraint – clashed with some journalists, including Surroi, as we shall see later when the issue led to serious confrontations in 2000.

TV21 made its start in the old, shabby high-rise building of the defunct Relindja newspaper, which we as OMIK tried to transform into a multipurpose Media House. It was run by Aferdita Sarqini in the simplest of circumstances, with just a few bare offices. A very enterprising lady, she also benefited from the American generosity that came with their ideological preferences in media development. Over the years her TV station developed into a very large and successful venture. Another journalist who found accommodation in the Media House, equally modest, was Blerim Shala. He ran Zeri, a daily newspaper more or less on par with Koha Ditore. I respected him greatly for his professional and personal integrity and independence. Always serious and never opportunistic, he had been politically active as well. He had been sympathetic to the 'third way' Parliamentary Party of Kosovo and had participated in the Rambouillet talks. Later he sold his newspaper and became a parliamentarian for a new 'third way' political formation, the Alliance for the Future of Kosovo (AAK). Other noteworthy, colourful and independent-minded journalists/writers in those early days were Baton Haxhiu (the outspoken Koha Ditore editor who much later also struck it rich with a TV empire of his own), Shkelzen Maliqi (who contributed prolifically to intellectual debate, also in junction with oppositional, progressive Serbs in Belgrade) and Dukagjin Gorani (another stalwart Koha Ditore journalist who also parted ways and later ventured into politics).

The UNMIK/OMIK media policy touched raw nerves where it came to ethical standards and sanctions in case of misconduct. Given the interethnic sensitivities and the risks associated with 'hate speech', internationals were deeply divided over the need for central oversight and sanctions. The United States, spurred on by American non-governmental media organizations such as Freedom House, was adamant about wanting to prohibit any semblance of government interference. The Europeans, on the other hand, were generally more mindful of the harm that wilful misinformation and hate-mongering could afflict. We in the OSCE, among others, pleaded for self-regulation and self-discipline by the media sector itself, on the basis of a jointly agreed code of conduct. In order to engage the Kosovo journalists and receive their feedback, we had created a Media Advisory Board with the former communist, but moderate, and widely respected politician Mahmut Bakalli in the Chair. This Board, in fact, had advised against the separate UN Blue Sky radio and had spoken out in favour of an Ethics Code for journalists. With help from the international Soros Foundation – always ready to support initiatives towards a more 'Open Society' – we organized a major conference in mid-October 1999 with international and local journalists and media experts. It called for an Association of Journalists and the drafting of a Code of Conduct.

The need for some self-control was obvious given the charged interethnic climate and the risks posed by inflammatory articles and hate speech. I remembered how years before, when heading a World Food Programme team in Ruanda, I had witnessed the devastating impact of hateful radio transmissions. As is well known, they had contributed to the genocidal Hutu terror over the minority Tutsi population, which left one million people dead. The Code of Conduct was supposed to discourage deliberate harm being inflicted on vulnerable persons and groups such as ethnic minorities. Its relevance was seen as even more pertinent since there were not yet any legal provisions for seeking recourse in court, which in normal circumstances is the appropriate procedure. We were sharply criticized by international purists who saw any code of conduct initiative as a serious threat to freedom of expression. We received a letter from the (American) World Press Freedom Committee, generally condemning OSCE's 'media control system'. I thought these responses misguided, as they completely ignored the special circumstances of interethnic conflict and violence in which the press operated in Kosovo at the time. They also ignored the fact that the code was not to be imposed from above but to be drafted and implemented by the most affected (Kosovo) professionals themselves. The issue was anything but theoretical as we were soon to see.

Political parties and civil society

From the very start of our international rule, the idea was – as per UN Resolution 1244 – to establish 'institutions for democratic and autonomous self-government'. That implied the organization of elections and creating a climate for political parties to compete for the popular vote. The latter was easy as the role of OMIK was simply one of facilitation. A few parties still had some infrastructure from before the war to build on, notably the LDK. There were also many newcomers, however. In order to provide some sort of a level playing field, we decided to establish Political Party Service Centres in several towns where aspiring parties were provided with office space and equipment as well as basic materials on party formation, democratic principles, political outreach, election procedures, etc. In a similar fashion we also set up NGO Resource Centres, with communications and meeting facilities, to enable the numerous NGOs to better establish themselves. Both initiatives were meant to give an initial boost to grassroots developments within the civil society. While many of these 'hundred flowers' – to quote Mao – never grew to bloom, the notion of popular participation and advocacy definitely gained ground through these efforts. The Norwegian OSCE chairman-in-office opened the first political service centre in Pristina, in mid-October. No less than thirteen parties and one coalition proudly took possession of their offices and equipment. They used the occasion right away to advocate the case for greater participation in government and for shared responsibility rather than mere consultations.

Obviously, everyone was interested to see how the KLA would enter the political arena. As mentioned earlier, it had been gradually built up in the beginning of the 1990s in the western regions of Kosovo by local strongmen in Kosovo such as Adem Jashari, the later resistance hero. It developed, more or less, as the armed wing of the Popular Movement for the Republic of Kosovo (LPRK) founded abroad by ex-students of Pristina University in Switzerland in 1982, renamed LPK in 1987. With the help of expatriate fundraising, 'Homeland Calling', the KLA had steadily gained strength to become an entity in its own right. The increased hostilities on the ground, with the massacre of the Jashari family in March 1998 as a tragic nadir, brought international attention. Its recognition received a boost when Demaci became its new general political representative. When he opted out of Rambouillet, Thaci as the political director took over the lead. In this capacity he had headed the Kosovo Albanian delegation during the negotiations in Rambouillet and, in its wake, had formed the provisional government of Kosovo (PGoK) in early April.

In the process the original LPK had been eclipsed. One of its early leaders, Bardhyl Mahmuti – together with other former KLA or LPK members such as Jakup Krasniqi and Pleurat Sejdiu – tried to revamp the LPK into a regular party immediately after the war. Under the name United Democratic Party it called on people to 'Think of the Future, Not Forget the War'. The initiative was not endorsed by Thaci who was still busy asserting himself as head of the PGoK and who was also involved in difficult negotiations with KFOR and UNMIK over the demilitarization of the KLA. By the first of October 1999, however, they were all ready to bundle forces and agreed to form a new party, as the political successor to the dissolved KLA. It so happened that I had scheduled a meeting with Thaci together with Ismije when this new party was being formalized. When considering possible names, I made the point that since Kosovo was not yet a true democracy, the party could best be presented as a harbinger of democracy. And thus the new party was named Party for Democratic Progress of Kosovo (PPDK), with Thaci as leader, Mahmuti as deputy and Jakup Krasniqi (also member of the PGoK) as general secretary. Half a year later the party was renamed Democratic Party of Kosovo (PDK), surely more for reason of easier use than to mark the democratic progress already achieved …

Kosovo Serbs representation

On the Serb side, the political organization in Kosovo had remained very much like it had been before the war, reflecting the national Serbian political spectrum with Milosevic's Socialist Party of Serbia, the Social Democrats of Zoran Djindjic and Boris Tadic, and the ultranationalists of Vojislav Sesjel all vying for prime position. With democratic elections still far off, the most urgent task now was to establish for the remaining Kosovo Serbs a representative body that could promote their cause with UNMIK and KFOR. The problem here was the different interests of the Serbs north and south of the Ibar, the river that divides the northern town of Mitrovica. The north was adjoining Serbia proper, inhabited overwhelmingly by Serbs and maintaining close ties to Belgrade, which continued to provide administrative and material support. South of the Ibar in Kosovo's mainland, the Serbs were clustered in enclaves, surrounded by Kosovo Albanians and heavily dependent on the international administration for security and support. Belgrade's long arm reached even here through the paying of pensions and various services. It was obvious, though, that the southern Serbs had a greater stake in coming to terms with their Kosovo Albanian neighbours and the international government than the northern Serbs.

The division within the Kosovo Serb community was reflected in their relationship to UNMIK and KFOR. In Kosovo's mainland, the leadership, headed by Bishop Artemije, with the sophisticated and articulate Father Sava as his right hand, and on the civilian side by Momcilo Trajkovic, showed an early preparedness to enter into dialogue. They participated in the Kosovo Transitional Council. They had their centre in Gracanica, not far from Pristina and the location of a beautiful orthodox church and monastery where the bishop and his 'cyber monk' Sava resided. At every visit to this place I made sure to have time to walk around and inside the fourteenth-century building. Unfortunately, large glass panels somewhat detracted from its external beauty, but the frescoes inside were as magnificent as those in the famous monasteries of Pec and Decanica.

The Kosovo Serbs north of the Ibar had a very different mindset. They were uncompromising in their rejection of the new reality. With backing from Belgrade they prevented UNMIK from taking effective control in the north and de facto ran a parallel administration. It had not helped, of course, that KFOR had not firmly secured the territory up to the northern border with Serbia immediately after the end of the war. The irresolute French troops assigned to the area and facing fierce Serb hostility, stayed put in south Mitrovica, basically leaving the northern area in the hands of the local Serbs. The latter would stay their own course, quite opposed to the more cooperative approach of Bishop Artemije and civic leaders in the South. One of the most articulate northern leaders was Oliver Ivanovic. Besides being a sophisticated private sector man (and karate champion), he was a likeable person who spoke fluent Albanian, which made him an unusually interesting interlocutor all around. However suave he was as a speaker, his stance was pretty hard-line, certainly in the beginning of the international rule. He did not favour participation in the KTC – they never took up the seat reserved for the northern Serbs – and did not really acknowledge UNMIK's authority in the north. Politically he was strongly anti-Milosevic, however, and allied with the Democratic Opposition in Belgrade.

I saw Oliver Ivanovic regularly, also in later years when he had joined the Social Democrat Government of Boris Tadic in Belgrade to deal with Kosovo issues. He remained committed to the Serb cause in Kosovo and was a popular figure in Mitrovica as was obvious when I was walking with him in the street. At one point, in 2014, he was arrested in Mitrovica, for alleged war crimes, on the instigation of an overzealous EU prosecutor. I thought it a very poorly timed, if not ill-advised, move to go against one of the few respectable, northern Kosovo Serbs who were interested in coming to terms with the government in Pristina and the international overlords. He was sentenced to jail for nine years in 2016, but the guilty verdict was annulled on appeal one year later. His political vision was one of a strongly autonomous Serbian community within an independent Kosovo. In that respect he clashed with right-wing Belgrade politicians and more radical leaders of the Serb community in north Kosovo such as Marko Jaksic and Milan Ivanovic. He was assassinated in January 2018. I happened to have shared coffee with him just a fortnight before. He told me at the time that he was concerned about Belgrade's political pressure and intimidation tactics to eliminate him politically. I have no doubt that the murderers should be found among Serbian extremist/criminal groups. For the Albanians there would be absolutely nothing to gain from his demise as he was basically prepared to reach accommodation with Pristina, over the objections from Belgrade.

Kosovar participation in government

With the post-war dust slowly settling, new institutions emerging, the KLA demilitarized and transformed into KPC, and the international government generally gaining traction, it became time by the end of September to make a beginning with the institutions of self-government as foreseen by the UN Resolution. The logical option was to expand the executive council of SRSG and Deputies, the international 'politburo', into a wider structure that would also include Kosovo political leaders. This expansion of the 'Interim Administrative Council' (IAC) was done roughly along the lines of the Rambouillet formula. Thus it was decided to bring on board one leader from each of the three political mainstreams in Rambouillet (LDK, KLA and LBD). Rugova and Thaci were obvious choices. So was Rexhep Qosja as leader of the LBD. A fourth seat was reserved for the Kosovo Serbs. There was a practical problem here, since the Serbs were just then in a non-cooperation mode with UNMIK. They felt they had been unjustly ignored on the issue of the KLA demilitarization and the formation of the Kosovo Protection Force, KPC. Also, the Kosovo Serbs were too divided among themselves to be ready to accept a formal association with the international government. For the time being their IAC seat was therefore left vacant.

It took some effort to bring all the Kosovo partners to the table. Rugova was, of course, more than willing. He saw this as another step towards his ultimate goal of becoming an officially recognized president of Kosovo. Qosja had hesitations. Professorial as he was, he had little clue about matters of administration. I had come to know him by then as a person of utmost integrity – a Kosovo Abraham Lincoln, indeed, if only by his stern looks. He taught Albanian and comparative literature at the Pristina University and had authored numerous books, including the novel 'Death Comes To Me From Such Eyes', a highlight of Albanian literature according to Albania's best-known author, Ismael Kadare. I think he accepted the role because he saw this as an opportunity to witness first-hand how history was being made and to be able to write about it with inside knowledge. And, indeed, he was to write profusely about his experience with the 'international protectorate' later on.

Thaci turned out to be the hardest nut to crack. Quite in keeping with his reputation from Rambouillet where he had also held out stubbornly until he got the maximum possible – to the chagrin of the international mediators and some of his fellow delegates. This time he was concerned about his credibility. As lead man of the armed resistance how could he join with a political rival (Rugova) in a common venture with the internationals? Also, participating in a government structure in a consultative rather than a decision-making capacity seemed a risky business and politically harmful. Was he not going to become an Uncle Tom or Bertold Brecht's tamed elephant that is used to lure and snare others? At the time he was involved in an inner party struggle over the leadership of the new party that was about to surface as the official, political successor to the KLA (the PPDK, later PDK).

When we learned that he was inclined to refuse the offer, Ismije and I went over to his office one evening in what had become the headquarters of his new party in Pristina's main street. We had considerable credibility with him and other emerging leaders because of our past role in Albania, our earlier encounters and the energetic and empathetic start we had made with the OMIK. We urged him to be constructive and seize this opportunity to be on the right side of history. For the benefit of a new Kosovo but also his own political future. This was a historic call that was not likely to come his way again, comparable to his Rambouillet challenge! It took a while – without rakija and cigarettes, unlike most such nightly meetings in Kosovo – before we had his consent in principle. The next day he confirmed his readiness to join. I won't claim that our intervention was decisive, but it probably did help to tip the scale as he himself acknowledged to me many years later.

The new IAC held its first meeting on 5 October. The dynamics turned out as anticipated. In the twice-weekly morning sessions with the four pillars' heads, presided over by Kouchner, our Kosovar IAC colleagues behaved true to their disposition. Rugova usually sat calmly and passively through the discussions, almost Buddha-like, without too much of an interest in the details of policymaking. I regularly visited him to discuss upcoming issues. He lived in a modest sized two storey villa in an ordinary street, with one LDK guard at the gate. He always received me cordially over tea in his main room with an imposing painting of Pjeter Bogdani (the fourteenth-century Catholic cleric and Albanian patriot and writer who had been the subject of Rugova's doctoral study) on the wall. And I could always expect him to listen patiently, comment kindly and let me depart with one or the other crystalline stone from his huge collection. Qosja also lived up to our expectation. During the IAC meetings he was mainly busy with meticulously penning down the gist of our discussions, to be of use in his later writings. To him, too, I paid many a visit, but more to tap into his wisdom and learn about past history and characters than to discuss administrative matters. Sober and dignified, he too lived in a modest house filled with books and paintings. I had earned his special gratitude when I had a bombed-out car in front of his house, a legacy from the war, removed by KFOR. Thaci was usually the most engaged in the IAC sessions, but also the most wary where policy proposals were concerned. Not a smooth talker, he did project the image of a man to reckon with, given his KLA/PGoK background and militant following. He could be quite obstinate if he did not agree or refused to understand. Overall, the chemistry of the meetings was quite positive, to the relief of us internationals. The serious differences of the past between, on the one hand, Rugova and, on the other hand, Thaci and Qosja, did not thwart their constructive participation. Clearly they felt that they were in this together and that there was enough of common ground. Again, this was quite a unique achievement and compares favourably with what has been witnessed in other post-conflict societies where civil and political strife continued or followed international intervention (the Nano-Berisha discord in Albania being the relatively mild case next door; Afghanistan, Iraq, Libya being some of the worst cases).

The new set-up was blessed by Kofi Annan, the soft-spoken but firm UN Secretary General, who came to visit Pristina on 13 and 14 October. He emphasized the urgency to build what was then still called a multiethnic, multicultural society and appealed to the Kosovo Albanian leaders to take positive action to end violence against non-Albanian communities. He also met with the 'Gracanica' Serbs and called on them to get involved in the governance, as many other prominent visitors did in that period. And, yes, they did make a move: on the eighteenth of that same month, Bishop Artemije founded the Serb National Council (SNC) in Gracanica, with Momcilo Trajkovic as the executive chairman, to liaise with UNMIK and to promote the Kosovo Serb interest. The problem remained that this SNC was not representative of the Serbs in the north who were still refusing to have anything to do with Pristina rule and had set up their own separate SNC.

Co-sharing administration

With the executive council 'Kosovarized' and continuing as IAC, it became time to also do the same with the actual administration. The underlying idea was to start co-sharing responsibilities in the various areas of governance. So in the course of November a blueprint for 'co-administration' was developed according to which some fifteen departments were to be established, each one headed by an international along with a Kosovar co-head. The departments were to be increasingly staffed with Kosovo employees, not only to take care of the expanding tasks but also to gradually replace the internationals. A precondition to this new governance arrangement was, of course, that existing parallel government structures be terminated – Rugova's presidency, Bukoshi's government-in-exile and Thaci's provisional government of Kosovo. The Serbian provincial government of Kosovo had by now completely dissipated, soon to be replaced by a special liaison office for contacts between Belgrade, and UNMIK and KFOR. Negotiations took a surprisingly short time and on 15 December the agreement on the Joint Interim Administrative Structure (JIAS) was signed by the three Kosovar IAC members Rugova, Thaci and Qosja. The new structure was to be operational from 31 January 2000. Simultaneously, it was decided that the Kosovo Transitional Council would remain a consultative body but in an expanded form so as to widen ethnic representation and to include more women.

The Kosovo Serbs, through their new SNC, voiced strong opposition to the Agreement, even though they had been offered a share of co-head positions in the JIAS departments while one of the four Kosovo seats in the IAC remained reserved for them. They felt again that they had not been properly consulted, just like they had felt bypassed on the issue of the KPC formation three months before. That earlier snub had led them to both reject participation in the IAC and boycott the KTC. The continuing ethnic violence also did not contribute to a more forthcoming attitude. This violence was a preoccupying issue, as stressed and condemned by the first Human Rights Conference organized by OMIK early in December, where the two 'Kosovo: As Seen, As Told' reports were also discussed. Yet, despite all objections and bitterness we did not give up the hope that sooner or later the Kosovo Serbs, at least the southern ones, would give in and join the new administration in their own interest. They did so, in fact, after a few months.

The Kosovo Serbs in the North were likely to stick to their guns, however, then and later. They never showed the slightest inclination to join. In their mindset they simply remained part of Serbia, as, in fact, their actual situation suggested. They were fully supported from Belgrade. Ever since the end of the war the Milosevic regime had done nothing to assist the international administration in Kosovo, least of all to effectively establish UNMIK's authority over the north. If anything, the regime kept feeding anti-UNMIK sentiments and undercutting its policies. To add insult to injury, on 12 December in Belgrade, Flora Brovina was sentenced to twelve years in prison on the spurious charge of 'terrorism'. Flora was a paediatrician and human rights activist who in the pre-war days had founded the Albanian Women's League. She had been one of the main organizers of a famous Women's March in early March 1993 when resistance to the Serb rule was mounting. After arrest during the war she had been taken to Serbia just days before the end of hostilities along with many other prisoners. Among them was also Demaci's assistant Albin Kurti who had been a vocal student activist and would become a political leader in his own right many years later. The sentencing caused an international outcry, but to no effect. It was not before November 2000 – after a change of Government in Belgrade – that Flora was released and allowed to return. Kurti had to wait yet another year before he was freed.

Happy ending?

While the human rights situation remained deplorable, the new IAC and JIAS developments in the direction of more participatory governance seemed to bode well for 2000. To end the year on a positive note, Kouchner wanted to add special drama to the New Year's Eve, taking advantage of the fact that it also marked the beginning of a new millennium. He persuaded Bajram Rexhepi, the much respected mayor of (south) Mitrovica, and Father Sava – together representing the former KLA and the orthodox church – to meet with Oliver Ivanovic, a key civil leader among the northern Kosovo Serbs. They met half way on the bridge to shake hands to symbolize reconciliation and cooperation. Everything, of course, in the glaring lights of TV cameras – Bernard's best friends – so that the whole world would be witness to this historic political encounter. It was an impressive event, worthy of being endured in the bitter cold of the moment. Unfortunately, as it turned out, the transmission to a world audience never took place because the satellite connection failed ... Was this predictive of the still difficult years ahead?

Note

1   A stunning example of such bias is the rescinding of the conviction for war crimes of the Croatian generals, Ante Gotovina and Mladen Markac, who had been found responsible for the massive ethnic cleansing of some 200,000 Croatian Serbs during Operation Storm in Croatia in 1995.

5

International protectorate II
Preparing for the next phase

Expanding the international reach

In the first few months of 2000, the new joint administration, through the Joint Interim Administrative Structure (JIAS), began to become operational, slowly but steadily. The Kosovo co-head positions of the fourteen departments were more or less rationally distributed among the major political factions. Not everyone was happy. I remember Nibike Kelmendi, the co-head of the Justice Department, complaining about under-representation of the LDK. Highly regarded in her own right, she was also respected for being the widow of the well-known human rights lawyer, Bajram Kelmendi, who had been murdered along with their two sons in the beginning of the war in 1999. Her problem was with regard to not only the departments but also at the municipal level. According to her, the same Rambouillet formula that was applied to the IAC – with 25 per cent for each political mainstream – should also be valid for municipal government where KLA had seized pre-emptive control in most areas. She definitely had a point, because an opinion poll at that time showed Rugova/LDK to be four times more popular than Thaci/PGoK. One probable explanation of this surprising outcome was dissatisfaction at the local level with the intimidating governing style of some of the local KLA bosses and the widely suspected implication of some KLA elements in criminal operations.

Most of the fourteen JIAS departments fell under the supervision of the UN and EU pillars. The only OMIK-related department was not subject to any institutional competition, probably because it was too innovative: the Department for Democratic Governance and Civil Society. I don't know of any precedents of such a department in other democracies, fledgling or not. I was lucky to find Vyosa Dobruna prepared to take on the job along with OMIK's Rob Pulver, the competent and mild-mannered American lawyer, whom I had lured from Albania to join me again in the Kosovo Mission. Vyosa, of course, embodied the perfect combination of political independence and womanhood. Together they formed a great team. In fact, of all the JIAS heads and co-head tandems, they were seen as the most functional one. There was plenty to do on both the democracy and the civil society fronts, albeit not always to everyone's taste. One of Vyosa's early disappointments was that Rugova did not want to publicly declare victims of rape during the war to be official war victims and be treated as such. He considered this too much of a 'feminist cause', although wartime rape had already been defined as a 'crime against humanity' by the post-Second World War Nuremberg trials. In present day Kosovo, and post-war Western Balkans at large, the trauma of wartime rape is still a big issue, with most cases remaining under the cover of silence, prejudice and shame.

The disbandment of the informal parallel government structures was a little harder. The LDK party showed some hesitation, which put its leader Rugova in an awkward position in the IAC. In the end the party did comply and held a convention to formally disband its government-in-exile (still headed by Bukoshi) as well as Rugova's 'shadow' presidency. The question of the remaining funds accumulated through the 3 per cent voluntary tax was never transparently resolved, however. Also, Rugova remained de facto president in the eyes of his many followers, emblematic scarf and all. And while the Thaci-led PGoK was correctly dissolved, many local KLA leaders were also loath to give up their entrenched positions. Some of them kept trying to throw their weight around and interfere in local affairs. This was, of course, especially true in areas where the KLA had had its main strength such as the Drenica, Gjakova and Llap regions. Informal power networks kept operating long after

UNMIK, through its UN pillar, had taken over a municipal government. It required constant efforts to enforce compliance with the new international rule, including respect for civil rights and property. On many occasions, the self-styled local chiefs had to be firmly reminded that it was the international government that was supposed to be in charge. Only by bringing in good international administrators could we effectively clip their wings.

One such case was Pec/Peja, where an excellent Frenchman, Alain Leroy, skilfully took over the mayoral responsibilities. In Prizren, we had a special situation. Originally this pretty town – clustered around a beautiful, orthodox cathedral and an equally impressive seventeenth-century mosque – was a very ethnically diverse area with Albanians, Serbs, Roma and Turks living side by side. The Serb and Roma minorities faced a very hostile environment after the war. Our field office reported massive and incessant house burning, targeting Serbs and Roma. By the end of 1999 only a few hundred of the initial 8,000-strong Serb community had remained while the numbers of the Roma community had also dwindled dramatically. The local KLA Commander – Ekrim Rexha, better known as Commander Drini – tried hard to stop the trend. Reasonable and constructive, he was an exemplary demilitarized KLA commander who stood for a civilized Kosovo. As an activist, he was OMIK's best ally in the area. To everyone's abhorrence he was murdered in early May 2000, obviously because of his tolerant and inclusive stance.

Preparation for elections

With the co-administration underway, civil society getting organized, political parties becoming more assertive and media displaying diversity and stridency, it was time to prepare for elections in earnest. They had to advance Kosovo to a new stage of self-government. And so we, as OMIK, readied ourselves to take on this huge challenge. Huge for two reasons: we had to compile a completely new voters' register and we had to build from scratch an organization that could prepare and deliver credible elections. The voters' register is normally extracted from the civil registry, but in post-war Kosovo 70 per cent of the municipal registers had been destroyed. The massive displacements of people had also added to utter administrative confusion. On the bright side, we could quickly come to an agreement in the IAC that the first post-war elections should be held at the municipal level. It was there that a representative government was not only most urgently needed but also easily achieved. Moreover, with Kosovo's status still undefined, central elections would be premature as there was no clarity yet as to what central Kosovo institutions – Parliament? President? – people were to vote for.

To guide the whole process, an Election Regulation was adopted by the IAC, on 7 March 2000, which also established a Central Election Commission. This CEC consisted of three internationals and nine Kosovars, including one Serb, to be nominated by the Kosovo members of IAC. Since OMIK was responsible for the organization and quality of the elections, I was appointed chairman. The Kosovo Serbs abstained as long as they had not committed to take part in the elections. I was not going to give up trying to engage them, though, and made it a point to share with them informally the gist and results of the CEC deliberations. To this end, I paid my occasional visit to Caglavica, a Serb enclave south of Pristina, where the civic leader Momcilo Trajkovic resided. The Commission needed, of course, the operational capacity for all the planning and day-to-day operations. In the shortest possible time, our Elections Department assembled an impressive staff, soon large enough to move out of our headquarters to their own building in the immediate vicinity. This proximity helped us to keep in regular touch, including after office hours for drinks in the nearby Bang Bang Room or dinner at the Tiffany restaurant. Especially the latter turned out to be a good, informal setting for election questions to be raised, (hotly) discussed and settled. Another favourite hang-out that served the same purpose was Antonella's Italian restaurant. I knew Antonella from Tirana, where she had run a similar restaurant that I used to frequent with friends and guests if we wanted a change from the good old Rogner hotel.

In order to raise awareness and kick off preparations for this major electoral test, we convened a much-publicized Round Table meeting under the heading 'Elections in Kosovo: Agreeing on Rules for a Clean Campaign'. It was moderated by James Rubin, Assistant Secretary of State from the US State Department and important Rambouillet player, and myself. The Kosovo Albanian participants used the occasion, understandably, to also raise the sensitive issue of Kosovo's interim status. How were these elections going to advance self-government? In the concluding, packed press conference, Rubin showed some guts by reproaching the Kosovo Albanian leaders for not showing leadership in clamping down on extremism and ethnic violence against Serbs and other communities. I publicly agreed with him but also called on the international community to better honour its commitment to adequate law enforcement (*see boxed text*).

From Notes of the press conference, on 12 March 2000, by Asst US Secr of State, James Rubin, and the Head of the OSCE Mission in Kosovo, Amb Daan Everts, re: Kosovo municipal elections.

…

Rubin went on to say that there are no winners and losers. 'This is a beginning of a process in which we don't choose sides. We choose for the democratic process. We are giving Kosovars the right to choose'. Amb Everts stressed that special provisions must be made to ensure participation of minorities so that they will be properly represented.

…

Rubin indicated that Secretary Albright had begun discussions about creating Kosovo-wide institutions for self-government. 'We shall see central elections before Kosovo's final status is determined, but we must expand on municipal elections first. The international community is looking to Kosovars to take more responsibility. The permanent status question is far away'.

…)

Ending on a somber note, Rubin mentioned that the purpose of his trip to Kosovo was not fun. 'We are deeply disappointed by the failure of the Kosovo Albanian leaders to use their leadership to make hard decisions and counter ethnic violence'. He stated that 'You cannot be leader and claim no responsibility when the time comes'. Shifting some of the blame from the Kosovo Albanians, Everts added that the International Community was at fault as well. Referring to the lack of a substantial number of deployed police officers and a fully functional judicial system, he said that the international commitment was falling short.

…

Prepared by Isidora Opacic for Media Action, 13 March 2000

The OMIK election team was headed by Peter Erben, a driven and highly competent little Danish Napoleon who would not take 'no' for an answer easily. Strong outside support was given by Jeff Fischer of IFES, the International Foundation for Election Support (IFES), headquartered in the United States. He periodically came over to give a hand, both in the design of the elections and operationally. Together we had two tough nuts to crack: the electoral system and the role of women. As to the electoral system, the choice was between voting for parties per municipality or voting for individuals per municipal district. In other words, municipality-wide proportional representation or individual mandates per municipal district (on the basis of who won the majority of votes). We had long discussions in the CEC and other platforms. We were wary that individual mandates per district would empower local bullies or worse. Proportional representation would strengthen, we hoped, the centrist forces that were prepared to cooperate with each other and the internationals. On the other hand, first-past-the-post election of individuals per district would allow for a more direct, personal link between the elected and the electorate. As a compromise, we opted for party representation through open lists that offered the voter the possibility to mark preference for an individual on the party's list. Thaci spoke out against this proportional system because he thought it 'less democratic'. Later also the LDK declared itself against it, no doubt for the same self-serving reason that proportional votes would enable small(er) parties to gain representation in the councils. This was, of course, likely to reduce the two main parties' dominance.

The second issue was about ensuring a greater role for women in politics. This required that political parties include more female candidates on their list, at eligible places. To that effect, we introduced the rule that one-third of the candidates should be women. And we added the requirement that these women candidates should take every third spot on the list in order to prevent their being grouped together at the unelectable bottom of the list. Thus up to 30 per cent of the elected could be female (unless voters mainly picked men on the open list). Like in the case of the police force, it took considerable effort to convince, first, the political parties, then the CEC and finally the IAC and KTC. It was, of course, quite revolutionary because no country in Europe had a similar candidate requirement. Very few states in the world had reached the 30 per cent target of women's participation in their parliaments or other representative bodies. I used this as a selling point. Kosovo was going to blaze the trail, in anticipation of the inevitable, worldwide development in this direction! In the IAC, it was Rugova who was most reluctant, referencing Albanian tradition. There was, however, strong support from inside Kosovo, by NGOs and women activists, as well as positive surprise and encouragement from abroad. In the end, everyone did agree, thereby creating an important precedent for the later, Kosovo-wide parliamentary elections of 2001. In subsequent years I have often been retroactively congratulated on this 'affirmative action'.

Now that the elections had become a real prospect, parties shifted into higher gear to get organized, attract a following and identify potential representatives. The LDK was historically well established with branches in all areas. They had in Ibrahim Rugova a lead man whose popularity among the masses, as shown by opinion polls, remained unshaken despite his past vacillation and indecisiveness. Thaci's PDK (they had dropped the word 'progressive' from the name to continue as Partie Democratike e Kosoves) with its KLA background and dominant role at the local level was also confidently anticipating the elections. It trusted that its liberation role would be rewarded by the electorate. Qosja's LBD coalition, on the other hand, remained more of a political gathering around a widely respected leader than a tightly organized political organization. Two promising newcomers appeared on the scene: the Alliance for the Future of Kosovo (AAK) and the Centre-Liberal Party of Kosovo (PQLP), both seeking to occupy the middle ground in the political landscape between LDK and PDK. The AAK was a coalition of several parties. It was founded in early April and headed by Ramush Haradinaj, the KLA commander of the first hour and later one of the three deputy commanders of the Kosovo Protection Corps. The well-established, centrist Parliamentary Party of Kosovo, earlier associated with the LBD, became its most important constituent party. It brought along high-profile members such as Mahmut Bakalli and Bajram Kosumi who became the AAK vice-president. The PQLK was created around the same time by another KLA Commander, Naim Maloku, who was soft-spoken and well regarded. His new party was widely welcomed, also by the internationals, for its appeal to reason and compromise.

Continuing ethnic tensions; role of the press

If over the course of the first several months of 2000 the international rule became more settled and daily life more adjusted to the new circumstances, this did not lead to improved interethnic relations. The official ethnic murder rate had come down considerably, but this was more likely a result of the reduction of targets than of an increase in tolerance. Ethnic violence remained ever-present. Serious incidents were still reported on a regular basis. Attempts to facilitate the return of displaced Kosovo Serbs to their original places of residence met with stiff resistance. Movement between Serb enclaves was hazardous and only possible with KFOR escort. Also, in Pristina the few apartment buildings that still housed Serbs needed constant protection. So did Serb employees of international organizations on their way to and from work. Tellingly, the international rhetoric had sobered from 'creating a multiethnic society' to 'promoting peaceful coexistence'. In fact, an 'Agenda for Peaceful Coexistence' was officially adopted by UNMIK in March. It was to ensure greater security and access to public services for ethnic minorities. To stress the point, Javier Solana, the EU High Representative for Common Foreign and Security Policy, paid a special visit to Pristina. He explicitly warned the Kosovo Albanian leaders that they should no longer just *talk* about peaceful coexistence and that they would be judged by their actions. His visit took place a day after the vitriolic Bota Sot newspaper, published in Switzerland and linked to LDK, had written that 'any Serb left in Kosovo is clearly a criminal'.

The Peaceful Coexistence initiative helped to bring the Gracanica Serbs back to the KTC, to have them agree to co-head two JIAS departments and to depute Rada Trajkovic to take the Kosovo Serb seat in the IAC. Despite her radical, hard-line past – she had been a member of the Serbian Radical Party of the infamous, convicted war criminal Sesjel – Rada, a medical doctor by profession, turned out to be another constructive member of the IAC. An early, positive result of this re-engagement was the adoption, by the KTC on 10 May, of a unanimous declaration condemning the mutual violence committed during and after the war. It did not change the negative attitude of the Kosovo Serbs in the north, however. Ivanovic called the decision to return 'a mistake' and, to our unpleasant surprise, he was backed in this by his political ally Zoran Djindjic, leader of the anti-Milosevic Democratic Opposition in Belgrade. The Serbian Government-sponsored Radio Gracanica went even further when it called for Momcilo Trajkovic to be hanged and Bishop Artemije to be defrocked because of their willingness to cooperate with UNMIK. This was one reason for Father Sava to ask for my urgent help in countering the 'dreadful' media situation resulting from Milosevic's near-monopoly of Serbian-language newspapers and radio stations. We did help him to establish an independent Radio Gracanica, but as OMIK we were in no position to meet his two higher priorities: better security for the Kosovo Serbs and more returns of their displaced. He was right, though, in warning that international failure to make progress on these two critical issues would tarnish the credibility of the Gracanica Serb National Council (SNC) and jeopardize its ability to cooperate.

Among the ethnic crimes, one murder in May especially tested any remaining confidence in ethnic reconciliation. Petar Topovski, a young Serb employee of the international administration of Pristina, was shot dead in broad daylight in the centre of the town. His murder followed the publication of his personal details in Dita, a nationalistic daily closely attuned to the PDK. Outraged and fearful of more ethnic crimes, SRSG Kouchner took the decision to close the paper for a week. He did so by executive order as there was not yet a legal basis for such action. I had problems with this extreme sanction in principle, but did sympathize with Kouchner since judicial recourse was not available and media self-discipline was still obviously lacking. Many others were, however, vehement in their condemnation of the SRSG decision. Local and international media representatives saw it as an act of unacceptable overreach. Baton Haxhiu, co-editor of Koha Ditore, offered Dita alternative printing facilities in the name of press freedom. Even the *New York Times*, in an editorial, took issue with the decision. What they all failed to recognize, was that the matter was anything but academic – as anyone witnessing an ethnically divided, conflict-ridden society could testify.

Both in the IAC and the broader KTC there was recognition of the need for a legal basis to counter hate-mongering in the media, apart from eventual self-discipline. It led the SRSG to issue an UNMIK Regulation a month later, in June, providing for a provisional code of conduct for the print media. This temporary code prohibited the publication of personal details about a person if that endangered his or her life. A companion regulation created, within OMIK, the office of an independent Temporary Media Commissioner (TMC) who was to oversee media policies, including issuing broadcast licences and preparing a new code of conduct. The regulation also established a Media Appeals Board consisting of two internationals and one local media expert. The new set-up was challenged almost immediately when Dita again started to publish a list of names of Kosovo Serbs whom it associated with war crimes without providing any evidence. The paper was given notice by the TMC and, when it did not respond, ordered to cease publication. When it kept surfacing – again with the help of Koha Ditore – it was heavily fined. Upon appeal, the Appeals Board agreed with the sanction, although it mitigated the fine.

In due course the TMC, as instructed, was to issue a new 'Temporary Code of Conduct for the Print Media', which applied to owners, operators, publishers and everyone with final editorial control. It laid out a number of rules and responsibilities on matters such as checking facts, protecting privacy and sensitive information, and separation of facts and opinion – all in line with European journalistic standards. This new code was broader in scope than Kouchner's preceding executive order, which only aimed to protect the safety of a person. The new system proved its worth as violations of journalistic standards under the new law were generally handled with fairness and even-handedly.

Minorities report

That the ethnic situation had not really improved since the beginning of the year – despite the efforts and rhetoric – became clear from the periodic OMIK report on 'The Situation of the Minorities in Kosovo' that we published on 1 June. It covered the period from February through May 2000 and reported that 'the security problems continue to be highlighted by incidents of harassment, intimidation, arson, assault, kidnapping and murder'. The lack of security and freedom of movement had remained fundamental problems affecting all minority communities in Kosovo. It noted that, with UNMIK police staffing falling short and a functioning and impartial judicial system lacking, criminal activity had remained unacceptably high. Minorities had been affected disproportionately. Kosovo Serbs were the hardest hit, with 105 incidents of arson, forty-nine incidents of aggravated assault, and twenty-five incidents of murder reported throughout Kosovo between the end of January and end of May. Given this gloomy picture, it was not surprising that the Gracanica SNC was having second thoughts about its cooperation with UNMIK.

It did not help that in late May an enormous, illegal weapons cache was found in the Drenica area, not far from former KLA strongholds: heavy machine guns, mortars, anti-tank rocket launchers and missiles, electronic scanners and receivers, and a large quantity of ammunition and explosives. This discovery, in combination with another spate of murders of Kosovo Serbs, was the reason for the Gracanica SNC to suspend participation in IAC and JIAS. On 5 June, in a letter to the UN Security Council, Bishop Artemije explained that without special protective measures, the Serb community would have to pull out of the peace process. Frantic negotiations followed, leading to a Memorandum of Understanding between the SRSG and the Bishop. Most notably, it referred to the creation of 'neighbourhood watches' and UNMIK 'community offices' in Serb-majority areas. The latter were to compensate for the lack of freedom of movement and to ensure equal access for Kosovo Serbs to public services. The Memorandum gave sufficient reassurance for the SNC Gracanica to decide to resume its participation in IAC and JIAS on 25 June. A decision that was condemned not only by Ivanovic and the even harder-line Jaksic in the north, but also by the more moderate 'southern' Momcilo Trajkovic who had walked out of the decisive SNC meeting. On the Kosovo Albanian side, Qosja and Thaci spoke out against the Memorandum of Understanding as they saw this as a step towards 'cantonization' and district autonomy along ethnic lines. For Thaci, it was even a reason to suspend his participation in IAC for a few weeks.

First anniversary

Although the security problems remained preoccupying, it was undeniable that notable improvements had been made on other fronts. Therefore, the first anniversary of UNMIK and KFOR's arrival seemed to give good reason for hopeful commemoration if not celebration. A big event was organized in June in the national stadium in Pristina. On the Kosovar side, Rugova and Thaci addressed a large crowd with many young people present. Being at their politically most correct, they both stressed the need for cooperation with UNMIK and KFOR and between the ethnic communities. To the dismay of the many assembled dignitaries, however, their words were also met with boos and whistling when references were made to the international community and Serbs. In another commemorative event organized by the Human Rights Council that he chaired, Adem Demaci gave an uplifting speech stressing the need for tolerance and reconciliation which, in his words, was 'not a concession to others'. Alas, his audience counted no more than fifty people. And when Father Sava made similar exhortations in Kosovo Polje, in a meeting commemorating the legendary battle of 1389, there were also only a handful of listeners. Coincidentally, it was in this same month that what we described as 'your friendly OMIK office' received its first bomb threat ever and had to be briefly evacuated. It all pointed to a resentment towards international rule that was starting to simmer – and would reach its boiling point much later in the ugly riots of 2004.

In an effort to counter the negatives and promote solidarity and cooperation across all dividing lines, we organized a high-profile event in Prizren, the ethnically diverse but torn area where Roma had been recent targets of harassment (and the popular ex-KLA commander Drini had been assassinated). Everyone was on board: Kouchner, Rugova, Thaci, Qosja, Surroi. They were there to reassure the Roma and other communities that the new government in Pristina was inclusive and would safeguard their rights, business and well-being. 'We have come here to tell you that we have lived together, we are living together and we shall live together', I remember Qosja saying in his solemn voice. All called for tolerance, cooperation and an end to the violence. Unfortunately, ethnic crimes are not stopped by condemnation and exhortation alone ...

More ethnic incidents

Soon, serious incidents took place in North Mitrovica, where Serb hardliners not only harassed the few remaining Albanians but also turned against KFOR and UNMIK. The disturbance started on 21 June around three apartment buildings, where Kosovo Albanian families lived, on the north bank of the river Ibar in central Mitrovica. The area formed part of a KFOR-protected 'Confidence Area' that was supposed to gradually expand, with increasing security, in the future. After a UNHCR water tanker was stoned by a group of Kosovo Serbs, a much larger number of them gathered to prevent the UNMIK police from making an arrest. A crowd of some two to three-hundred people started to attack the police. They overran a KFOR post and damaged a number of UNMIK police vehicles while threatening to enter the apartment buildings. Rather abruptly, the crowd moved away towards the main bridge and started pelting KFOR troops and UNMIK police with stones. From there they went on to surround the main UNMIK police station in the centre of North Mitrovica for hours. By the end of day, nine UNMIK police officers had suffered injuries, eleven UNMIK and several other international vehicles had been burned or stolen, while several apartments of international staff in North Mitrovica had also been looted. All the while the UNMIK police had been under instructions from their highest command in Pristina to stay inside the station and their colleagues in south Mitrovica not to cross the bridge. The idea, of course, was to avoid escalation, but to any outsider it appeared as a complete abdication of duties and yielding to mob rule.

Within a month, violence struck again in the same area, this time solely aimed at the international presence. Following the arrest of one of the infamous 'bridge watchers', a large crowd gathered around the UNMIK police station demanding the release of the detainee. Some gunfire erupted and one UNMIK police officer was taken hostage for several hours. Shops were forced to close and roadblocks erected. Some apartments rented by international police officers were looted and a vehicle burned. Again, the international response was very timid, at best. When challenged, the Mitrovica Serb National Council – through Oliver Ivanovic – did condemn the violence. At the same time, it sided with the troublemakers, however, by calling on them to refuse to rent apartments or sell goods to the UNMIK police. Together, the incidents and blatant defiance formed a stark reminder of the lack of effective international rule in the north. As I reported to the OSCE headquarters in Vienna at the time: '(If) the current erosion of authority is to be halted, both UNMIK Police and KFOR must ensure that there is a robust response to this violence directed against it. Time seems to have come to restore UNMIK authority, a forceful establishment of law and order, and to review the entire governing structure in the north in order to break the grip of existing parallel structures linked to the regime in Belgrade'.[1] These were, as time would tell, words blowing in the wind ...

Not all news was bad in those summer months, though. After all, the JIAS structure had made a promising beginning with 'Kosovarizing' the governance. The earlier complaint that the Kosovo co-heads were merely advisers to the international heads of the departments was addressed by giving the co-heads more substantive roles. The bi-weekly meetings of heads of departments were expanded to include the co-heads. The Kosovo Police was continuing its success story, to both international and domestic acclaim. The school had delivered its 2,000th graduate and the KP force was gradually taking on more responsibilities from the UNMIK police, such as patrolling in the capital. The divisive media issues had been brought to a more or less satisfactory resolution. The Ombudsman institution was being firmly established. The NGO community was booming and the Political Party Centres buzzed with activity in anticipation of the upcoming elections. In fact, elections had become the talk of the town and I myself became increasingly preoccupied with their preparations as our OMIK reputation was very much on the line, in Kosovo, in Serbia and beyond.

Preparations for elections moving forward

In order to build a complete and reliable Voters' List we had made massive efforts, in good coordination with the civil administration (under the UN pillar), to convince the population to go and register themselves with the municipal offices. As there was a potential electorate of over a million, we hired as many people as possible under the budget to cope with the enormous caseload. Even plane-loads of UN volunteers were brought in to help. The number of people registering had rapidly climbed in the last few months. In June a Gallup poll showed that 67 per cent of the people surveyed had registered while 80 per cent had declared themselves to be 'well-informed' about the procedures, with no less than 93 per cent calling the registration 'important'. To urge those who had not yet answered the call, we organized a widely publicized one kilometre run in Pristina, 'The Race to Register', with the SRSG and me participating. True to form, Bernard asked me before the start not to run too fast lest I should arrive ahead of him ... I had an unfair advantage, admittedly, because ever since my arrival I had been running three times a week on the jogging trail in Germija Park, always accompanied by a loyal bunch of co-runners from among the OMIK staff. We liked to navigate the winding path up and down a steep hill, past bomb craters, minefields (fortunately, properly flagged) and a destroyed former building of the Serbian police. Twenty years later, I found it difficult to recognize the old track in what had become a nicely groomed strolling path with benches for the tired and retired.

On 9 July, Kouchner signed the Municipal Elections Regulation, which set the parameters for the elections, including the requirement of thirty female candidates. A week later, the voters' registration formally ended. The end result was spectacular: over 900,000 people had registered. This number covered 90 per cent of the Kosovo Albanian electorate. The Kosovo Serbs, however, had not responded to our many appeals to join. While the Gracanica SNC was not opposed to the elections, the combined opposition from hard-line Kosovo Serbs and the government in Belgrade, still under Milosevic, had dissuaded any intent to participate *(see boxed text on discussions with Kosovo Serbs from the north)*. When a breakthrough seemed imminent in Leposavic, where the local mayor had convinced quite a few villagers to sign up, an intimidating visit by 'bridge watchers' from Mitrovica effectively halted the initiative. Given the likely absence of Serb participation in the elections, the SRSG proposed that he would appoint Kosovo Serbs in the councils of those municipalities where their numbers were sizeable. He could justify this by pointing to the lack of freedom of movement and the fact that so many eligible Serb voters were displaced outside Kosovo.

Discussions with Kosovo Serbs from the north, re: participation in elections and registration (Leposavic, 7 July 2000)

(... intro ...)

D(aan) E(verts): This is the time to secure the future. You can only gain by participating. Those who opt out, will be bypassed, marginalized. If you make clear you want to be part of Kosovo society, the Int Comm will give you more than proportional political power. You cannot lose by being included in a voter register. Don't be mistaken, there definitely will be self-government in Kosovo. You better be part of that.

Nenad (Mayor of Leposavic): ... We should participate in municipalities with majority Serb inhabitants to stop others taking over, but elsewhere conditions are not right.

DE: in other areas from where Serbs have been displaced, we will take all measures to include them by reaching out to the IDPs wherever they are.

Oliver Ivanovic: One year has passed. 500 of our people murdered and much territory has been left. But we want to live in Kosovo and cooperate. What we need is physical, legal and economic security. This is only way you can get Serbs to participate and to legitimize yourselves. You must explain to the Kosovo Albanians that Kosovo is not independent. ... No registration and no elections on the Serb side without Serb return.

DE: ... We are the first to criticize ourselves for the lack of security. Determination of Int Comm to restore normalcy is stronger than ever. Things will improve faster and better if you participate. You cannot wait for this to happen because registration is NOW.

Marko Jaksic: We listened to your promises, those from Michael Jackson and Kouchner. Promises, promises, while houses burned and people killed. In all our history no one has cleared us of a territory the way the Int Comm has. With your experiment we are now living one without the other. One nation has success, the other tragedy. That reality cannot be hidden by elections. Could you tell us one instance of a place where elections happen without Freedom of Movement, when one nation lives in an enclave, can't speak or live. Those are abnormal living conditions, let alone election conditions. We will give the Int Comm the opportunity to stop the violence and bring back the IDPs. When this happens we can discuss elections and registration. ...

DE: we have acknowledged the lack of progress on security and returns. However, the Int Comm also does not want to continue with self-appointed leaders. They must be replaced by democratically elected ones. This is the reason for the elections now. By the way, elections have happened in Bosnia Herzegovina without freedom of movement and with IDPs participating. Main question (to Jaksic and Ivanovic) is: what are you offering as an alternative?? Nothing, isolation, marginalization, no economic benefits. This is unfair to your own people.

Nokic (from the South): we are supportive of a democratic initiative like registration. It will show how many Serbs are here, how many gone and how

> *many Albanians have illegally crossed the border. But we agree that there are no free elections without security and freedom of movement.*
>
> …
>
> Ristic (municipality of Zubin Potok in the North):
>
> *You say you want to make the situation of the Kosovo Serbs better and that without participation it will get worse. That reminds me of Holbrooke before the NATO bombardment: take it or leave it. The Serbs ARE participating with the Int Comm, just can't participate in registration and elections.*
>
> DE: *I hear you, but keep asking what is your alternative? If the Serb community is seen as non-cooperative, non-participatory, this will only reinforce the negative stance on the other side. Moderates will be weakened, extremists reinforced. …. You cannot lose by registration. It makes your presence, incl. IDPs, official and non-ignorable. It confirms also rights to property, houses, etc. We cannot just debate the past. Vital interests are at stake.*
>
> …
>
> Excerpts of notes prepared by Isidora of the OMIK Serb Outreach Task Force

With the registration basically achieved and hence the precondition for holding the elections met, a new chapter in Kosovo's history was about to begin. To provide context to the developments, Kouchner went on the road and used town meetings to sell his concept of a new 'Pact for Kosovo'. Now that true representation was about to be achieved at the municipal level, it was time to think beyond Rambouillet and also define more clearly what 'substantial autonomy' meant at the central level. The imminent discrepancy between grassroots and central democracy needed to be addressed. The United States took the initiative to bring the leaders of both the Kosovo Albanians and Serbs to a retreat in Virginia. This Airlie House gathering was a follow-up of two earlier meetings in 1999: with only Kosovo Albanians in the USA (September) and with only Kosovo Serbs in Bulgaria (December). The new talks produced the joint 'Airlie House Declaration' of 23 July 2000. It acknowledged the problem of 'continuing violence' and recognized the necessity of tolerance and cooperation, while conceding that the road to reconciliation would be slow. It also referred to the need to counter hate-mongering. It welcomed the Code of Conduct for the print media as a step towards self-regulation by the media, to be incorporated in Kosovo's legal and penal codes. It asked for the release of political prisoners in Serbia and stressed the urgent need to find the many missing persons on both sides. Significantly, it also approved of the idea to have Kosovo Serbs appointed in municipal councils in the event that the Serb community declined to participate in the elections.

In mid-August, the election date was chosen to be 28 October 2000. By now, everyone was seized by the prospect of Kosovo's first truly democratic elections. Political parties readied themselves for the election campaign. We had to scrutinize their lists of candidates to make sure these met the eligibility requirements and included the prescribed number and ranking of women candidates. Municipal Election Committees had been appointed but now needed training. Political Party Centres and Voters' Voices forums were mobilized all over Kosovo to identify local issues of concern for political debates and to acquaint parties and voters with electoral procedures. The latter included the unfamiliar option of 'conditional ballots', meant to compensate for errors in the Voters' List so that no eligible voter would be deprived of the right to vote. After all, inadequacies were bound to appear, even if we were to subject the still provisional Voters' List to an intensive period of confirmation, additions and challenges. There was also a downside to the electoral excitement. There were incidents of election-related hostility, most often directed at local LDK officials. We regularly received complaints about militant behaviour by supporters of the parties linked to the former KLA. In an effort to reduce the political strife, the youth wings of the main Kosovo Albanian parties organized a 'Project for Tolerance' from 1 September through to September 13, the day marking the official start of the election campaign. During this period a youthful, multiparty delegation went around to meet with various citizens' groups, organizations and institutions. Also, as a follow-up to the Airlie House Declaration, all main political actors joined in a 'Day against Violence' on 9 September, including the representative of the Gracanica Serbs, Rada Trajkovic.

Kosovo Serbs opposed

Despite all good intentions and signals, the plight of the minorities, especially the Kosovo Serbs, remained grim. Ugly attacks continued to happen, such as a hand grenade attack on a playground near Obilic that left ten kids injured. A spontaneous protest demonstration followed, blaming UNMIK police and KFOR for failing in their protection duties. In Mitrovica, the rule of law was again severely tested when fifteen Kosovo Serb prisoners, all suspected of war crimes, escaped. They had been in pre-trial detention for over a year, by itself indicative of the poor administration of justice. It was also then that in Pristina the murder of Rexhep Luci, the Municipal Planning Director who had ordered the demolition of an illegal hotel construction, took place. It was worrisome evidence that organized crime, in its pursuit of illegal economic and financial gains, had become a major source of violence, besides ethnic hostility and political rivalry.

The continued lack of effective law enforcement and dim prospects for reconciliation were reasons for the Kosovo Serbs not registering for the municipal elections. In contrast, they did decide to participate in the presidential elections of the Federal Republic of Yugoslavia, scheduled for 23 September, which, of course, the Kosovo Albanians did not recognize. Many Kosovo Serbs saw these elections as a chance for regime change in Belgrade. SNCs in both Gracanica and Mitrovica actively supported the presidential candidate of the joint Democratic Opposition, Vojislav Kostunica, thereby resisting the heavy-handed pressure from Milosevic's Socialist Party. The UNMIK position on these elections was ambivalent. Given the official requirement to respect the FRY's 'territorial integrity', it could not prevent Belgrade from holding elections on Kosovo territory. On the other hand, it did not want to be in any way associated as they were not relevant to the governance of Kosovo. So, no support was given to its organization. We did want to make sure, however, that the FRY elections were not used by the Milosevic regime to fraudulently boost the turnout and claim a massive pro-government vote from Kosovo (as had happened in the past). Hence, we made sure that the polling stations in the north and the scattered few in the southern enclaves were closely monitored in order to check the number of people who had voted. As it turned out, some 44,000 Kosovo Serbs did vote in this election that marked the end of the calamitous Milosevic era. Whether the change of president would significantly alter the relationship between Belgrade and Pristina remained to be seen and would also depend on the outcome of the FRY parliamentary elections that were to follow in three months.

Readying for election day

The election campaign for the Kosovo municipal elections officially began on 13 September, forty-five days before E-Day (28 October). No less than twenty-six parties had registered. The two main contenders were Rugova's LDK and Thaci's PDK. In early opinion polls, the LDK scored well, thanks also to Rugova's enduring popularity. The LDK was especially strong in rural areas, while the PDK seemed to appeal to the more sophisticated urban voters. Qosja's LBD had opted to compete together with the small Albanian Liberal Party under the name Coalition for Independence (KP) but remained rather inconspicuous. Among the many others, the AAK of Ramush and PQLK of Maloku were the most noticeable. All of these hopefuls kicked off their campaigns in mid-September with well-attended rallies. In contrast, the LDK initially maintained a low profile. Rugova also refused to be drawn into television debates. When I asked him about the reason for this relative silence, he mentioned fear of intimidation and pointed to the hostility that LDK members had experienced. Among the examples mentioned were several local LDK officials who had been violently confronted. One notable case involved the regional KPC (and former KLA) commander in Skenderaj, Sami Lustaku, who had made a threatening appearance in the LDK office. Others questioned this explanation, however, as a convenient excuse. They suggested that the low-key strategy had more to do with reliance on LDK's traditionally strong support base combined with the lack of an up-to-date electoral agenda. When by the end of September the LDK did finally decide to organize a main event, it did succeed in mobilizing many thousands of supporters in a march through Pristina.

While the politicians were vying for attention, we in OMIK had to continue the tedious work of improving the Voters' List, still called 'Provisional'. Corrections and additions had to reduce the number of errors to no more than 5 per cent, which could then be accommodated through conditional ballots on election day. To our dismay, Veton Surroi's Koha Ditore tried to throw a spanner in the works when – one month before the election! – it published an article stating as a matter of fact that the voters' registration was a 'catastrophe'. I had to go all out to contradict the article. It had confused the civil registration, which required more detailed information (about marital status, colour of eyes, etc.) with the more simple voters' registration. While the former had met with difficulties, for various reasons, the latter was on the way to being successfully completed. After my emphatic complaint, Koha did publish the full OMIK rebuke in a subsequent edition, thus undoing the 'fake news' it had started. We felt much reassured when a major, last check just before election day showed that only 4 per cent of a sample of 80,000 voters could not find their names on the final voters list. We created a supplementary voters list so as to further lower the percentage. A remarkable 85 per cent indicated that they had 'complete or general trust' in the election process.

The final weeks before election day were full of excitement. In the IAC and KTC, politicians started to look further ahead. The election of Kostunica in the FRY elections had made the Kosovo Albanians somewhat edgy. They worried that, with the demise of Milosevic, the international community might become less interested in Kosovo and its future status. They asked for assurances that Kosovo-wide elections would be held in 2001 and that, further to Kouchner's idea of a 'Pact for Kosovo', work would commence on drafting an interim constitution that would bring the promised autonomy and self-government. On the municipal elections themselves, the KTC concluded that the electoral campaign had gone well and that the level of violence had remained 'remarkably low'. In a report to an anxious Permanent Council of the OSCE in Vienna I confirmed this, calling the electoral campaign 'encouraging' given the special post-war context. I attributed this to the presence of KFOR, the police and the obvious wish of parties and politicians to impress on the world that they were ready for self-government. In a show of solidarity all parties committed themselves – in a 'Declaration on the 28 October elections in

Kosovo' – to respect the legitimacy of the elections' outcome and to cooperate peacefully in establishing municipal boards. Foreign VIPs, among whom was Richard Holbrooke, made last-minute visits in order to stress the importance of this electoral test for Kosovo's international goodwill. By this time we had trained 10,000 local polling station members and mobilized almost 1,500 international PS supervisors. Being an OSCE offshoot we could not rely on the election capacities of OSCE's Office for Democratic Institutions and Human Rights (ODIHR), but had to do this in our own right. The OMIK mission itself had burgeoned into a huge undertaking with 750 international and 1,850 local staff members. For the independent observation of the election process other institutions such as the Council of Europe and NGOs had recruited 200 international and 6,000 domestic observers. Everyone and everything seemed poised for the great day.

Election day

The 28 October Municipal Elections did turn out to be a success. On the sunny autumn day, Kosovars came out in hundreds of thousands to vote in their first-ever democratic elections. Early in the morning queues, 300- to 400-strong, began to form calmly outside polling stations even before they had opened at 7.00 am. I made an early round, quite thrilled, to witness the opening procedures but became worried when I saw some Polling Mega Centres being overwhelmed by the massive, early response. These were large public buildings, often schools, which co-located seven to ten individual polling stations, accommodating up to 7,500 voters. Swift action was called for from the Election Operations Department to supplement materials and increase both international and national staff. UNMIK police and KPS were asked to increase their presence to control crowds, just in case. The latter proved to be hardly necessary, as voters showed remarkable patience while waiting for their turn to vote. By mid-morning technical and logistical problems had been resolved and voting had settled down to a steady rhythm. Early in the afternoon, the CEC announced that some polling stations would stay open after 7.00 pm to absorb any late rush of voters. The day remained virtually free of security incidents. In fact, KFOR stated later that it had been 'the least violent day since its arrival in June 1999'. A number of factors contributed to the positive event: a general desire to conduct these elections in line with international standards; the attitude of the political party leaders in urging their followers to behave with dignity and tolerance; the call of the international community on Kosovars to demonstrate their aptitude for democracy; and the omnipresence of the UNMIK police and KPS officers (by then over 2,200), as well as KFOR soldiers.

Not only was the turnout impressive, but there were also very few official complaints and reports of (attempted) fraud from our election supervisors and the 200 international and 6,000 domestic observers. A few of us went all around Kosovo by helicopter to check the situation at different places. Everywhere an almost festive atmosphere prevailed. People obviously took great pride in this democratic exercise and many came to vote in their best outfits. At the final press conference late in the evening, before some 300 journalists and staff, I had the opportunity to congratulate the Kosovars on passing the test of democracy with flying colours. After all, the elections had met the three basic conditions: free of fraud, free of violence and high turnout. All the more remarkable, I added, since they had to be organized from scratch, in a society in institutional shambles, with no voters' register, no experience in transparent election management and little democratic awareness. My recent, rather boastful, prediction that these elections would be the best in the Balkans, seemed vindicated. SRSG Kouchner reiterated the celebratory remarks, declared the day an overriding success and thanked OMIK for the excellent organization. In his typical English he praised the 'obstination' that had ensured the success. For the Kosovo Serbs he had a special message. Under pressure from the Milosevic regime they had not registered and, therefore, had not been able to vote. As had been agreed by all in the joint Airlie House Declaration, he announced that fresh elections would be held in the Kosovo Serb-majority areas as soon as practicable. (Other minority communities, notably the Turks and Goranis, had voted in significant numbers).

Forty-eight hours after the elections, the 'partial' results were released, based on 90 per cent of the ballots. On 7 November, the final results were announced, with some impressive statistics. They confirmed the success of these elections: the turnout was a record 79 per cent; only 3.4 per cent of all ballots were invalid. Blank votes numbered only 1.4 per cent, a remarkably low figure in a first post-conflict election, also considering the system of open lists, which had made the voting more complex. Obviously, the voter education campaign OMIK had undertaken since the beginning of September, had worked. Another indicator, the number of conditional ballots cast, showed that the Voters' List – containing a high percentage of errors even in August – had been effectively cleaned up by the OMIK technicians. The final number of these ballots was 5.8 per cent of the total number of ballots cast, well within international norms. After verification, the vast majority (87 per cent) of them were included in the count, an achievement in any society, let alone a post-conflict society with no prior voter registration. Other criteria that enhanced the credibility of the elections included the fact that all who wanted to vote could vote. As the international observers reported, many polling stations stayed open late into the evening to allow everyone still in line to cast his or her vote.

Implementing election results

The distribution of votes among the parties showed three main political forces emerging from these elections: Rugova's LDK was the clear winner with an impressive total of 58 per cent of the votes cast; Thaci's PDK received 27.3 per cent; and Ramush' AAK 7.7 per cent. Of the 920 seats in thirty municipalities, the LDK captured 504, the PDK 267 and the AAK 71. The fifty-one seats of the three Serb-majority municipalities with no or negligible turnout – Leposavic, Zubin Potok and Zvecan – remained vacant and would be temporarily filled through appointment by the SRSG. On 11 November, the new Municipal Councils were officially inaugurated. As Kouchner stated on that occasion, it was 'a first step towards the establishment of institutions for democratic and autonomous self-government' and as such the beginning of a progressive transfer of administrative responsibilities by UNMIK. He made it clear, however, that he had the right to veto any decision that was in contradiction with the UNSC Resolution 1244. He ended with a warning and emphatic plea:

'The enemies of peace and democracy, the militants of intolerance, have not given up. Do not accept this image of Kosovo that is so detrimental to your future. Stand up, Democrats!'

The implementation of the election results went relatively well, considering that many self-styled local leaders had to make place for the newly elected. The LDK had become the controlling factor in twenty-one municipalities, the PDK in six. The newly elected LDK municipal assembly (MA) members seemed to be quite awed by the expectations of the electorate and the complexities of municipal government. Like all newly elected councillors they were not accustomed to governance by a democratic process, instead of executive fiat. They had, of course, been used to an internal party culture that discouraged dissent. Although the party had indicated a willingness to work with others, in practice they were still inclined to go it alone in the municipalities where they had obtained the majority of seats. So were the PDK in the areas they dominated. Success at the polls did not come without a downside: incidents of political violence kept occurring. Most often LDK officials were the target. Among them was Xhemajl Mustafa, a widely respected journalist and writer, who was assassinated on 23 November. Coincidentally, the murder happened one day after a bomb had exploded in front of the residence of Belgrade's chief representative in Kosovo, Stanimir Vukicevic, who remained unhurt. Together with other incidents, these were indications that despite the calm campaign period and an almost incident-free election day, the potential for violence was still very much present.

The PDK was understandably disappointed and in several areas quite bitter and angry about the election results. Party members even accused the OMIK of manipulating the process or the timing of the election so as to facilitate an LDK victory. They conveniently ignored the fact that the disappointing outcome was partly due to disenchantment over the way in which some local KLA/PDK militants had abused their municipal powers during the previous year. The PDK leadership, on the other hand, officially recognized the results and pledged to cooperate constructively in municipal governance. In reality, this was not very visible at the local level as they declined to offer power sharing in places where they had won such as Shkenderaj/Srbica and Gllogoc/Glogovac. Although the LDK did not do much better in its areas of dominance, there were cases where the PDK refused the appointments offered by LDK, for example in Rahovec/Orahovac and (south) Mitrovica where the PDK had scored sizeable minorities. It seemed to me at the time that the PDK had somewhat lost interest in municipal administration. Instead, it refocused on Kosovo-wide issues such as further steps towards self-government, central elections and, of course, independence.

The AAK of Ramush Haradinaj (with 8 per cent of the popular vote) adopted a more genuine will to cooperate, congratulating the LDK on their victory and pledging to work together in the new assemblies. The AAK's ready acceptance of the new political reality could be attributed to the moderating influence of the Parliamentary Party, its most important constituent party. All other parties fared very poorly. The main casualty of the elections was Rexhep Qosja, the LBD leader whose Coalition for Independence (KP) failed to make even the 1 per cent minimum. As a consequence he decided to leave politics and vacate his IAC seat. The PQLK of Naim Maloku, also a noticeable public figure, did not do well, either. Within a few months he would leave his party and join the AAK coalition, thus reinforcing its moderate, centrist wing.

It was up to the SRSG to appoint representatives of minorities to the municipal assemblies where they had not turned out to vote or where their numbers were too insufficient to secure a seat. With the smaller minorities such as the Roma, Goranis and Turks, this went generally well, but the issue remained controversial with the Kosovo Serbs. When I broached the option of by-elections in Serb-majority areas, Bishop Artemije voiced strong reservations unless three conditions were met: potential voters who had left for Serbia should be registered, the return policy for them should be intensified and, generally, the security of movement, life and employment should be higher on the UNMIK agenda. In several mixed areas south of the Ibar, Kosovo Serbs did accept appointments to municipal councils, though. At the same time all leaders, in the north and the south, urged their communities to vote in the FRY parliamentary elections, scheduled for 23 December. Their message was, basically, to 'leave no misunderstanding that Kosovo is part of Serbia'. The outcome of these FRY elections showed not only a narrow win for the Democratic Opposition of Serbia (with Zoran Djindjic as the front runner), but also a surprisingly strong runner-up result for the SPS of Milosevic despite his recent loss in the presidential election. How much of a change a Djindjic government would bring in Belgrade's Kosovo policies was still to be awaited, but at least he himself had proven in the past to be prepared to enter into dialogue, with the internationals as well as the Kosovo Albanians.

It did not come as a surprise, of course, that the Kosovo Serbs in the north were the hardest to engage throughout these months. North Mitrovica remained a scene of frequent unrest and open defiance of UNMIK authority. It even happened at one point that seven (Belgian) KFO soldiers were briefly taken hostage. Generally, the continuing ethnic violence Kosovo-wide reinforced the position of hardliners. In a particularly ugly incident in November, four members of the Ashkali minority were murdered. They had tried to return, from Serbia, to their original place of residence. It was a stark reminder that the political climate, at least on the ground, was anything but welcoming for returning IDPs.

Also on the Kosovo Albanian side, not everyone was happy about the appointment of Serb council members. Why be so generous to the Kosovo Serbs when they showed no loyalty by abstaining from the elections? And why be so forthcoming when the international community had already 'rewarded' the election of President Kostunica with the lifting of sanctions and re-admittance to the UN and OSCE without even demanding the release of political prisoners? This latter issue remained a constant source of anxiety and regularly triggered demonstrations by family members and others concerned. Calls for their release fell on deaf ears in Serbia, although Belgrade made one concession when it freed Flora Brovina, the human rights activist, on 1 November. As mentioned earlier, she had been brought to Serbia just before the end of the war and imprisoned following an outrageous twelve-year terrorism conviction. Coincidentally, her release came one day after a remarkable visit by Adem Demaci to Belgrade, where he met with journalists, youth representatives and intellectuals. He showed his usual frankness by declaring, in the lion's den, that he personally had no problems with the Serbs but that 'independence of Kosovo is imperative if the two communities were to live in peace'. His visit did not lead, however, to the release of his former collaborator, Albin Kurti, another well-known prisoner of war. It gave me reason to write an official letter on behalf of the OSCE asking for him to be set free.

In yet another noteworthy attempt to amend the poor interethnic relations, the local NGO, *Kosovar Association for Analysis and Civil Initiative* (KACI), held a round table meeting on the subject 'Serbs in Kosova: perspectives for the future' in late December. Discussions centred on the importance of protecting individual basic rights as well as minority group interests. From the Kosovo Albanian side all the main parties were represented at the highest level. Also, we internationals gave *acte de presence* in full. The Kosovo Serb presence was less stellar in the absence of Momcilo Trajkovic and Oliver Ivanovic, but still forcefully represented by IAC-member Rada Trajkovic. She stressed that building new democratic institutions could not succeed unless the overall security environment was significantly improved. One conclusion all talking heads agreed upon was that irrespective of the final status the two communities should be able to establish better relations and that the security situation for the Kosovo Serbs should be improved. A bold and hopeful conclusion that, over time, would be seriously challenged.

Mixed feelings at year's end

Thus the year 2000 ended with the ethnic issue remaining an overriding concern both in and outside Kosovo. It was clear that the uncertainty about the final status was not helpful. As long as this continued, the two communities would not give up their respective dreams of (for the Kosovo Albanians) independence and (for the Serbs) reintegration in FRY/Serbia. I reported to the OSCE Permanent Council that this limbo status energized the more radical factions in both communities, to the detriment of the more moderate and conciliatory.

Our favourite Serb interlocutor, Father Sava, announced that he would withdraw from politics and retreat to the Decani monastery, that magnificent fourteenth-century monastery, with the finest of Byzantine frescoes. It surely was a great place for meditation and delicate icon painting, but I could not help suspecting that he had been ordered to go there because of his good standing among both internationals and Kosovo Albanians. Besides the continuing ethnic tension, the year's record in crime fighting and law enforcement in general had been quite poor. The police and judiciary were still too short in numbers and quality to end the persistent sense of impunity. On the bright side of the balance sheet there was the success of the elections and the promise of democratic self-government at the local level. There had also been notable progress on other fronts. (Re) construction of houses and roads had been impressive. The economic pace was picking up, stimulated by international transfers, remittances from Kosovars abroad and local industriousness. December also saw the introduction of the much anticipated ID cards and travel documents. And the rehabilitation of the terrestrial transmission network helped to expand TV coverage to reach ever-increasing numbers of people.

As far as OMIK was concerned, we looked back at a highly productive year 2000, with the successful elections being an obvious culmination point. The Central Election Committee was disbanded, to be replaced in 2001. Its successor committee had to reflect the changed political landscape. It would be in charge of the organization of the first-ever, democratic Kosovo-wide elections. Within the Joint Interim Administration Structure our unique Department for Democratic Institutions and Human Rights had found its bearings and, as an inside watchdog for good governance, had started to take over part of the OMIK agenda. The police school was still going strong, reaching nearly 3,000 graduates by the year's end. RTK, the public broadcaster, was also expanding and had its studios further improved, thanks to generous donations from various donor countries that believed in a Kosovo BBC. It had been awarded a prize by the independent Journalist Association of Kosovo for its professional coverage of the election campaign and election day itself. Generally, the media situation had matured, with a functioning Temporary Media Commissioner and Media Appeals Commission. Tens of newspapers, weeklies and magazines had sprung up, while dozens of radio stations and no less than three Kosovo-wide TV stations made themselves heard and seen. On the legal side three new institutions had come to life. The Kosovo Law School and the Kosovo Judicial Institute were engaged in research, training and advice, while the Ombudsman looked into administrative neglect or abuse. Hopefully, they would contribute to what was so direly needed, a better rule of law. As long as that was lacking our OMIK Human Rights department would have to continue monitoring the volatile human rights situation and remind people of the stark realities on the ground.

Overall, we felt that we were well poised to help the international protectorate consolidate the gains while addressing both its shortcomings and new challenges in the year to come.

Note

1 Spot Report OMIK, 17 July 2000.

6

Transition to self-rule I
Preparing a constitution and central elections

A new beginning

The year 2001 came with a major change of the guard: SRSG Kouchner left, to be succeeded by Hans Haekkerup, a former defence minister from Denmark. A greater contrast in terms of personalities was hardly imaginable. A colourful Frenchman, passionate but impulsive, versus a colourless Dane, impersonal but disciplined. Whereas flamboyant Kouchner could be unpredictable in his work habits, Haekkerup was a man of no surprises, who valued his privacy and literally tried to stick to a nine to five work schedule. Their egos were correspondingly dissimilar, the one eager for acclaim and publicity, the other trying to do the job without fanfare.

The farewell speech of Kouchner, during a ceremony on 12 January, was impressive. Of course, he could not let the opportunity pass to aggrandize the achievements during his reign – 'the fastest ever progress made in a UN mission' – but, to his credit, he did acknowledge the failure to contain the ethnic violence. He pointed out that this issue could cost Kosovo dearly in terms of international sympathy and support. He referred to 'the wall of blood' between the Kosovo Serbs and Albanians and called on them to reject intolerance, isolate the extremists, stop the killings and end the violence.

Before he left Kosovo, we had him sign as his last act as SRSG a Regulation on the Prohibition of Trafficking in Persons. This was a follow-up on the work OMIK had done in helping to address this growing problem of human trafficking, especially women who were exploited in bars and sex houses. Together with UNHCR and IOM (the International Organization for Migration), we had opened several 'safe houses' to rescue the victims and help them return to their home countries. A month earlier, in Palermo I had participated, on behalf of UNMIK, in a signing ceremony of the International Crime Convention and its Optional Protocol on Trafficking in Human Beings. The problem proved, of course, to be far too persistent to be solved by protocols and regulations. In fact, the international presence itself was implicated in this sordid business. I remember giving one of my middle-level staff members a stiff warning after he was caught by the UNMIK police in one of those sleazy bars. In later years, the UN at large came under fierce criticism for negligence with regard to involvement of its military and civilian staff in the exploitation of women in crisis situations. So did large international NGOs, which proves that international crisis response may come with moral deficiency. The issue remained a preoccupation of our Human Rights Department throughout the year. While there was occasional success in rescuing women from the clutches of human traffickers, the problem persisted because many other victims did not dare to come forward or press charges, leaving the traffickers out of judicial reach.

Haekkerup started his first IAC session with a clear message. He was to give high priority to the drafting of a 'legal framework' – a euphemism for the constitution that the Kosovo Albanians were clamouring for. This would have to define the powers of an elected Assembly (read Parliament) and an executive body (read Government) that would bring substantial autonomy 'without prejudice to the final political settlement'. He made it clear that Adoption of the Framework was a prerequisite for holding the general, Kosovo-wide elections in 2001. I seized the occasion to point out that whatever the time line, preparations for these elections would have to start right away, given the long lead time. Also, I stressed the need for concerted efforts to get the Kosovo Serbs on board if we wanted the elections to be all-inclusive and the future parliament to be truly representative. The IAC at that time was still incomplete, with Rexhep Qosja's seat still vacant. His natural successor would be Ramush

Haradinaj as the president of the third largest party, but Rugova and Thaci were not particularly keen on him, or any Kosovo Albanian for that matter, joining and sharing influence and limelight. I remember arguing repeatedly with them to justify the move, which only materialized by mid-February of that year.

Ethnic tension, again

It did not take long for Haekkerup to be reminded of the most pernicious and emotional issue that he would face during his tenure. Ethnic violence flared up again in the last week of January, also involving the international presence. Not surprisingly, it happened in Mitrovica and this time on both sides of the Ibar river, in the so-called confidence zones where the international community had tried to promote peaceful coexistence. It started with an attack on a UN bus that killed two Kosovo Serbs, followed by violence that left eight Kosovo Albanians dead. To end clashes, the SRSG, the KFOR commander and local Kosovo Albanian leaders signed a joint *Declaration on Mitrovica*, calling for expansion of the confidence zones, with a stronger presence of KFOR and UNMIK police, freedom of movement and return of the displaced. It was of little avail. The declaration was received with great suspicion by the Kosovo Serbs. They had not been consulted and saw it as a devious way to force the return of Kosovo Albanians to the northern side while their own numbers south of the river were rapidly dwindling. In response they created a 'Political Committee for the Defense of Mitrovica'. Headed by hard-liner Milan Ivanovic – unrelated to his namesake Oliver – it was quick to come out with a counter-statement rejecting the intent of the Declaration.

The nature of the clashes – with shots fired; hand grenades, petrol bombs and stones thrown; vehicles damaged; and staff threatened – had a disturbing impact on the international presence. KFOR had no less than twenty-three French soldiers injured, while UNMIK staff members had not just been harassed but also assaulted. A further troubling aspect of the violence was that the perpetrators apparently had nothing to fear from the UNMIK police. No one was arrested despite positive identification. The result of it all was a prevailing climate of impunity, with little trust in the ability of the international presence to uphold the law and protect those under threat, whatever their ethnicity. The surge of hostilities featured highly on the agenda of the IAC meeting on 6 February. When SRSG Haekkerup optimistically discussed the promise of the Mitrovica Declaration, both Rugova and Thaci were sceptical; they blamed KFOR and UNMIK for not being robust enough in maintaining law and order.

The confidence zone south of the Ibar, which had been more or less suspended during the week of unrest, was re-established on 9 February. On that same day, however, the 'Political Committee for the Defence of Mitrovica' organized a demonstration against the extension of the confidence zone north of the river. Between 4,000 and 5,000 Kosovo Serbs participated. I went up to our Mitrovica field office to learn more about the issues at stake and received quite an earful. The Kosovo Albanians demanded the return of displaced families to their homes in the northern part of the town and the establishment of a unified municipal assembly and government for the whole of Mitrovica. For the Kosovo Serbs, on the other hand, the notion of a return of Kosovo Albanians in an expanded confidence zone was totally unacceptable.

They accused the 'international community' of being concerned solely about the freedom of movement and return of Kosovo Albanians to the north. Oliver Ivanovic, who by then had been declared *de facto* persona non grata by UNMIK and KFOR, berated me for not consulting the Kosovo Serbs regarding the Joint Declaration. In his view the confidence areas were actually 'ethnic cleansing areas', since Kosovo Serbs had left those areas shortly after they were set up. He mentioned as an example an ethnically mixed, protected zone ('Bosniak Mahalla') where of the initial fifty Serbian families less than five had remained. In short, according to him, the confidence zones should be abolished completely. Unifying the governance of Mitrovica was, of course, completely out of question. He warned that more, active resistance would follow, with roadblocks and boycotts, if we internationals 'did not recognize their plight'.

While rancour reigned in the north, the Kosovo Serb political climate further south was somewhat clearing up. That same February, Momcilo Trajkovic – who had become the chairman of a new *Kosovo Commission*, created and guided by the new Djindjic government in Belgrade – gave official, political clearance for Serb participation in the UNMIK structures. And Rada Trajkovic, the IAC member, came to ask me how to register her new Christian Democratic Party of Serbia with UNMIK, obviously with a view to future elections. Bishop Artemije also made a constructive move by announcing that he would formally register the SNC (Gracanica) as an NGO with UNMIK. We saw these overtures as hopeful signs for the elections later in the year. Of course, given the uncertain future status of Kosovo, we knew that all Kosovo Serbs were apprehensive about any central institution in which they would be far outnumbered. It was therefore obvious to us in OMIK that we should come up with an ingenious electoral formula to convince the Serbs to register to vote and participate in the elections. At the same time we had to leave no doubt that a well-designed electoral system offered them the best – and only – opportunity to promote and defend their interests.

'Nish express' attack and its aftermath

With the impasse in Mitrovica still unresolved, a horrendous new blow struck not far from there in the Pudujevo municipality. On 16 February, seven Kosovo Serbs were killed and forty-three wounded (ten critically) in an attack on the weekly convoy from Serbia – the so-called 'Nish express'. The blast completely destroyed the first bus in the KFOR-escorted seven-bus convoy, which was transporting a total of 200 Kosovo Serbs from Serbia back to the southern enclaves. The explosive, hidden in a drain underneath the road, was detonated by a remote-controlled wire device located in an abandoned house nearby. The bomb left a crater that was 6 by 10 metres wide and 2 metres deep. It was precisely timed because it left the escorting KFOR vehicles – in the front, middle and back – intact. The remaining six buses immediately turned back to Serbia, while the wounded were flown by KFOR helicopters to hospitals.

Upon hearing the news of the attack, an angry crowd of some six hundred gathered in Gracanica demanding to know the identities of those killed and the injured and protesting against the overall lack of security for Kosovo Serbs. Demonstrations started in other enclaves as well, some of them targeting international vehicles. KFOR/UNMIK declared a security stage BLACK for the whole of Kosovo, restricting movement to only the essential. The attack was the most lethal, single attack on the Kosovo Serb community since July 1999, when fourteen Kosovo Serb farmers had been killed in Gracko. To make matters worse, it came at the heels of a sniper attack against a KFOR-escorted bus with Serb passengers earlier that week near Strpce in southern Kosovo, which killed one and injured three passengers. Attacking such convoys was striking at the lifeline of Kosovo Serbs living in the enclaves, since they depended on them for basic supplies and for travel to other Serb-inhabited areas and Serbia itself.

Of course, the terrorist attack on the 'Nish express' elicited the strongest possible condemnations. KFOR described it as an act of 'ruthless premeditated mass murder designed to achieve mass casualties' and added that this would 'alienate and polarize the communities on both sides'. SRSG Haekkerup contacted all IAC members and other prominent interlocutors urging them to strongly condemn this incident and help to bring the perpetrators to justice. As in the past, the Kosovo Albanian leaders were quick to denounce the bombing, and join in what had become standard public statements on such occasions. More than routine compassion was displayed on the pages of Koha Ditore and Zeri. Baton Haxhiu of Koha called the attack a 'black day for Kosovo' and stated that 'there is a new noose, which the Kosovars themselves are tightening'. Blerim Shala, the editor of Zeri, lamented that Kosovo 'had lost its image before the world. Despite the mystery behind the killings, the consequences will fall on the Kosovo Albanian majority'.

The mood among the Kosovo Serbs, in the north and south, remained grim during the following days. About a dozen demonstrations brought many places to a standstill. The memorial service for the victims in Gracanica's monastery on 21 February proceeded with dignity and without incident. I surely was not the only one present feeling awkward to represent an international authority that had failed terribly in the eyes of the mourners. Demonstrations continued for a few more days. In Mitrovica over 1,000 Kosovo Serbs gathered at the initiative of the Committee for the Defence of Mitrovica, which called for the creation of a self-administered municipality and the return of Serbian police and security forces to Kosovo. The frustration about the lack of protection was also voiced in Belgrade by the new Serbian deputy prime minister Nebojsa

Covic, who suggested that the Serbian government and KFOR should work together 'for the security of Serbs in Kosovo'. He would later expand on this notion by suggesting that Kosovo be organized along two identity lines: a 'historic' Serbian Kosovo and an 'ethnic' Albanian Kosovo[1]. It would recur in different shapes and forms in times to come. It was, of course, strongly rejected by Kosovo Albanians and internationals alike. For UNMIK and KFOR it was clear, though, that the existing security arrangements for non-Albanian Kosovars needed urgent review. The increased levels of organization and sophistication of the attacks were a direct challenge to the way the rule of law was upheld. Why, for instance, had there been so few convictions for attacks on non-Albanian residents?

Another worrying aspect of the events was that the attacks, by their timing and synchrony, seemed to be premeditated attempts to obstruct the return of displaced Kosovo Serbs to their home areas. The issue of return had become more pertinent since a beginning had been made with implementing the so-called *'Framework for Return 2001'*. This was a return strategy earlier prepared by UNMIK, UNHCR and, on the Kosovo Serb side, Bishop Artemije of SNC Gracanica and Oliver Ivanovic of SNC Mitrovica. In January, there had been some small-scale return of Kosovo Serbs in the south and west. A successful return programme, however, depended vitally on safe movements between places of return, (other) enclaves and Serbia. The convoy attacks threatened these lifelines, reinforcing the vulnerability of Kosovo Serbs and adding to the pressure on them, and other ethnic minorities, to abandon their places of residence. It was clear that the very prospect of IDP return and peaceful coexistence was at risk.

By the end of that fateful February, Kosovo hosted its third Donors' Conference with representatives from thirty countries in attendance. It was made very clear that Kosovo should address the problems of violence more effectively if donor interest and funding were to be maintained. I remember Kosovo Albanian politicians, including those from the three main parties, feeling slighted at being collectively blamed for the ethnic attacks. They had a point. After all, Western countries themselves had not been able to stamp out racist/ethnic violence among their own populations, not to speak of regions elsewhere. Also, they felt that they were being held responsible for the failure of KFOR and UNMIK to provide a secure environment as they were supposed to do. In fact, some of them argued, the Kosovo Albanians themselves were victims of these brutal attacks since they undercut their efforts to build a democratic society. Many a commentator also made a link between the uncertainty about Kosovo's future status and the violence: the fight for independence was not over yet. This was a theme that would be recurring with increasing intensity in the future.

Drafting a constitution; anticipating elections

During March the situation calmed down and the daily business of rebuilding Kosovo resumed its pace. A joint 'Working Group on the Principles for Provisional Self-Governing Institutions in Kosovo' was set up to draft the legal framework. Chaired by a representative of the SRSG, it consisted of six internationals from the 'Pillars' and seven Kosovar members: one each from LDK, PDK and AAK, one Kosovo Serb, one Kosovo Bosniak (to represent all other ethnic minorities) and two independent Kosovo Albanians (the always reliable Blerim Shala and the equally respected, legal expert Blerim Reka). This Joint Working Group (JWG) went about its work professionally and made rapid progress. Since Haekkerup had officially notified OMIK that general elections would be held in 2001, I made an intensive round of briefings together with Peter Erben, the Director of the Elections Department. We informed the political parties and the JWG on various electoral issues. Besides voter eligibility, proportional or district representation and open or closed lists, these included the key question of 'reserved seats' in the future Assembly for Kosovo's various ethnic communities. Without guaranteed seats it would be impossible to make the Assembly inclusive of all segments of the population. That same month also, the new Central Election Commission was established with twelve members, among whom were three internationals and one Kosovo Serb – who had left it vacant for the time being. I myself was appointed to the Chair.

One big, if not the biggest, issue for the elections was going to be the participation of the Kosovo Serbs. So, in the middle of March (2001), I went to Belgrade with Peter to discuss the registration of IDPs from Kosovo and, generally, the involvement of the Kosovo Serbs in the elections. We were convinced that without support from the FRY/Serbian authorities it would be impossible to mobilize them to participate. It was the first time I visited Belgrade since before the Kosovo war. On that earlier occasion, in 1997, Yugoslavia had just emerged from the Dayton Accords and Belgrade's appearance was gloomy and sombre. I was on an official visit as head of the European Monitoring Mission, then called ECMM. We stayed in the iconic Moskwa hotel that clearly had lost most of its lustre. I remember the breakfast as wartime spartan: a few pieces of stale, white bread, a few slices of tomato, cucumber and local cheese, some indistinct sausage and hard-boiled eggs. The only coffee was 'domaci', domestic Serbian (I made the grave mistake of calling it 'Turkish'). Going out towards the pedestrian Mihailova Street in the evening was no joy either, with shops boarded up and minimal street lighting. Belgrade's famous, fun-loving 'jeunesse dorée' was conspicuously absent. Zoran Djindjic, who then was the mayor of Belgrade, was the bright exception. He received me in his office. Unlike the sober and sombre surroundings, he appeared spirited and open-minded, embodying Serbia's best qualities of sophistication, drive and wit. As I had witnessed before and would experience later, the Serbian sense of (self-deprecating) humour is unparalleled in the Balkans.

I met Djindjic again in 1999 in Pristina, soon after the Kosovo war. He had exiled himself to Montenegro after he had come under personal threat at the beginning of the war. When we learned about his return to Belgrade via Pristina, I organized an OSCE Round Table meeting for his travelling party together with prominent Kosovo Albanians. From Belgrade also came Stojan Cerovic, the courageous chief editor of the anti-Milosevic weekly Vreme. We were then still hopeful that forward-looking, progressive individuals on both sides of the fence could foster a climate of reconciliation and help to overcome the traumas of the past. The cordial, even jovial way the participants behaved towards each other seemed to confirm our presentiment. Restaurant Tiffany had to stay open deep into the night to serve massive quantities of food and drinks in celebration of the rediscovered friendship. Alas, later reality would prove to be a lot less malleable than we foresaw in those late hours. And little did we foresee then that a few years down the road Djindjic would be assassinated in Belgrade.[2]

On this new visit to Belgrade in March 2001 we stayed again in the Moskwa, which had not improved visibly since my last stay in 1997. Neither had the Mihailova Street. Generally, the mood was not uplifting. A decade of war, isolation and sanctions had left its mark, physically and mentally. Much potential development had been lost because of Milosevic's chauvinistic hubris. Whereas in the past Yugoslavia had been in the vanguard of eastern European countries in terms of economic standards and quality of life, now it had sadly fallen behind. The NATO bombing and the massive influx of displaced persons from Kosovo had added to bitterness and a sense of victimization. Many young people had left or were trying to leave for greener pastures abroad. The sentiment in the street was to blame the big, bad outside world for all the woes rather than engaging in some honest self-critique. Although Milosevic was sidelined and soon to be delivered to The Hague to the war tribunal, his political legacy was still very much alive. So much so that his political party maintained a forceful presence and his collaborators such as Alexander Vucic and Ivica Dacic could later resurface in dominant ruling positions, with their authoritarian tendencies still intact.

During our two-day visit we met, on the Yugoslav side (Serbia and Montenegro were still together in the Federal Republic of Yugoslavia, the FRY), President Kostunica, Foreign Minister Svilanovic and Minister for the Interior Zivkovic and on the Serbian government side, with Prime Minister Djindjic out of town, our key interlocutors were the Serbian deputy prime minister, Nebojsa Covic, and Commissioner for Refugees and IDPs, Sanda Raskovic-Ivic. We were well received; it was clear that the new government in Belgrade was interested in cooperation with UNMIK, at both the political and operational levels. Everyone seemed to acknowledge that the international administration of Kosovo was there to stay for a considerable length of time. They supported UNMIK's efforts to establish a legal framework with provisions for self-governing institutions, provided this was done with proper consultations and strictly within the context of UNSCR 1244. On registration and elections also, there were positive signals. Belgrade was prepared to facilitate OMIK's tasks, on the condition that key concerns about security in Kosovo and the return of IDPs were addressed. Following our departure, Prime Minister Djindjic, after a meeting with Oliver Ivanovic (on behalf of SNC Mitrovica, who was also a political ally), issued a statement that 'taking part in the general elections in Kosovo is a way for the Serbs to protect their interests and have their positions presented to the international administration'. Several other Serbian politicians also called on their affiliated parties in Kosovo to consider positive cooperation with UNMIK and participation in the Kosovo political process. It seemed clear that the key politicians in charge of the new government in Belgrade were distinctly better disposed towards the international rule in Kosovo than the hardliners among the Kosovo Serbs in the north, even if they were party affiliates. It made us wonder whether the latter would soften their opposition and become more cooperative.

Unrest in Macedonia

While the framework was under construction and all UNMIK pillars were busy with nation building, ethnic conflicts in neighbouring regions demanded international attention. The Presevo Valley in South Serbia, with its Albanian majority, had been restive ever since the Kosovo war. Recently unrest had flared up, causing many people to cross the Kosovo border for refuge. The EU had stepped in to help contain the Serbian–Albanian hostility and seek peaceful settlement of grievances. In next-door Macedonia (then formally known by the ridiculous misnomer of Former Yugoslav Republic of Macedonia, FYROM, in 2019 renamed North Macedonia), the situation was becoming even more threatening with armed groups of ethnic Albanians confronting the government in Skopje. Clashes near the Kosovo border brought an influx of displaced persons into the southern parts of Kosovo. When Macedonia closed the border to all traffic in the beginning of March, both the local and international community became really concerned because of Kosovo's dependence on vital imports through this border. Kosovo Albanian political leaders were of two minds. They did not want trouble at their borders but were not without sympathy for the cause of the Macedonian Albanians who were rebelling against what they felt was systemic discrimination. In several Kosovo towns there were spontaneous demonstrations in support of the Albanian insurgents. Students were also actively protesting, making comparisons with the historic student uprising in Pristina exactly twenty years earlier against (Serbian) Slav dominance. The two situations were far from identical, though, because the Kosovo Albanians constituted more than two-thirds of the Kosovo population in 1981, while the Macedonian Albanians formed a minority of one-fourth by best estimates.

The international community had little patience with the Macedonian unrest. It did not want any disturbances next door to Kosovo that could exacerbate a situation already difficult to handle. It demanded public condemnation of the armed rebellion. Under pressure, the IAC had issued a statement on 6 March, denouncing 'the extremist actions that destabilize the situation in FYROM'. Also, the KTC had appealed for a peaceful solution. That was not enough, apparently. A top-heavy mission on behalf of the EU came to visit Pristina on 22 March to discuss the 'FYROM situation' with UNMIK, KFOR and Kosovo political leaders. It was made up of Javier Solana, responsible for the EU's Common Foreign and Security Policy, Chris Patten, EU Commissioner for External Relations and two foreign ministers representing the European Council, Anna Lindh from Sweden and Luis Michel of Belgium. The EU wanted a signed, joint declaration condemning the insurgency. The Kosovo Albanian leaders balked, loath as they were to publicly comment on a situation in a neighbouring state involving their ethnic kin. There were strong indications that some former commanders of the KLA, now senior officers of the KPC, were implicated in the rebellion. A US blacklist would later identify five of them, among whom – not surprising, given their reputation – were the familiar names of Sami Lushtaku (strongman in Drenica area), Rrustem Mustafa ('commander Remi' in the Llap region) and Daut Haradinaj (brother of Ramush, in Gjakova/Djakovica).

A tense meeting followed in which the EU linked its continued support for Kosovo to a more compliant attitude. Under such threats, Rugova and Thaci gave in. Ramush remained hesitant, however, probably because he knew more about what was going on and who was involved. As there was a lot at stake in terms of European support for Kosovo, I took it upon myself to make a last-ditch attempt to persuade him. Not long before I had enjoyed his hospitality in a forest restaurant near the Batlava lake, where I had tasted my first (and last) piece of wild boar, with considerable quantities of local beer and rakija. Together with Ismije I went over to his AAK office in the evening. It took many hours of arguing, and not a little of rakija, to get him to yield and sign a piece of paper on which I had reproduced the exact wording of the draft declaration. I informed Solana and the next day, 23 March, the joint statement was signed by the three leaders calling on the insurgents to end the fighting and return to their homes. They also urged the FYROM Government 'to show restraint and to address and resolve the grievances through peaceful and democratic means'. Although the situation remained tense for many more months, with thousands of people seeking refuge in Kosovo, in the end a political solution was found that removed this external threat to Kosovo's stability.

By the end of that same month of March I happened to find myself in Washington in the company of NATO's Supreme Allied Commander in Europe, General Ralston, and a Special Envoy of the State Department, Ambassador Pardew. We had been called to testify before the Senate Foreign Relations Committee to shed light on the complex situation in Kosovo. There were some nine senators, and staff, listening attentively. I was asked to explain the OMIK's role in building the police force, media development, human rights reporting and the organization of the upcoming elections. When it was time for questions and answers, another senator suddenly made her entry under the glare of television lights. Hillary Clinton apparently needed public attention. To my astonishment she was not interested in hearing anything about Kosovo from her fellow senators or our delegation, but just delivered a prepared speech in which she sang her own praises about her experience with the Balkans and peacemaking. Immediately after delivery she left and with her, the television cameras. I felt somewhat short-changed by this gallery play, but was later comforted by the assurance that our testimony would be duly entered into the Congressional Records for her to read ... The visit to the United States was capped by meetings at the UN headquarters in New York. Most memorably, there was an encounter with Ambassador Serge Lavrov, the later Russian Foreign Minister, who was mainly intent on hearing whether UNMIK/OMIK were doing enough for the Kosovo Serbs. I could tell him truthfully that we were leaning over backwards to engage the Serbs and promote peaceful coexistence.

Milosevic to The Hague; constitution finalized

April started with some spectacular news. Milosevic had been arrested by the Djindjic government and was soon to be transported to The Hague to face the Yugoslavia Tribunal. Having lived near the prison in Scheveningen, I could give a vivid account of his future, luxury residence to eager listeners. How different his conditions were going to be in comparison with those that the Albanian Abnori, the Montenegrin Djilas and the Kosovar Demaci had had to endure for many, many years in communist jails! The political reaction in Pristina was rather muted. Kosovo Albanian leaders shrugged their shoulders and thought that other issues with Belgrade deserved more attention such as the search for missing war victims and the release of political prisoners. The Kosovo Serbs also did not show great surprise or excitement. Bishop Artemije told me that he hoped that the Serbs would finally recognize Milosevic for 'the criminal' he was. We in OMIK were at that moment preoccupied with the '7th Joint Assessment of the Situation of the Minorities in Kosovo', which we brought out together with UNHCR. Its contents were, again, disquieting. The report noted a still prevailing lack of security for non-Albanian communities, seriously hampering their freedom of movement. Apart from violence against individuals, attacks on property and illegal occupation of houses had not abated. Access to public services remained difficult for minorities in municipalities with an ethnically mixed population, necessitating special community offices. As before, we were complimented all around with the quality of the reporting and, of course, the findings were noted with concern. However informative it was about the human rights and general security situation, the report had little practical impact. Improvement of conditions on the ground remained elusive. In terms of (no) consequences, it shared the fate of the six preceding reports ...

Meanwhile, intense efforts by the Joint Working Group and the involvement of members of IAC had achieved good progress with the drafting of the legal framework. Unfortunately, the Kosovo Serbs had not taken part as they had kept waiting for instructions from the new government in Belgrade. By the middle of April most of the text had been hammered out. The draft, which stayed strictly within the limits of UN Security Council Resolution 1244, covered the powers and responsibilities of the new institutions of self-government, the competencies and (veto) powers remaining with the SRSG and details of an Assembly, an executive and a judicial system. Other sections covered human rights, community rights and various independent bodies and offices (such as the Ombudsman). As expected, the Kosovo Albanian members of the JWG had advocated the maximum possible transfer of authority to domestic control. On four issues they fundamentally disagreed with the international position. The Kosovo Albanians wanted a self-standing, elected president instead of a president chosen by the Assembly; they wanted a Constitutional Court instead of a Panel of the Supreme Court to address constitutional issues; they wanted the right to hold popular consultations on the final status (read 'referendum') and they wanted to rename legal framework as 'Temporary Constitution'. Their proposals were reflected in the text within square brackets, to be decided at a higher, political level. To the relief of us in OMIK, full consensus had been reached on all electoral provisions, in line with our recommendations: a Kosovo-wide single constituency; proportional representation; closed lists; cut-off date for voter eligibility; and reserved seats for ethnic minorities.

Since the Kosovo Serb representative in the JWG had joined only two days before the end of the seven-week process, he was given a copy of the draft and asked to provide his comments in writing. One day before the draft text was to be submitted to the IAC on 17 April, a bizarre incident occurred. It started with the publication of the draft in the *Zeri* newspaper of Blerim Shala, one of the two independents in the JWG. The purpose of this leak was, obviously, to reveal to the Kosovo Albanian population the text proposals from the Albanian side on the four sensitive issues before the SRSG would decide and rule them out. It was, in other words, a pre-emptive move in self-defence against accusations of a sell-out. The trick did not work, however, as the Kosovo Albanian members of the JWG came under fierce attack in the local press, principally *Koha Ditore*. They were accused of giving in to international demands that the legal framework not go beyond the limits of the old UN Resolution 1244. To make matters worse, Surroi printed a version of the draft framework without the text in brackets. In this way the readers were left ignorant of the four key proposals that the Albanian drafters had fought so hard for. Dismayed, Shala promptly resigned from the JWG – along with Blerim Reka, the other independent member – only to continue what became a bitter feud in the columns of the two newspapers.

On 20 April the Serb side came with their detailed comments. They agreed that the title should be 'Legal Framework' and that the President should, indeed, be elected by the Assembly. They demanded that ten seats should be set aside, to be allocated, to each of the Kosovo Albanian, the Kosovo Serb and the other communities. These special thirty seats were to be reserved for deputies of national communities with the right to request a special procedure for any disputed proposals or issues of vital interest to their national community. Effectively, this would create a second chamber within the Assembly. The judicial provisions in the draft were also to be deleted, according to the Serb side, but they joined the consensus that, for the purpose of the elections, Kosovo be treated as a single constituency and that proportional representation be the rule. The Kosovo Albanians in the working group were quick to refuse to discuss any of the counter-proposals. This meant that the final draft (with bracketed text) and the Serb comments now had to be reviewed together and decided upon at the higher, political level: the IAC and, ultimately, for decision, the UN in New York.

The IAC and KTC discussed the draft legal framework on 24 and 25 April, respectively, without reaching full agreement. Another week of intensive consultations with IAC members and legal experts followed, to find compromises and text adjustments. In the process an important consensus was reached on the guaranteed seats for non-Albanian communities: no less than 20 on top of the 100 regular Assembly seats. Ten out of the twenty were to be reserved for the Kosovo Serbs, three for Bosniaks, three for Roma, two for Ashkali and Egyptians (two small, but distinct, ethnic communities often confused with Roma), and two for the Turkish community. This by itself implied a considerable overrepresentation, which could still be augmented if any of the 100 regular seats were gained through proportional election. We internationals were most impressed that the Kosovo Albanian leaders went along with such a generous seat allocation formula. By all standards, this was a major political concession and quite unprecedented in similar post-conflict situations. As such, it did and still does merit praise.

After a last IAC meeting on 5 May, with the bracketed text still in dispute, Haekkerup announced that he would forward the draft to the UN headquarters for the final review and decision. And thus it happened. He himself joined the discussions in New York, including in the Security Council. After his return from the UN, Haekkerup explained in a televised address that 'lack of courage (on the Kosovar side) to compromise' had forced the international community to decide on the four politically sensitive issues. He gave an overview of the basic provisions of what was now called the 'Constitutional Framework for Self-Government in Kosovo'. The Assembly was to have 120 elected members. The task of the Assembly would be to adopt laws on all matters of self-government. There would be a seven-member presidency of the Assembly, with representation of the principal political parties and communities. The Assembly was to elect the president of Kosovo who, in coordination with the SRSG, would take action in the field of external relations and guarantee the democratic functioning of the government. To implement the laws of the Assembly, a government would be formed. One hundred of the 120 seats within the Assembly would be distributed among all political formations in proportion to the number of valid votes they received in the elections. The other twenty seats were reserved for *additional* representation of non-Albanian Kosovo Communities. The SRSG would retain reserved powers and responsibilities, including the protection of the rights and interests of all communities, dissolving the Assembly and acting on international matters. UNMIK would still be responsible for justice and law enforcement as well as the Kosovo Protection Corps. KFOR would continue to ensure a secure environment but would itself not be bound by any provision of the Constitutional Framework. Finally, in this address, Haekkerup also announced 17 November as the election day for the new Assembly.

After concluding a meeting with the members of the IAC, Haekkerup signed the Constitutional Framework as an UNMIK Regulation on 15 May. During the signing ceremony, the SRSG reiterated that the Framework did not address the final political status of Kosovo and that the provisional institutions of self-government must exercise their authority in accordance with UNSCR 1244. All three Kosovo Albanian IAC representatives were present at the signing ceremony and pledged respect for the provisions of the Constitutional Framework. Rugova and Ramush noted that significant powers and responsibilities were going to be transferred to the people of

Kosovo and its elected leaders. Both added that the document represented a fair compromise. It left a few politically sensitive issues open such as a final status referendum, but these they would continue to pursue separately. Thaci took more distance, deploring that the document was not meeting 'the aim of the people of Kosovo, which is political independence'. The Kosovo Serb IAC member, Rada Trajkovic, did not attend the signing ceremony. She had stated in the preceding IAC meeting that the Framework gave de facto independence to Kosovo, infringing on the vital interests of the Kosovo Serbs.

Getting the Kosovo Serbs on board

With the Constitutional Framework adopted and the election date set, the greatest political challenge now was how to integrate the Kosovo Serbs in the future, self-governing Kosovo and thus preserve the unity of governance over the whole territory. The final text of the Framework had been badly received by all Kosovo Serb leaders since they had not been part of the drafting and none of their last-minute amendments had been adopted. Their position was backed by Belgrade where Prime Minister Djindjic spoke out in their support. On the proposed elections, the views were more diverse, however. Momcilo Trajkovic basically endorsed participation, as he had always done with me; Oliver Ivanovic maintained a kind of non-committal middle ground whereas his hard-line rivals in the north flatly rejected the idea. A special 18 May gathering in Belgrade, however, produced a semblance of unity: a joint statement declared that the attitude towards the 17 November elections would depend on whether the 'International Administration would ensure the return of Serb expellees and displaced persons "in a foreseeable future"'. For OMIK, and me personally, it meant that, in addition to all of our other nation-building tasks, we had to embark on a dedicated campaign to reach out to the Kosovo Serbs, both in and outside Kosovo. If they were to become part of the democratic process, we would have to persuade them to first register to vote and then to actually participate in the elections, something we had not been able to achieve a year earlier with the municipal elections.

A fundamental problem to overcome was the different interests of those living north and south of the Ibar, each accounting for roughly half of the remaining Kosovo Serb population of some 100,000. The northern Serbs basically rejected integration and wanted to remain part of Serbia for all intents and purposes. It was safe to assume that most of the 100,000 plus IDPs in Serbia and Montenegro would share their animosity towards UNMIK and KFOR and, hence, would not be very receptive to our message. In contrast, the Serbs in the centre and south of Kosovo were prepared to come to terms with UNMIK and become part of the new Kosovo provided their vital interests – cultural, educational and economic – were protected. A secure environment that allowed full freedom of movement and the option of return for those displaced was their primary demand. The north–south divide had become even more marked since the middle of April when the Serbs in the north had embarked on a new collision course with UNMIK – this time over a tax it was trying to impose on goods coming in from Serbia through the northern border. Since UNMIK had been unable to enforce the existing Kosovo-wide sales tax of 15 per cent in the north, local Serbs there enjoyed an inflow of goods free of taxes from either Belgrade or Pristina which, in turn, enabled lucrative trading.

To put a halt to this thriving 'free' (black) market, UNMIK wanted to introduce a 15 per cent customs duty at the various border crossings. The new tax policy triggered vehement protests; road blocks were erected that severely hindered traffic and hampered KFOR and UNMIK operations in the north. With civilian life disrupted, including Kosovo Serb children impeded from attending schools, the anti-Pristina feelings grew to new heights. The Serbian government had initially voiced no objection to UNMIK's corrective tax measure. However, the Serbian National Assembly – then still hoping to influence the Legal Framework negotiations – had adopted a motion demanding strict respect for 'territorial integrity' and better protection of the non-Albanian population in Kosovo. In response, the Djindjic government abruptly changed course and came out in support of the protests. Hardened in their resistance, the northern Serbs even established a Crisis Committee to issue certificates for people to get supplies from Serbia free of taxes or customs fees. Spokesmen of this Committee were, unsurprisingly, the ever-present hardliners Milan Ivanovic and Marko Jaksic. It was not before June that the protests finally subsided, the roadblocks disappeared and the tax collection points began to function. One consequence of the turmoil was that the same Ivanovic and Jaksic persuaded the northern Serb National Council to oust Oliver Ivanovic, its Executive Council President. Along with two other, moderate members he was accused of 'solo performances' not in sync with SNC (north) policies. It did not affect his stature very much, since he remained a popular and influential public figure in Mitrovica. He also remained the first-choice point of contact for us internationals.

When June arrived, a commemoration of the second anniversary of KFOR's arrival and UNMIK's beginning was deemed appropriate. The celebration proceeded without incident – except for an anti-demonstration in northern Mitrovica that drew some 2,000 Kosovo Serbs. The high point in Pristina was a festive music and dance event in the Pristine stadium on 11 June, with political leaders including Thaci and Haradinaj as well as KPC commander Ceku attending. To show interethnic progress a Roma dance group also gave a performance. On that same day Blerim Shala's *Zeri* organized a memorable Round Table meeting with the Heads of German, US, UK and French Liaison Offices in Pristina, and Kosovo political leaders and me on behalf of UNMIK/OMIK. We were asked to give an account of the biggest achievements and failures of the past two years. Sitting informally with our sleeves rolled-up in the non-air-conditioned editor's room, we had a remarkably frank discussion. Achievements cited included the unprecedented return and re-absorption of the expelled Kosovo Albanian community, the massive (albeit unregulated) reconstruction, the creation of the Kosovo Police Service with police officers from all ethnic communities, the organization of free and fair municipal elections, the media development and the adoption of the Constitutional Framework (albeit less than wholeheartedly). Among the biggest failures were the situation of the non-Albanian ethnic communities, the lack of ethnic tolerance, the ineffectiveness of the law enforcement system and the continuing problems in the north. The international participants noted that in the outside world sympathy for Kosovo was waning because of the incessant intolerance and continuing ethnic violence. The conclusion in the end was that although there was much to celebrate about the progress achieved in two years, the commitment to the establishment of an open, multiethnic, democratic Kosovo was still far from fulfilled.

Progress towards a more inclusive, tolerant and democratic society was also the primary demand of various high-level visitors around that time. They were all briefed on the security situation and the efforts – and obstacles – to promoting the rule of law and building democratic institutions. An ambassadorial delegation of the UN Security Council, consisting of fifteen members from all parts of the world, came to visit both Pristina and the north. So did the dynamic OSCE Chairman-in-Office Mircea Geoana, who emphasized the regional, Balkan context and in that connection warned against illegal trafficking, including in women and children. The President of the Russian federation, Vladimir Putin, also came over for a day, but only to meet with the international side and mainly to express concern about the Kosovo Serb situation. And there was President George W Bush, in the company of his National Security Advisor, Condoleezza Rice. We met over a beer in one of the containers-turned-office at Camp Bondsteel. I explained the preparations for the elections and the difficulties in getting the Kosovo Serbs on board. I remember Rice raising some intelligent questions; the President seemed mainly interested in good-news stories. These international visits followed the usual routine and ended with predictable press statements. The UN Ambassadors' message was slightly different, though. It concluded quite starkly that reconciliation between the Kosovo Albanian and Serb communities was being held back by the extremists in their midst. It urged community leaders to resist these pressures and reach out to the other side, not only in formal settings but also in informal ways.

Cautious optimism and more outreach

Given the high stakes involved in the elections, we paid a new visit to Belgrade in June. The main goal this time was to secure support for the massive voter registration efforts. Without registration the Kosovo Serbs would not be able to vote in the elections at all. Potential voters among the IDP population in Serbia and Montenegro could, of course, not be reached without formal clearance and administrative cooperation from the FRY/Serbian and Montenegrin governments. Since there was no commitment yet to participating in elections, I made it a point to disassociate the registration process from the actual voting. Decisions about the latter could be deferred to a later stage, but the decision to start the voter registration was urgently needed given the long lead time. The tactics seemed to work. Our operational counterpart in Belgrade, the Serbian Commissioner Raskovic-Ivic, turned out to be responsive and constructive. After two days of intensive talks we left the city in an upbeat mood; with her promised help we would be able to do the job. The good feelings must have bordered on overconfidence judging from the description of Jackie Rowland of the BBC after an interview in my office in Pristina: 'Mr Everts twittered blithely about how the elections were going to be a big success and how he was sure that the Kosovo Serbs would abandon their opposition to the vote and take part. I became aware of another blithe twittering in his office: two budgerigars, one blue and one green, in a cage on his filing cabinet. The various twitterings merged into each other'. Little did I, or Jackie, know that fifteen years later Twitter would rule the world!

The general voter registration was to start on 30 July, so we stepped up our efforts to coax political leaders of all communities into mobilizing the potential voters to register. Simultaneously, we had to alert political entities, whether parties or coalitions, to get organized and obtain certification from the Central Election Committee if they wanted to be part of the elections. The Kosovo Albanian politicians needed little prodding, they were more than eager to begin the run-up. It was the non-Albanian part of the political spectrum that needed convincing, especially the Kosovo Serbs. So, again, we went to Belgrade in mid-July, this time to also encourage the political parties that were active in Kosovo but had their headquarters in Belgrade (almost all) to speak out in support of voter registration and to urge them to seek certification in Kosovo. Deputy Prime Minister Covic, now formally in charge of Kosovo policy but also leader of one of the ruling democratic parties, had no problem in supporting registration publicly and unequivocally. On party certification he was less determined. He was aware that Kosovo Serb voters would be left with little or no choice in the elections if no Serb party applied for certification with the Kosovo CEC. He mentioned his intention to seek an inter-party, common strategy to enter the elections as one block but was not sure others would agree. In a similarly constructive meeting, Boris Tadic, the later president of Serbia but then defence minister and vice-president of the leading Social Democratic Party, recognized the need to join forces. Other politicians we spoke to in Belgrade also seemed receptive to the idea of forming a common front. Everyone cautioned, however, that without progress on issues of vital interest to the Kosovo Serbs, they would not be able to sustain a positive attitude towards election participation.

On two of these vital issues UNMIK was, in fact, trying to move forward. The first one was the return of IDPs. Haekkerup had the 'Framework for Return 2001' – a policy document produced earlier by UNMIK and Kosovo Serb leaders – updated and reconsidered in the IAC. The Kosovo Albanian IAC members were cautiously constructive in their response. They endorsed the 'principles of return' although they expressed doubts about their practicability. The principles affirmed the right to return as a fundamental human right for all displaced persons, both inside and outside Kosovo, irrespective of ethnicity. Return to the displaced person's place of origin had to be voluntary and conducted with safety and dignity. It had also to be sustainable in terms of accommodation, access to public services and social and economic opportunities. And returnees had to enjoy freedom of movement. This renewed policy was to be tested during a first, low-profile phase with Kosovo Serbs returning to a few carefully selected, low-risk locations. A pilot project was to start in the Osojane area in the Istog/Istok municipality.

The other, equally long-standing and sensitive issue had to do with persons who had gone missing during the war and its immediate aftermath. This was a source of great anxiety and resentment for both the Kosovo Albanian and Serb communities. Most of those missing had been killed and buried in unmarked (mass) graves. As long as their fate was unknown, some bereft families kept up their hopes of reunion. Others, more realistically, wanted to take possession of the remains so that they could at least prepare for a proper funeral. The families often staged demonstrations, with pictures of their missing loved ones, to demand more effective action by the government. Now, with the new urgency to improve the political climate, UNMIK decided to speed up the action. It created – surprise, surprise – a special Working

Group, the bureaucratic answer to an intractable problem. On the Kosovo Albanian side 3,620 bodies had been exhumed since the end of the war, under supervision of the ICTY, of which 1260 had not yet been, identified. On the Kosovo Serb side approximately 1,300 were known to be missing. The uncertain fate of the latter had been the reason for an extended hunger strike in Gracanica in July, in which up to 200 people participated on and off for several weeks. It had needed the personal intervention of Covic, with a message from President Kostunica, to end this strike. Demonstrations kept recurring from time to time, as they did on the Albanian side. Again, despite all good intentions, this issue would also continue to haunt the international rule for many more years to come.

For the outreach to the potential Kosovo Serb electorate, we went all out using all available means and channels. We created a special Serb Task Force within OMIK consisting of Serbian-speaking internationals, divided in mobile teams to tour around Kosovo and visit IDP communities in Serbia and Montenegro. The unquestionable star of this little, dedicated group was Isidora from New York – with a Yugoslav background – who had caught my eye earlier as a young journalist working for the NGO Media Action. She had gone back to the United States to complete her master's degree at Columbia, but I enticed her to return to work in the OMIK's Elections Department. For daily contact with the Serbian authorities we now also opened a liaison office in Belgrade. I sent the best man available for the job: my chief of staff in the Pristina headquarters, Andrew Jocelyn, another fine specimen of that impressive breed of British senior military officers who combine superior education with great operational skills and discipline. I had benefited from them before in Albania in the person of Tim Isles as deputy head of Mission. And again in Pristina in the person of Martin Drake who seamlessly took over the job of chief of staff. Andrew himself set up camp in Hotel Jugoslavia, a Soviet-style building in the Zemun suburb of Belgrade, right on the banks of the Danube. Another occupant of this uninviting building was Zeljko Raznatovic, better known as Arkan, the notoriously criminal Serbian paramilitary who had caused so much suffering and bloodshed with his 'Tigers' in the Kosovo and earlier Yugoslav wars[3]. He would later meet his own violent death in front of another socialist-style hotel in Belgrade, the falsely named Intercontinental.

The main mantra early in our campaign to sway the Kosovo Serb voters was that voter registration was not a commitment to actually voting but rather a step that would keep all their options open. I usually added, slightly creatively, that their political masters in Belgrade were supporting the elections and agreed with the need to register. Of course, we assured them that the registration drive would also include their kin who were currently living as IDPs in Serbia and Montenegro. It helped a great deal that in all these promotional meetings we could point out the twenty guaranteed seats that offered an unprecedented opportunity to be (over)represented. As we soon learned, the IDP population was not easy to communicate with. On a first tour through Montenegro we visited clusters of them, often in depressing settlements. The reception was wary if not outright unfriendly. Understandably so, because most of them had lost their property, livelihood and hope. They demanded – rhetorically – to know what the hell international rule, or I for that matter, had done for them thus far. It always took a good deal of the Serbian-speaking team's time and mine to overcome the initial hostility and convince them of our good faith. We kept repeating that there was no alternative for improving their prospects than participating in the democratic process and making best use of their disproportionate share of seats in the new Assembly. We left no illusion that there was any chance of a return to the pre-war past.

In Serbia the meetings with IDPs were even more difficult, if anything. I recall a large crowd gathering outside a theatre in Nish where we were to make our presentations. Against the advice of my security detail, I stepped out to meet the assembled people. In a tense situation, amid lots of shouting and unprintable cursing, I managed to identify some spokesmen. We exchanged enough sentences for them to accept my invitation to continue our dialogue in a more civilized setting inside. It did lead to a serious review of issues and arguments. As always, it was crucial to show sincere empathy with their hardship and then move on to discuss what was realistically feasible in the given, admittedly awful circumstances. The meeting was followed by TV interviews and a chat session with journalists on a widely viewed Serbian channel. When we left there were still people outside but this time politely making way for us to leave the scene. Wizened by this and other outreach experiences, we started to produce specific radio and TV spots for the Serb language media and disseminated lots of leaflets, in both Cyrillic and Latin, explaining the composition of the Assembly, the voting system and the seats reserved for the Kosovo Serbs. And, of course, we had an endless supply of posters printed, exhorting people to *'Register, Keep Your Options Open'*.

During his own Kosovo round trip in July, Covic had appealed to all Serb political parties to form a single coalition. He repeated, several times, his call to Kosovo Serbs to register as voters in order to keep all options open for polling day. His positive interventions were somewhat tempered by comments from the north. Marko Jaksic of the SNC (north) kept insisting that Kosovo Serbs had nothing to gain from the elections. Oliver Ivanovic was only slightly more constructive; his refrain was that Kosovo Serbs would not participate in the 17 November elections if no progress was made on vital issues. The most cooperative leader among the northern Serbs, Nenad Radosavljevic from Leposavic, fell more in line. He reinforced Covic's call by making it clear that his local New Democracy party would participate in the elections but only in unison with other Kosovo Serb political entities.

Voter registration

The voter registration began on 30 July and was to run through to 8 September. During this period, a total of 173 Voter Service Centres functioned within Kosovo, of which forty-eight were fixed centres and 125 mobile that went from place to place. Their task was to update the 2000 Municipal Elections Voters' List comprising almost one million voters divided over polling stations. They had to add those Kosovo Albanian residents – an estimated 100,000 – who had newly been included in the UN civil registry but still needed to be included in the Voters' List. They also had to enlist members of the non-Albanian communities in Kosovo who had chosen not to register before, also estimated to number up to 100,000. For eligible voters outside Kosovo a separate Voters' List had to be compiled. We contracted the IOM, International Organization for Migration, for this job. In Serbia and Montenegro, where the number of IDPs was at least 100,000, they opened eighty-one and nineteen registration sites, respectively. For the unknown number of eligible voters in other countries they organized registration by mail. Five Voter Information Offices (VIO) were set up in countries with the largest concentrations of Kosovars (Germany, Belgium, Italy, Switzerland, and the United States), some of them covering neighbouring countries as well. Each office had information hotlines to answer questions from potential registrants. An Election Coordination Office in Vienna dealt with all countries not covered by a VIO. This office was also the central place to process all registration forms (against supporting documents) and in due course receive the sent-in ballots and count them on election day.

The registration got off to a slow start. The first week produced less than 4,000 new registrants in Kosovo, some 2,000 in Serbia/Montenegro and just under 6,000 applications by mail. When the speed did not pick up in the following weeks, we started to get worried and stepped up our efforts to inform and motivate all potential registrants. I made another round among the Kosovo Albanian leaders and persuaded Rugova, Thaci and Ramush to record messages for broadcast media calling on all communities to register. Our greatest concern was the low number of registrants from the non-Albanian communities, notably the Kosovo Serbs, because without them the credibility of the elections would be seriously diminished. Although President Kostunica, Prime Minister Djindjic, and Vice-Premier Čović had endorsed the registration process earlier, Kosovo Serbs were apparently still hesitant and awaiting clearer signals from their political and spiritual leaders.

The situation changed for the better towards the end of August. Local leaders, among them Bishop Artemije and Momcilo Trajkovic, registered in person, often with wide media coverage. And prominent Serbian political and religious leaders, including the Orthodox Patriarch Pavle and, again, President Kostunica, came out with strong statements in support of registration. Following these signals, the turnout at sites serving Kosovo Serbs within Kosovo jumped to thousands a day. Registration in Serbia and Montenegro also increased dramatically. To capitalize on this late spurt, I announced a two-week extension of the registration period, until 22 September, 'because of the quite spectacular surge in the demand to register'. We deployed extra staff and re-assigned mobile teams to accommodate the wave of late customers. Evidently, the message had sunk in among the Kosovo

Serbs that they could only gain politically by standing up and being counted. Some overzealous leaders might have taken it even too far, because towards the end of the period we received a number of complaints, from both in and outside Kosovo, that people had been forced to register under threat of losing their jobs or social benefits.

On 22 September, the official 'Voter Service and Civil Registration period for the 17 November 2001 Kosovo-wide Assembly Election' came to a close both in and outside Kosovo. More than 197,000 people had newly registered in Kosovo, Serbia and Montenegro. As we did not collect ethnic data on registrants, we could not give exact numbers of Kosovo Serb registrants. But more than 173,000 people registered at centres serving primarily Kosovo Serb communities, of which 70,000 were in Kosovo, nearly 98,000 in Serbia and almost 6,000 in Montenegro. In Kosovo, the number of newly registered Kosovo Albanians was a disappointingly low 25,000 (out of an estimated potential of 100,000), but this was partially explained by their temporary residence abroad. Mail-in registration applications in Vienna numbered about 50,0000. On the registration process the Election Observation Mission of the Council of Europe, responsible for the international monitoring of the electoral process, would later report that 'overall, the registration process has been conducted in a manner which is in accordance with international standards, and (the Observation Mission) pays tribute to the work of OSCE, UNMIK and the CEC [Central Election Commission]'.[4] With the registration ended, OMIK was now set to turn the raw data collected into the 2001 Voters' List. Thereafter registered voters would be invited to inspect and challenge this list before its finalization. There were some rumblings among the Kosovo Albanian parties, also voiced in the KTC, that the number of Kosovo Serb registrants was unrealistically high. I had to explain that the figure of 170,000 non-Kosovo Albanian registrants included an undetermined, but not insignificant, number of Kosovo Roma, Bosniaks, Goranis, Turks, Ashkalis, Egyptians and Croats.

With the registration of all ethnic communities brought to a good end, we had reached our first goal and precondition for successful, inclusive elections and self-government.

Notes

1 OSCE, Spot Report OMIK, 17 July 2000.

2 See footnote 1 in Chapter 2. In the case of Djindjic's murder the timing, again, was most suspicious. He was murdered in 2003 very shortly after he had made his interest known in a direct meeting with Hashim Thaci (in Budva, Montenegro) to search for a joint solution of the Serbia–Kosovo problem. It also seems increasingly likely that the murder of Oliver Ivanovic, who favoured dialogue with Pristina, in North Mitrovica in 2018 is attributable to these same extremist, right-wing circles. Evidently, throughout the years there have been well-connected forces at work to prevent any rapprochement and problem-solving between Belgrade and Pristina.

3 Arkan was also the self-styled strongman who ominously argued in public, in 1994, that 800,000 Albanians should be deported from Kosovo.

4 OSCE, Spot Report OMIK, September 2001.

7

Transition to self-rule II
Handing over governance

Birth of a party

The impressive turnout of Kosovo Serbs for registration would have had little significance without a Kosovo Serb political entity on the ballot to vote for. We had received some piecemeal indications of interest in late July, but the situation became more momentous when the political masters in Belgrade began to show interest. They figured – rightly so – that with a united front all Kosovo Serb votes could be pooled for maximum result. Yet, by the middle of September, two months before the elections, there was still no clarity about the form this joint approach would take. We had postponed the certification deadline to enable the complex negotiations to be completed, but now time was running out. The lottery to decide under what number each party was to compete on election day was set for 25 September, by which time the list of all participating parties had to be finalized. So, in order to drive home the message that the window of opportunity was soon to close, I again went with my key election staff to Belgrade on 15 September. Together with Nebojsa Covic and Kosovo Serb party representatives, we reviewed the coalition building efforts and the party certification requirements. In a final round on 17 September the Office of President Kostunica also became involved. At the request of Covic we agreed to postpone the deadline one more time until 21 September when, he promised, the certification papers would be handed over.

On that very last application date we went to Covic's office late in the afternoon to pick up the signed papers. We were asked to wait as he was busy attending to his Deputy Prime Minister's duties. After waiting for more than half an hour I asked the secretary to remind him of our presence. Another half an hour passed. Several visitors went in and out. Through the opening door we saw him behind his desk as he certainly saw us sitting in the antechamber. I sent in another message, still polite, that we would have to leave shortly to go back to Pristina. Through the door we saw that he was just continuing with his desk work as before without making the slightest gesture to acknowledge our presence, let alone apologize for the inordinately long wait. I was starting to get visibly upset. After all, here we were, having come from Pristina and delaying our return for the sole reason of safeguarding the interest of the Kosovo Serbs. And that, to add insult to injury, after so many months of strenuous efforts to reach out and create the best possible conditions for their electoral success and political strength in a future, self-governing Kosovo. When my OMIK colleagues wondered aloud how much longer this ridiculous waiting game was to go on, I decided to give it one more half hour. The secretary, quite disconcerted by now, again conveyed the message. Not even the semblance of a response. This was too much of an affront; furiously we stormed out of the building, jumped into our two waiting Pajeros and drove back to Kosovo.

All past labours seemed to have gone to waste. The election would have to be held without Kosovo Serb parties, its democratic value tarnished as a result. On the highway to Nish, somewhat calmed down – but only slightly – I decided to make one last move to turn things around. After all, there was too much at stake to let hurt pride stand in the way. I called the American Ambassador in Belgrade, Wes Montgomery, whom I had met several times before when briefing Belgrade diplomats about the elections and Serb participation. The US, of course, had an enormous stake in the success of the elections given their decisive role before, during and after the war. Montgomery answered the phone and I spilled no niceties to tell him that we were completely fed up with the way we had been treated. The game was over, the Serbs had refused to play by the rules, the deadline for certification was deliberately missed and the chances for Kosovo Serb participation in Kosovo's democratic governance were squashed. And, by the way, as UN/OSCE representatives we had been treated in an unacceptably rude manner that I surely would make known to all and sundry, in Kosovo, New York, Vienna and his own Washington. Montgomery was clearly taken aback, and he asked me to pause at the next gas station while he would contact the Government. Within half an hour he called back. It was all a misunderstanding: could we please return and pick up the papers? So we did. I did not bother to ask for explanations or apologies, but just took possession of the papers and departed instantly for Pristina ... greatly relieved. Uncle Sam's reach evidently also extended to Belgrade.

The newly created Kosovo Serb coalition was named *'Koalicija Povratak'* (Coalition Return, KP) and represented a mixture of some twenty Serb parties, mainly of the anti-Milosevic type, and NGOs. It was certified by the CEC just in time for it to participate in the ballot lottery on 25 September, which determined the order of parties on the ballot. Being a broad-based 'Citizen's Initiative' initiated and concluded by the Serbian deputy prime minister, the KP clearly reflected the intention to reaffirm Serbia's governmental stake in Kosovo politics. It meant that the Kosovo Serb centre of gravity had now firmly shifted to Belgrade, instead of fluctuating between various leaders and factions in Mitrovica, Gracanica and Belgrade. If it were to turn out as encompassing as intended, KP could, indeed, be a new, authoritative Serb force in Kosovo's political spectrum. It would also, uniquely, represent IDPs. As the only Serb political entity taking part in the Kosovo-wide election, it was likely to 'de-legitimize' other Kosovo Serb political initiatives such as the hard-line Committee for the Defence of Mitrovica which strongly opposed cooperation with UNMIK. Much depended, of course, on how the relationship between the Belgrade-based members of KP and its Kosovo-based representatives would evolve and what 'political profile' it would develop.

Conditions improve for participation

Neither the successful registration nor the certification of KP automatically implied a commitment to voting on election day. As all Serbian officials and Kosovo Serb leaders kept repeating, the final decision on voting was contingent on progress regarding the key issues of security, returns and the missing.

Happily, just at that juncture several positive developments were occurring that hinted at a better general political climate. There were, for instance, signs that the participation of Kosovo Serbs and other Kosovo ethnic communities in local administration, public utilities and public education was improving. The Kosovo Serbs decided to finally fill their vacant seats in the Pristina Municipal Council and cooperate in the municipal administration. Also, the latest (8th) *OSCE/UNHCR Assessment on the Situation of Minorities,* covering the period from March through August, reported that the situation of ethnic communities had generally improved – for the first time since 1999. Serious violence against them had declined, although daily incidents of low-level harassment remained common. In many locations a tentative improvement in freedom of movement had been noted. Paradoxically, this had a downside as well insofar as members of ethnic minorities now faced discrimination in the access to employment and administrative services. The report warned that democratic development would be undermined if these discriminatory practices were not addressed.

Significant progress had also been made in the preparations for the interim self-government that was to take over many of the UNMIK's responsibilities. According to a Regulation signed by Haekkerup on 13 September, the future Provisional Institutions of Self-Government (PISG) would comprise nine ministries, one of which was to be headed by a Kosovo Serb and another one by a member of another ethnic minority. The existing twenty departments of the JIAS (Joint Interim Administrative Structures) were being clustered to fit this new PISG structure, a process that would be completed by the time of the elections. Some key responsibilities remained under the authority of UNMIK, like the maintenance of public order and peace, international relations, the appointment of judges and fiscal policy. A proposal by Ramush to create an extra department for Euro-Atlantic relations did not make it. Also, plans for the new Assembly to start functioning by early December were being finalized, including rules of procedures and support services that duly recognized the ethnic diversity of its members.

It was helpful, too, that the issues of both missing persons and IDP returns were being actively addressed in that period of time. Something of a breakthrough had occurred through an agreement with the International

Committee for the Missing Persons to enable DNA testing and identify remains. And the first IDPs had returned to the Osojane valley. There was hope that more would follow. Also, a Regulation had been promulgated that aimed at monitoring sales of property owned by ethnic communities. The idea here was to prevent dubious transactions that would be to the detriment of minority members and threaten the multiethnic character of specific areas. (Unfortunately, one can only conclude – with the benefit of twenty years of hindsight – that this return programme never really took off, although some modest, initial returns were achieved. Local resistance proved to be too widespread and persistent. As a matter of fact, throughout these years the net outflow of Kosovo Serbs never halted.)

There was other positive news as well. On 15 September the Kosovo Police School reached its original goal of delivering 4,000 locally recruited police officers. Its latest class of graduates counted 259 cadets, of whom twenty-six represented minority communities and twenty-nine women, numbers that more or less followed the historical trend. A new target of 5,700 officers was set by the end of 2002, with higher-level training programmes added to the curriculum.

The media scene also brought good tidings. Radio Television Kosovo was, through an UNMIK Regulation, formally established as a legal, public entity. By then RTK had seven hours of television programming daily, in Albanian and Serbian, and two Kosovo-wide radio stations. With the European Broadcasting Union support phasing out – with many thanks for its crucial, initial role – Agim Zatriqi became the inspired and tireless new general manager in September. As prescribed by the Regulation, a nine-member board of directors was installed to ensure the independent public character of the broadcaster and shield it from political and commercial interference. It was made up of six representatives from Kosovo and three internationals. The Kosovo members were to be appointed from nominations by non-political bodies, namely the Senate of Pristina University, the Assembly of Kosovo NGOs, the Association of Kosovo Journalists and the RTK Workers Union. To avoid conflict of interest they could not hold elected public office, be a member of the executive body of a political party or have financial interests in the telecommunications or broadcasting industries.

During the first board meeting that I was asked to chair, the members elected Adem Demaci to the Chair, with Vjosa Dobruna and Blerim Reka as vice-chairpersons. All three were known for their inclusive, tolerant outlook and each of them had responded readily to my entreaties to stand as candidates. Coincidentally, an independent Kosovo Media Institute *Gani Bobo* had just then published the results of a media survey in Kosovo. As far as the electronic media were concerned, 85.1 per cent of those surveyed regularly watched RTK, with KTV and TV21 more or less equally trailing behind. Also, in response to a question on which TV station viewers watched for information, 86.6 per cent answered RTK, 3.6 per cent KTV and 1.2 per cent TV21. It was, for me personally, very heartening to note that this OMIK brainchild had developed into the most watched and trusted TV station in Kosovo. Our efforts to professionalize its staff (with help of the EBU), to safeguard its editorial independence from all political influences and to increase Kosovo participation in its management and journalistic activities were clearly paying off.

The political contenders

Thus, given the overall state of affairs, a modest sense of optimism was spreading and it seemed, by the end of September that conditions portended well for Kosovo's first free, general elections. Among the twenty-six certified parties, all ethnic minorities were represented: the Serbs with one, the Turks with one, the Bosniaks and Goranis with two, and the Roma, Ashkali and Egyptian communities with three parties. On the Kosovo Albanian side the main contenders were, of course, the three parties that had emerged victorious from the municipal elections of 2000. First-placed was Ibrahim Rugova's LDK with 58 per cent of the votes in 2000 and in control of twenty-two municipalities. Although it had not organized a party congress for more than three years, its party structure on the ground was still relatively unscathed. Ibrahim Rugova's popularity had remained unrivalled. To his many followers he was still 'the President'. Like other internationals I had personally experienced over many meetings that, after his success in the municipal elections, he had become more communicative and confident. Unlike in 2000 he was now intent on going out and campaigning in all the municipalities. Nevertheless, he did face some internal challenges. Rugova had placed academics and party loyalists at the top of the candidate list without much consultation, leaving out members like Bujar Bukoshi and his supporters who had been critical of his (lack of) leadership.

Hashim Thaci's second-placed PDK had won 27.3 per cents of the municipal vote and was in control of just five municipalities. After this unexpected, disappointing outcome, Thaci had somewhat changed his operating style. He had become increasingly active, visiting municipalities, encouraging newly elected representatives to leave aside political quarrels and be more inclusive. The party had also made efforts to improve its image in relation to the international presence. Although Thaci had not endorsed the Constitutional Framework for Provisional Self-Government, he had not rejected it outright and was only critical of certain provisions. On elections, for instance, he still disagreed with the chosen electoral formula preferring the majority (district) system to proportional representation – this in spite of my many attempts to convince him that a 'first past the post' district system would be at the expense of small parties and hence to the detriment of the ethnic minorities. The PDK candidates' list for the November elections was interesting. Thaci, probably inspired by his SP allies in Albania, put many non-politically affiliated persons on the PDK candidates' list. Some of these were prominent and popular like Flora Brovina and several well-known artists and writers. While these names could widen PDK's appeal, their inclusion also brought on an internal struggle, with some members from the first hour like Bardhyl Mahmuti opting out. On the other hand, to the party's credit, some other, quite prominent PDK members were excluded from the list because of their suspected association with corruption.

The Alliance for the Future of Kosovo (AAK) of Ramush Haradinaj, founded only in April 2000, had obtained 7.7 per cent of the votes cast in the municipal elections, making it the third largest party. This coalition had lost two of its member parties after the 2000 elections – the LPK (Popular Movement of Kosovo) in December 2000, when it wanted stronger support for the Albanian rebellion in the Presevo Valley, and the LKCK (the Popular Movement for the Liberation of Kosovo), the most radical wing of the coalition, in January 2001 after disagreements over AAK's leadership. Both the LPK and LKCK contained some allegedly 'extremist' elements and several of their candidates for the November elections were denied certification by the CEC. This followed an executive decision by the SRSG 'on the ineligibility of candidates', which targeted persons who were on a US 'black list' of people implicated in the violence in Macedonia. Unaffected by the defections, the AAK had remained a well-organized party with a strong, centralized management. It followed a centrist course, middle-of-the-road between LDK and PDK, as advocated by its main constituent, the Parliamentary Party, and reinforced by people like Naim Maloku who had joined earlier in the year. Ramush himself had become a very 'visible' politician, frequently visiting municipalities and meeting with people throughout Kosovo. He had proven to be especially popular among the youth while at the same time being on good terms with both other political parties and the internationals. In competition with the PDK, the AAK also placed well known, public figures on its candidates' list. The most prominent among them was Mahmut Bakalli, the moderate, communist stalwart from the 1970s turned political activist in the 1980s (and, at my request, member of the Media Advisory Board that helped us shape the media policy).

Since the other Kosovo Albanian parties had little chance of gaining any seats, the Kosovo Serb coalition Povratak (KP) was likely to be the only serious fourth contender. It could compete for the regular Assembly seats and was also assured ten out of the twenty extra seats reserved for the ethnic minorities. Its certification factually made it the main player on the Kosovo Serb political scene. It was the KP that was to determine who would be 'in' and 'who' out among Kosovo Serb leaders and who would or would not be authoritative interlocutors of the internationals. It still remained to be seen whether KP could, in the time available, develop a Kosovo identity, with a Kosovo centre and a decision-making process that would counter the perception that it was remote-controlled from Belgrade. It needed a strong, geographically diverse candidates' list with candidates from mainland Kosovo, the north and from among the IDPs in order to be credible as the dominant Kosovo Serb political factor, both within and outside Kosovo. As far as the other ethnic communities were concerned, they all basically had their own representative party that stood no chance to gain more than their guaranteed seats: three for Bosniaks and Goranis combined, three for the Roma, two for Ashkalis and Egyptians and two for the Kosovo Turks.

Electoral campaign

3 October saw the start of the electoral campaign. The day before, the KTC had its last meeting because many of its political members were going to be actively campaigning. It would be replaced by the new Kosovo Assembly after the elections. The campaigning period was to last forty-five days. It was going to be closely monitored by several observer organizations, both domestic and foreign. International interest was intense. The UN Secretary General, Kofi Annan, issued a special appeal for a violence-free electoral campaign. So did the UN Security Council, which also called on the Kosovo Serbs to join in the voting on election day. From many capitals came similar exhortations for a multiethnic and violence-free election.

I organized a visit of all four Kosovo members of the IAC – Rugova, Thaci, Ramush and Rada – to Vienna, to be heard by the Permanent Council of the OSCE. They gave off the impressive signal that, at the least, communication if not yet full-fledged cooperation between the four main factions in Kosovo politics was viable and ongoing. How favourably this compared with other post-conflict societies was not left unnoticed by many of the Permanent Representatives of this intergovernmental security organization.

The campaign's beginning showed that the international appeals had filtered through. All three Kosovo Albanian front runners struck a tone of moderation and inclusiveness. Rugova made a direct link between the elections and independence, but at the same time he called for an integrated Kosovo with guarantees for ethnic communities as spelled out in his LDK programme. The PDK platform while aiming at 'freedom, independence, and democracy', also stated a commitment to creating ethnic tolerance and integration. Thaci called on Kosovo Serbs to 'unite with the other people of Kosovo to produce a highly tolerant society', and stated that the PDK would 'stand by all citizens in the region, regardless of their ethnicity or political orientation'. Interestingly, the

PDK proposed Flora Brovina for the post of President, a sign of support for the emancipation of women but surely also a provocative slight directed at presidential-hopeful Rugova. Unlike its two main competitors, the AAK did not mention independence as an explicit goal in their platform, but referred to it in an indirect way by calling for the 'development of a democratic state'. It also stressed the importance of good relationships across ethnic lines and promoting cooperation and political understanding. True to form, Ramush was also the first Kosovo Albanian leader to hold a political rally in a Serb-dominated area (Leposavic in the north with its UNMIK-friendly mayor, Nenad Radosavljevic).

In terms of programmatic substance, there was not much that distinguished the different parties. The choice for the voters was basically between the individual leaders. Who could they best trust to be in charge of the new Provisional Institutions for Self-Government (PISG) and lead Kosovo to more prosperity and, sooner or later, independence. To the internationals, also, there was not much of a programmatic difference between the various main parties or, for that matter, the three front runners Rugova, Thaci and Ramush. They had all shown to be constructive partners in the IAC. Therefore, the internationals voiced more interest in the electoral process itself than the outcome, hoping that the massive efforts that had gone into the preparations would pay off and that the elections would be free of violence, fraud and manipulation. As OMIK we went out to various party rallies, always bringing the message that above all DEMOCRACY should win and voters should have an unimpeded choice. When I was spotted at an LDK rally with an LDK scarf, Veton Surroi wrote a nasty editorial in his Koha Ditore, accusing me of partisanship while ignoring the fact that I made similar 'empathetic' appearances at other parties' rallies. According to one of his co-editors, Dukagjin Gorani, a prominent journalist in his own right, this personal attack was probably triggered by the fact that we had collided in the past over some sensitive issues (access to public premises, RTK acces to commercial revenue, code of conduct).

If the election campaign got off to a smooth start for the Kosovo Albanians, the Kosovo Serbs were still struggling to determine their course of action. The KP was in its formative stage and had yet to establish some sort of a corporate entity, while the relations between the Belgrade-based members and the representatives in Kosovo still needed to be better defined. The party's political agenda was clear, though. It focused on security, freedom of movement, fate of the missing, return of property and the return of IDPs – all of this to be achieved 'through mutual dialogue and tolerance of all ethnic communities'. During a general meeting early in October in Gracanica, hosted by Bishop Artemije, guest speaker Covic reiterated the need for full and transparent cooperation with UNMIK within the framework of UNSCR 1244. He cautioned, however, that a decision on Kosovo Serb participation in the 17 November vote had not yet been made.

In a step towards building confidence among ethnic communities ahead of the elections, the Princeton University-based *Project on Ethnic Relations*, with support from OMIK, held a special Kosovo Review Session. There were participants from all communities in Kosovo, from Belgrade and from the foreign offices and international agencies in Pristina. It was the first encounter of the Kosovo Albanian political leaders with Serbian deputy prime minister Covic. Rugova, Thaci and Ramush were *unisono* in urging the Kosovo Serbs to participate in the elections while acknowledging the legitimate demands of the Serbs for better security, freedom of movement and returns. Covic, in response, expressed his hope that the situation would soon be normalized in Kosovo. He added, though, that everyone should accept that the elections did not come with a mandate to change the status of Kosovo. The Kosovo Serb representatives confirmed that they understood the importance of the electoral process while reiterating the need for the internationals and Kosovo Albanians to do more to meet their concerns. The international participants, on their part, emphasized the responsibility of the (Kosovo) Serb leaders to inform Kosovo Serbs about the irreparable harm to their community that would result from their non-participation. Although this Round Table meeting did not produce concrete results, it marked the beginning of direct communication and exchange of views between senior Belgrade and Kosovo Albanian leaders.

Final effort to engage the Serbs

Meanwhile, the CEC had verified all but a few of the candidate lists. Each party was allowed to field up to 110 candidates. Among the various criteria was also the one that had been so successfully introduced the year before, namely that every third candidate had to be a woman (in the first two-thirds of each list). By the middle of October, the KP was the only one that had not yet submitted a complete candidate list. This meant that again special efforts were needed to engage the Serbs in general and to motivate the Kosovo Serbs to vote. This is exactly what we set out to do. On 25 October a crucial encounter was set up in Belgrade between a top-level UNMIK delegation and FRY/Serbian officials led by President Kostunica. The immediate aim was to persuade the Belgrade leadership to encourage Kosovo Serb participation in the 17 November election, as well as permit election preparations in Serbia and Montenegro. We were not alone in that quest. A week earlier the UN Secretary General had also requested support from the FRY and Serbian governments for the Kosovo-wide election. So, in fact, had US President Bush.

The broader purpose of the talks was to reach a cooperation agreement between UNMIK and the FRY/Serbian Governments. To this end UNMIK had prepared a document 'On The Protection And Promotion Of Kosovo Serb Interests: Current Situation And The Way Forward'. It provided a detailed overview of the measures that were already in place or being planned to protect the rights and interests of Kosovo Serbs. The idea was that follow-up negotiations should produce a Joint UNMIK/FRY Declaration on all the main issues and give their endorsement for the elections. The meetings were held in the huge presidential building in New Belgrade, a massive structure clearly designed to impress and reflect the socialist ambitions of Tito's Federal Yugoslavia at the time. The atmosphere inside was quite positive. However constructive, the first meeting did not yet provide OMIK with the much needed go-ahead for the preparations of elections in Serbia and Montenegro. We needed this official clearance to proceed with the setting up of polling centres and the recruitment and training of staff. For me it was reason to issue a press release, on 26 October, expressing concern that – with less than three weeks to election day – approximately 100,000 eligible Kosovo Serb IDPs risked becoming disenfranchised.

During a marathon meeting on Friday, 2 November, a joint document was discussed that reflected a great deal of agreement but left three key issues unresolved. On security, the judiciary and the police, Kostunica could not accept the proposed texts. It became clear that a final agreement would take more time. In order to salvage the elections I suggested that the endorsement of Kosovo Serb election participation be decoupled from agreement on the joint document as a whole. This pragmatic solution was widely supported. We even got the UN headquarters to intervene. UN Secretary General Kofi Annan telephoned Kostunica urging him to endorse the elections and continue discussions on two of the three outstanding issues. The third issue of security calling for the return of the Yugoslav army and police, the SG ruled out as totally unacceptable to the UN. By the end of the day, President Kostunica went along and stated so publicly in a late-night press conference. The next day, Saturday 3 November, saw confirmation of this outcome, with clear signals to the public that Kosovo Serbs should vote. In a TV interview Kostunica repeated the message that non-participation was the greater evil that would lead to isolation of not only Kosovo Serbs but also of the FRY/Serbia and, secondly, that defending and promoting the interests of the Kosovo Serbs would be better done inside the new Kosovo institutions. There was no more time to waste now, so on that very same day I met with Covic and Raskovic-Ivic (the Commissioner for Refugees and IDPs) to review the arrangements and finalize a formal agreement, needed to organize the elections in Serbia and Montenegro. This covering Memorandum of Understanding, already prepared by us in Pristina, was signed a day later.

The 'Common Document'

Work on the basic agreement also progressed sufficiently for Haekkerup and Kostunica to formally sign, on 5 November, what was now named the 'UNMIK-FRY Common Document'. Strictly in line with UNSC Resolution 1244, it stressed that UNMIK remained the only body responsible for the administration of Kosovo while leaving the Constitutional Framework and the future Provisional Institutions of Self-Government (PISG) intact. The document also identified areas of common interest for cooperation with Belgrade and a series of activities aimed at improving the lives of Kosovo Serbs. A working group would be formed with Belgrade representatives, on one side, and representatives of UNMIK and the PISG, on the other. As an important step towards rebuilding mutual confidence, FRY/Serbia-UNMIK cooperation would be pursued with respect to the missing persons, the detainees and the judicial system. And, indeed, OMIK was given the green light to begin work on election preparation in the republics of Serbia and Montenegro.

Throughout Kosovo, the reaction to the Common Document in the Kosovo Albanian press was highly critical. Even more moderate Kosovo Albanian dailies strongly denounced it as going against Kosovo Albanian interests. The main concern was the (perceived) suggestion of greater influence of FRY/Serbia in the governance of Kosovo, which contradicted the tenets of UNSCR 1244. Within hours after Haekkerup's return from Belgrade, he convened a special IAC session although Thaci and Rada Trajkovic were both out of town. The SRSG presented the UNMIK-FRY Common Document, reminding the attending IAC members that the document enjoyed unanimous international support. Rugova and Ramush were not impressed. Rugova noted that though UNMIK had the right to sign such a document and though the LDK would not obstruct it, Kosovo Albanians did not like it. He added that the proposal to form an UNMIK – FRY – PISG working group was not necessary since its areas of interest would be part of the competence of the new Assembly. He did, however, welcome the decision in favour of Kosovo Serb participation in the elections and their involvement in the PISG. Ramush Haradinaj described the document as 'unnecessary'. As it had also been signed by UNMIK, it opened new inroads for Belgrade interventions, which were strongly opposed by the Kosovo Albanian population. Although he also welcomed Kosovo Serb participation in the election, he wanted it to be made clear that Kosovo would never be 'returned to Serbia'. In the regular IAC session the following day (6 November), the SRSG once again presented the Document. With Rugova and Ramush absent, it was now Thaci who made short shrift of the Document. He denounced it as 'unacceptable' since Kosovo Albanian leaders had not been consulted. Rugova's substitute, Fatmir Sejdiu, supported Thaci's comments. Randel Nokic, who substituted for Rada Trajkovic as Kosovo Serb representative, could be little more than a hapless bystander, visibly uncomfortable with the situation.

While the Kosovo Albanian leadership's reaction to the Common Document had been intensely critical, the Kosovo Serb leadership also appeared to be divided on the 'Common Document', especially the call for Serb participation in the elections. Some prominent Kosovo Serb leaders such as Rada Trajkovic and Nenad Radosavljevic spoke out in support. They argued that the elections were only a first step in a long democratic process, which they were now willing to take. Others such as the northern hardliners, but also a relative moderate like Momcilo Trajkovic disagreed because in their view the Document provided no guarantees that the minimum conditions for participation would be fulfilled. Their position did not change with the special visit by NATO Secretary General, George Robertson, who welcomed the Common Document, urged all Kosovo Serbs to vote and reminded them and everyone else that NATO was committed to a 'multi-ethnic Kosovo and would not tolerate the creation of another mono-ethnic state'.

Pre-election final days

While the agitated debate on the Common Document was going on, Kosovo Albanian political parties continued to reach out to voters through rallies and town-hall meetings. The AAK was running a modern, well-organized campaign, distributing extensive campaign literature at large rallies attended by Ramush and other senior leaders like Naim Maloku and Mahmut Bakalli. In order to portray itself as a party of the centre, the AAK used the slogan 'Neither left, nor right, just straight ahead' and emphasized economic development. The LDK campaign was less intense and outreaching, with scattered rallies capitalizing on the personal popularity of Rugova. The tenor of speeches here was more general and nationalistic, focusing mostly on LDK's role in the 'fight for Kosovo's independence' and the sacrifices it had made before, during and after the war. Surprisingly, in comparison with the LDK, the PDK was using quite moderate language explicitly mentioning, for example, the need for integration of ethnic communities, especially the Kosovo Serb community. True to their preference for district representation, the PDK had placed candidates from the municipalities, outside of Pristina, high up on the candidates' list. This was to send the message that municipalities would have their 'own representative' in the Assembly if people voted for PDK. In general, all campaign events were conducted 'in a calm and peaceful way', in the words of the international observers.

Koalicija Povratak (KP)'s election campaign began only after the signing of the 5 November Common Document and FRY President Kostunica's call for Kosovo Serb participation in the election. It submitted a list of sixty candidates, comprising a mix of academicians, teachers, doctors, journalists and politicians. They included several familiar personalities like Rada Trajkovic from Gracanica, Randel Nokic from Kosovo Polje and Nenad Radosavljevic from Leposavic. More of a surprise was the candidature of Oliver Ivanovic from North Mitrovica, even if he had, indeed, become more cooperative with UNMIK. He had, for instance, been active in organizing the return of IDPs under the 'Framework for Return 2001' (that he had co-authored). As expected, Momcilo Trajkovic was not part of the list. Although in August he had been among the first to register and had urged others to do the same, he had reached the conclusion that conditions were not right to vote. He was now actively calling for non-participation.

KP's difficulties in presenting itself and rallying for the Kosovo Serb electorate became soon apparent, an indication of how divided the Kosovo Serb community still was. When conducting 'town hall meetings' KP candidates and Belgrade delegations were confronted with a long list of grievances and frustrations by Kosovo Serbs. Touring Kosovo Serb areas to promote KP, Deputy Prime Minister Covic himself faced criticism and disapproval of Belgrade's decision to endorse the electoral process. On a visit to the Patriarchate in Pec/Peja – a medieval architectural wonder with fine Byzantine frescoes – even the monks turned against him and expressed their unwillingness to participate. On a similar visit there around the same time, I was myself rather rudely reminded that I was not a very welcome foreigner. In the north of Kosovo, where KP actively distributed flyers and put up posters displaying *'Vote for Povratak! For the return of our Army and Police'*, its campaign material was quickly torn down in most places. When I asked Oliver Ivanovic about the poor reception of 'his' party, he mentioned that Kosovo Serbs were still confused over the contradictory messages coming from various political centres in Belgrade. That included President Kostunica's own party, of which the hostile Marko Jaksic was the Kosovo spokesman. Mastermind Covic also blamed the poor

Kosovo Serb response to the Povratak campaign on unnamed, obstructionist (Serbian) party and state officials. Still, it was not clear how effective this opposition would turn out to be or, inversely, how successful KP would be in swaying the Kosovo Serbs to their side. Only the election results could tell.

In order to ensure the best possible quality of the voting process, I had successfully asked the OSCE Permanent Council for 100 per cent international supervision, which required the participating states to provide 1,600 International Polling Station Supervisors. These supervisors were trained in Greece in the week prior to the election day. It was probably one of the largest OSCE election staffing efforts ever. It was quite exhilarating to address this huge crowd of keenly interested men and women in the largest assembly hall of Thessaloniki. I fed their excitement by stressing the historic significance of their mission: assisting the birth of a nation at a critical juncture. Russia and other Slavic countries had also responded to the call for staff so that many of their supervisors could usefully become part of the multinational teams deployed in Serbian-speaking polling areas.

E-day

17 November 2001 – E-Day – turned out to be a great day. Members of all of Kosovo's communities cast ballots for the new Kosovo Assembly. Neither the boycott of Kosovo Serb voters nor the early logistical difficulties that affected the 2000 municipal elections were repeated. The election was observed by 200 short-term and 20 long-term international observers under the umbrella of the Council of Europe. Among the short-term observers were parliamentarians from the OSCE Parliamentary Assembly, the Council of Europe Parliamentary Assembly and the European Parliament. As important, if not more so, were the 13,286 domestic observers, from political entities and non-governmental organizations, who had registered to observe the elections. They played an irreplaceable role in ensuring the transparency of the process to the voters and the acceptance of the results. As such, they set an important precedent for future elections.

Nearly 65 per cent of the 1.25 million registered voters went to vote. Although the percentage turnout was higher for the 2000 municipal elections, more people voted in the 2001 Kosovo-wide elections as a result of the fact that many more eligible voters had registered. Approximately 810,000 votes were cast, some 13 per cent more than the year before. Again, OMIK did not collect ethnic data about voters, so there was no precise information about the ethnicity of the voters. However, based upon the locations of the polling centres, it could be fairly estimated that some 67 per cent of voters residing in predominantly Kosovo Albanian areas and 47 per cent of those living in predominantly non-Albanian areas had voted. As for out-of-Kosovo voters, 58 per cent and 57 per cent voted in the republics of Serbia and Montenegro, respectively, whereas 53 per cent of the by-mail registrants sent in their ballot.

The Kosovo Albanian turnout of 67 per cent appeared to be lower than was the case in the 2000 municipal elections (79 per cent). This was partially due to the absence of registered voters who had gone abroad. The natural decline in participation seen in post-conflict elections and cold weather explained much of the rest of the decline. That said, the turnout was still much more than achieved in most mature democracies. Given the fact that the FRY/Serbian governments and Kosovo Serb leaders had endorsed the electoral process only twelve days prior to the election, the turnout among Kosovo Serbs was truly impressive. Especially so, when considering the anti-election intimidation in some Kosovo Serb areas, notably in the north, as reported by international and domestic observers. A remarkable achievement was pulled off in Serbia and Montenegro where the IOM, together with the respective Commissariats for Refugees, succeeded in managing an orderly election with a high turnout of the IDPs within the twelve-day time frame (most parliamentary democracies need at least one month to conduct an election). Generally, polling procedures and management of polling stations, especially large polling centres, had improved considerably compared to the municipal elections and queues were short, fast and orderly.

By the end of the day, it was clear that the OMIK had delivered on its commitment to provide the right electoral conditions to all voters and communities, and that Kosovo had peacefully adhered to the electoral rules. In a joint press conference that evening SRSG Hans Haekkerup, KFOR commander, General Marcel Valentin and myself on behalf of OMIK lauded the success of the elections and the democratic spirit of the voters. As I reported to the OSCE headquarters: 'Election Day was conducted in the same atmosphere of calm that marked the campaign. 20,000 OMK staff, including almost 9,000 local Polling Station Committee members and 2,000 International Polling Station Supervisors, served the electorate in an expeditious and professional manner. The political entities and the voters respected the Electoral Rules. Turnout was high, even on a cold day, and even among communities which chose not to participate in the 2000 Municipal Elections.' The international observers of the Council of Europe, the OSCE and the EU issued a joint, very positive, statement, stating that 'the Electoral Code provided conditions for free and fair elections ... registration was carried out successfully ... the elections were conducted in an efficient manner (...) the organizing authorities performed their duties in a constructive and professional manner'. Bruce George (UK MP), speaking on behalf of the OSCE Parliamentary Assembly observers, said, 'The election yesterday was conducted to the very highest standards, not only in comparison to recently emerging democracies but against older democracies ... election observers, staff and public can feel immensely proud.'[1]

Election results and aftermath

While the electoral process was being praised all around, the obvious next question was whether the results would be respected and implemented. The first indicative results showed that the LDK had won approximately 46 per cent of the vote, the PDK 26, Coalition Return (KP) nearly 11 and the AAK nearly 8 per cent, while four small parties had each received roughly 1 percent of the votes. With the final outcome still pending, the Kosovo Albanian leaders already came out with public statements lauding the elections and claiming success. Rugova announced, rather prematurely, a 'landslide victory' of 70 per cent for his LDK and declared himself the future president of Kosovo. Calling on the world for immediate recognition of Kosovo as an independent state, he reassured the Kosovo Serbs that they would have all the rights enjoyed by ethnic communities in other states. In addition to their seats in the Kosovo parliament, he promised them a ministerial post in the future government. Ramush Haradinaj praised the electoral process and stated that 'we are very happy for the elections yesterday, because the AAK supports the institutions that will be created after 17 November (...) we are very honored to be in the future parliament of Kosovo'. He noted that the Alliance had achieved a solid result, claiming to have doubled the number of voters they had had in the municipal elections. Thaci also joined the chorus by overestimating PDK support, claiming to have obtained more than 33 per cent of the votes.

When on 19 November, the more definitive results confirmed the initial figures and it became clear that the Kosovo Serb citizens' initiative KP had obtained over 10 per cent of the vote, the reactions of the Kosovo Albanian leaders became less positive – about the results, that is, not the process. They realized that their number of seats in the Assembly would be less than expected and that the Kosovo Serbs would obtain, besides their share of regular seats, an additional ten seats as guaranteed by the Constitutional Framework. They started to have second thoughts about the system of reserved seats. In their view, this had been adopted in anticipation of a Kosovo Serb boycott of the elections. Now that the Kosovo Serbs had actually participated and won regular seats, they would be vastly overrepresented. As a result the Assembly would not fairly reflect the ethnic composition of the Kosovo population. There was, however, little they could do but abide by the jointly agreed rules, which – to their credit – they did.

The Kosovo Serb reaction to the conduct of the election, the turnout and the results was largely positive, as was to be expected with the KP gaining nearly 11 per cent of the votes. FRY President Vojislav Kostunica, noting the high turnout of Kosovo Serbs, stated that the Kosovo-wide elections represent the 'political wisdom, resolve and responsibility' of Kosovo Serbs and that cooperation with the international community was the only way ahead. Serbian deputy prime minister Nebojsa Covic also noted that these elections were a step towards democracy (though he deplored, not very realistically, the fact that a fierce 'anti-election campaign' by Serb obstructionists had cost the Kosovo Serbs seven to ten more seats in the Assembly). This positive sentiment was echoed by most Kosovo Serb leaders. It was a bit disconcerting, however, that some of them saw the electoral success not so much as a ticket to join the new self-governing institutions but, rather, as a step towards restoring

Belgrade's participation in the governance of Kosovo. How loyally the KP would participate in Kosovo's self-rule remained to be seen.

The SRSG certified the election results on 24 November and announced that the inaugural session of the Assembly would be convened on 10 December. Though fourteen parties had obtained regular seats, only three Kosovo Albanian parties had won more than one elected seat in the Assembly. The LDK had gained forty-seven, the PDK twenty and the AAK eight elected seats. The *Koalicija Povratak* (KP), in addition to the ten seats set aside as provided for in the Constitutional Framework, had won twelve elected seats with their percentage of the general vote and thus become the third largest faction in the Assembly. Despite the second thoughts about the seat allocation system, the fact remained that these first, democratic Kosovo-wide elections had proven to be inclusive and reflective of the diversity of Kosovo. All communities had participated in the electoral process and, thanks to the reserved seats, all would be heard in the Assembly. Moreover, thirty-four women had been elected – almost 30 per cent of the Assembly. And the elected candidates were registered in twenty-one different municipalities, representing a wide geographical spread. No single party would be able to dominate. Cooperation would be the practical necessity of the future. Only time could tell how the different cooperative, competitive and even obstructionist tendencies would play out.

The elections marked the end of the important first phase of nation building. As I concluded at the time (*see boxed text*), the international intervention had brought some notable achievements. Despite the undeniable tragedies, shortcomings and setbacks, the Kosovo intervention was a 'relative success', in comparison with situations elsewhere in the world emerging from bitter ethnic strife and civil war, whether nearby Bosnia and Herzegovina, Israel and the Middle East or Cambodia, Ruanda and Afghanistan. Surely, ethnic reconciliation – the hardest of all challenges, anytime anywhere – seemed to remain a fata morgana, but the foundation had been laid for Kosovo to further develop into a democratic state within and akin to the European family of nations. Whether and how this was going to be sustained and expanded was, of course, far from clear, given the continued uncertainty of its status and the inherent risks thereof.

At the end of my stay I summarized in a personal note, for 'future reference', how Kosovo under international guidance had met five main challenges in the first phase of post-conflict stabilization and rehabilitation:

1. Return of refugees
Kosovo has succeeded in re-absorbing and reintegrating well over a million refugees and displaced persons – some 80% of the population – in a matter of months under the worst possible conditions, when the administration, the economy and the infrastructure were still in tatters. Important also, the usual 'collateral damage' of huge refugee flows remaining in third countries had not occurred. On the negative side, the successful return was partly offset by the failure to prevent an exodus of Kosovo Serbs and Roma, amounting to around 8% of its population.

2. Ethnic strife
Post-war ethnic revenge by Kosovo Albanians has caused an estimated 500 deaths and 100.000 refugees/displaced persons among the Kosovo Serbs. However tragic and condemnable, this was crucially different from the earlier Serbian ethnic cleansing of Kosovo Albanians – and the Croatian ethnic cleansing of Serbs in Croatia in 1995 – in that it was individually motivated and enacted. It was not officially sanctioned and systematically executed by organs of state such as the military, police and paramilitary. While unpardonable, this human toll should be weighed against the 10 to 15,000 dead and around one million refugees and displaced on the Kosovo Albanian side before and during the war. It should also be assessed in the light of failing (international) law enforcement in the first months after the war.

Sadly, the initial stated goal of a harmonious multi-ethnic society never stood a chance in a (former) Yugoslavia that had already succumbed to a vicious and infectious nationalism. Developments tended towards mono-ethnic nationhood in spite of all international pressure, governmental measures and moral persuasion. The new Kosovo proved no exception to the rest of the (Western) Balkans – or the world for that matter. Yet, despite the virulent ethnic enmity, in the far and recent past, the Kosovo Albanian leaders – whether for political opportunism or conscience or both – did consistently call for moderation and reconciliation from day one after the war. They might have done more to discourage the ethnic vindictiveness but they could certainly not be accused of stoking ethnic hatred. In fact, it was quite unprecedented how far they went along with appeals and measures to protect minority rights.

3. Demilitarization and police
The way the KLA guerrilla force was demilitarized and transformed into a civil defense corps was most impressive, given the liberation claims and expectation of corresponding rewards. Both the low numbers absorbed in the KPC and its restricted mandate came as a huge disappointment if not humiliation to the KLA fighters. It is a major, and quite unprecedented, political achievement that the KLA foremen, notably Hashim Thaci and Agim Ceku, were able to pull this off.

Similarly, the creation of a domestic police force has been a widely acclaimed success, inside and outside Kosovo. It is the one new state institution with a significant participation of minorities and an unprecedented share of women. Starting from scratch and still in formation it could not, and still cannot, be expected to compensate for the serious shortcomings of UNMIK's international police force.

4. Political accommodation
From the start the Kosovo Albanian leaders went along with far-reaching formulas of sharing power in governing institutions, at the municipal and central level. Similarly, they agreed to more than fair shares of minorities in other bodies such as the police, the judiciary and the Central Election Commission. They contributed to very successful, first general elections by abiding by the electoral rules and accepting the outcome even in the face of disappointing results. They accepted a formula of guaranteed seats in Parliament that was heavily skewed in favor of the minorities, notably the Kosovo Serbs. There are, world-wide, few if any examples of such generous power sharing with former adversaries.

5. Media landscape
Critical for any democracy is a media climate that fosters diversity and freedom of the press. Through legislation and wide support, from private and public sources both national and international, Kosovo can boast of a robust presence of independent press, electronic and printed. Quite unique for an emerging democracy, it has a public broadcaster, widely watched, that is legally shielded from governmental and political interference.

With OMIK having delivered credible elections, I felt that my own mission had come to completion. Although the international role was far from over, it was time for me personally to hand over the baton. And so the end came, not without an exuberant, emotional farewell party.

I left a new Kosovo that was hugely different from the one I had entered in June 1999 : full of promise but also of risk and challenge.

Note

1   As quoted in OSCE Spot Report OMIK, November 2001.

8

Concluding remarks
Lessons not learned

When looking back at the two missions, the obvious question is whether there are any lessons to be passed on. There may well be, but I have few illusions in this regard. History shows that every foreign intervention has its own dynamics and makes its own mistakes, both old and new. I have witnessed quite a few interventions, from within and from afar, but seldom have I seen 'lessons' learned and applied. In practice, institutional memory is stored away and the wheel ever so often reinvented. Admittedly, neither situations nor the people involved are ever identical. What I can offer, therefore, are some comparative observations on key issues that may or may not be relevant for future interventions.

Simple versus complex

The intervention in Albania confirms the obvious: a simple mission that is limited in size, duration and mandate has far better chances to succeed than a complex one. In the Albanian case the conditions were exceptionally benign. The intervention was widely welcomed, inside and outside the country. The Italian-led military 'coalition of the willing' – ALBA – was never challenged, nor was the lead role of the OSCE. There was no plethora of international organizations vying for dominance or a larger share of the responsibilities. The

UN had a very modest and quiet presence, the Council of Europe just one person co-located with the OSCE. The OSCE mission was comparatively small, with some twenty internationals in Tirana and another twenty in ten field offices spread over the country. Also, there was no 'invasion' of NGOs preoccupied with their own, often donor-driven agendas, however well-meaning. In short, Albania did not witness the overbearing international presence that over time tends to cause local frustration, impatience and resentment.

From the start, the military role of ALBA was defined to be short-lived, not open-ended. It was to defuse the civil conflict, to enable fair elections and to quit. It did so in six months. The command structure and duties were clear-cut and not questioned. There was not the obfuscation with civilian tasks that bedeviled military deployments in other crisis areas, straining relations with civilian agencies and NGOs (as I witnessed in Afghanistan, for example). On the non-military side, the OSCE was also well scripted: to assist in stabilizing the situation and to usher in a new era of democratic governance while cementing a stronger linkage to Euro-Atlantic structures. The code to success in the Albanian intervention may therefore well be summarized as clarity of purpose, clarity of tasks and clarity of actors.

The Kosovo intervention was the exact opposite. It resulted from a war that was disputed and had deepened ethnic trauma and division. The mandate was inherently ambivalent, with irreconcilable objectives: preparing Kosovo for self-government while insisting that it had to remain an integral part of the Federal Republic of Yugoslavia/Serbia. Instead of supporting national governance as was the case in Albania, in Kosovo the 'international community' itself had to exercise governance and run a protectorate – something it had never done before. To further complicate matters, it had to do so through two separate, independent multinational institutions, NATO/KFOR for the military and UN/UNMIK for the civilian tasks.

The military force was under unified NATO command but only up to a point, since the various troop contingents remained under final control (Rules of Engagement) of the contributing nations. As a result, widely divergent practices of peacekeeping were followed in different regions. Some of these reflected differences in style such as patrolling the streets in vehicles and heavy armour (the US) or on foot and lightly armed (the UK) – with obviously different impacts on local perception. Other differences were more consequential. The

French troops in the north, for example, were notoriously reluctant to take on the militant Kosovo Serbs, having given up that northern region to the latter's control. The German troops in the south were under instructions from their capital to avoid lethal confrontations. So much so that during the ethnic riots of 2004 they withdrew from the scene of violence in Prizren, to the outrage of the then (German!) commander of KFOR.

The civilian lead role of the UN was also hampered by complexity insofar as its leverage over the other constituent UNMIK partners – notably the EU and OSCE, with their own mandates – was limited and dependent on mutual agreements and personal chemistry. This handicap was only partially overcome by a formal, central coordinating body, with the UN Special Representative of the Secretary General presiding over the four 'Pillar Heads', who also served as his Deputy SRSGs. In the crucial area of law enforcement the UNMIK police, unlike KFOR, did have a clear central command, but its problems were with the rank and file. Policemen (never women as far as I have noticed) came in national contingents supplied by member states from different regions of the world. Cultural differences, language and communication problems as well as (very) frequent rotations and time lags detracted UNMIK police from becoming an effective force. Inadequate skill levels and a general tendency towards risk-avoidance often compounded the problem.

Legitimacy versus legality

After the Second World War the United Nations was created to prevent or settle conflicts between nations in what was becoming an increasingly interdependent world. By implication a foreign intervention in any state should be sanctioned by this highest body if might is not to prevail arbitrarily over right. The Albanian intervention was consensual, internationally and domestically. The OSCE had obtained proper authorization from the UN Security Council through a supporting Resolution before the intervention was launched. On the other hand, the Kosovo intervention, at least its beginning, was *illegal* in the strict sense of international law. The NATO bombing campaign was not formally sanctioned by the UN Security Council, although it did receive an endorsement of seventeen members of the Security Council against three (among which was the veto-wielding Russian Federation, Serbia's long-term ally). Nevertheless, there are strong arguments to consider the intervention *legitimate*.

International efforts to resolve the long-simmering conflict in Kosovo through peaceful means had been many and multifarious, spanning several years: special envoys, resolutions in different multilateral forums and bilateral appeals. Twice in 1998, in March and September, the UN Security Council issued strong-worded warnings to the Yugoslav government to refrain from oppressive policies and seek political solutions. It even imposed an arms embargo and, in its September resolution, warned of 'additional measures' if troops were not withdrawn and displaced people allowed to return to their homes.

Also, by way of censure the OSCE maintained Yugoslavia's suspension as a participating state, dating from the earlier Bosnian war. NATO had issued warnings on two occasions that it was preparing for air strikes in case Belgrade did not heed international admonitions. The response of the Milosevic regime to all entreaties, exhortations and warnings was, consistently, outward defiance and internal repression. Two final diplomatic efforts tried to stop the violence and massive expulsion of Kosovo Albanians: the Holbrooke–Milosevic agreement of October 1998 and the Rambouillet peace negotiations of February–March 1999. Even if considered only a 'Band Aid' solution by the Americans, the first one could have offered a way out of the conflict if only the Serbs had been more prepared to compromise and if the Europeans had acted more decisively. Neither of these happened and the agreement was soon breached in both spirit and action. The second, final effort in Rambouillet was practically doomed from the start, with Western patience running out, Serbian intransigence continuing, the US keen to force regime change in Belgrade and conditions on the ground in Kosovo worsening.

With diplomatic efforts exhausted and the humanitarian disaster unfolding, an international military intervention became unstoppable. Inaction was no longer an option, especially in light of two earlier ethnic dramas that had been enabled by international passivity: the nearby Srebrenica massacre of 8,000 Muslim men and boys in 1995 and, even far worse, the wanton killing of almost one million Tutsis in Ruanda in 1997. In both cases the UN had had to stand by haplessly because of the lack of international consensus: this was the main reason for the US and the UK insisting on NATO rather than UN boots on the ground in Kosovo. If there were also ulterior motives at play such as regime change in FRY/Serbia – as I am sure there have been – they were by themselves not decisive enough to trigger the war. By ignoring the international concerns and defiantly dealing with the conflict as an internal affair, the Belgrade regime basically brought the war onto itself. Not unlike it had fomented the armed resistance by the Kosovo Liberation Army by disregarding peaceful attempts in Kosovo to seek political accommodation from within.

The legitimacy of the intervention was in a way confirmed by the same UN Security Council when it took formal charge of the post-war situation through its Resolution 1244. The Russian Federation, while opposed to the UN sanctioning the war, actively contributed to the peace settlement. So much so that a Russian military contingent was integrated in KFOR while Russia also took part in the civilian UNMIK. In other words, the outcome of the war – transfer of Kosovo's administration from Belgrade to the 'international community', meaning the UN – was based on consensus.

The tangled history illustrates the predicament of 'legitimate' versus 'legal'. The Independent International Commission on Kosovo, the so-called Goldstone Commission, concluded in 2000 that the Kosovo war had been legitimate even if formally illegal. It went on to recommend that international law be expanded and refined to close this gap between legal and legitimate. A good 'lesson learned', indeed, if the defence of human and democratic rights is an international concern and, in principle, a common responsibility. In fact, as mentioned in the Context Chapter, all Heads of State and Government at a World Summit in 2005 affirmed the Responsibility to Protect populations from genocide, ethnic cleansing and crimes against humanity, also for the international community in case an individual State flagrantly fails to protect its population. I am afraid, though, that sanctioning of military interventions by the UN Security Council will remain rare, and imaginable only if not in conflict with the geopolitical interests of the veto-wielding members – as had been the case with the Albanian intervention.

International protectorate

In Albania the international assistance came to support existing governmental structures and elected representatives. For post-war Kosovo, the UN

Resolution 1244 stipulated a uniquely different set-up: an international civilian administration under UN auspices to provide for interim governance while preparing institutions for self-government. There was no viable alternative. Contrary to what some Kosovo commentators have argued, the option of immediate self-rule with international backstopping was completely out of question. As we have seen, Kosovo had basically imploded. No trained human capacities were at hand since in the preceding decade Kosovo Albanians had been largely excluded from governing responsibilities or they had gone abroad. Politically also, self-government was to be ruled out. Apart from the perilous situation of the minority populations, notably the Kosovo Serbs, there was a vast divide between the two main Kosovo Albanian political factions, Ibrahim Rugova's LDK and Hashim Thaci's KLA (claiming the Provisional Government of Kosovo). Forging a united government from these divergent forces was simply inconceivable. Internationally speaking, instant self-government was also out of question if only because Kosovo's constitutional status had been left undefined. It was a matter of principal disagreement between the Kosovo Albanians and Belgrade, which was echoed at the higher international level between NATO member countries and Russia and, less prominently, China. The latter two were opposed to the separatism that Kosovo exemplified. Even among NATO countries there were differences of view on the future relationship between Kosovo and Serbia, ranging from more or less autonomy to semi- or full independence. This lack of international consensus was, of course, the main reason why Resolution 1244 had left Kosovo's final status vague, to be decided at an unspecified later date – a sure recipe for continuous tension and conflict.

Limbo status

With the benefit of hindsight one could reason that the very premise of the international administration of Kosovo was flawed. The end goal had been left deliberately vague: self-government within Yugoslav borders. The key notion of 'independence' was only obliquely referred to as 'the will of the people' and never upheld as a foreseeable end status. Independence from

Serbia was, of course, the historic, shared objective of all Kosovo Albanians – just as it had become a reality for the other constituent people of Yugoslavia: Slovenes, Croats, Bosnians, Macedonians and, lastly, Montenegrins. Being an elusive goal, many in Kosovo felt – after the war – that it was still to be wrested from Serbia and the international community. To them, the struggle for independence was not yet over, a cause of the continuing militancy. One can only wonder how much of the violence – the ethnic cleansing, the war and the violent aftermath – could have been avoided if, in an alternative scenario, agreement had been reached in Rambouillet, or better still, earlier, on a time path to independence with effective safeguards for all.

This notion of 'conditional independence' had been advocated by the Goldstone Commission. Its eleven expert members came from all parts of the world, including the US and Russia. On the status of Kosovo the Commission acknowledged the inherent contradiction between 'preparing for self-government' and the 'territorial integrity of Yugoslavia'. It had determined that a return to Serbian supervision would be complete anathema to the Kosovo Albanians, the overwhelming majority of the resident population. It recommended, therefore, a 'conditional independence' within an international framework that would ensure the rights of all Kosovo minorities. Unfortunately, their thoughtful analyses and recommendations fell on deaf ears.

In later years the international community introduced the idea of 'Standards before Status', meaning that basic democratic and human rights standards should be met before independence could be granted. Being the special representative of the OSCE chairman-in-office at that time, I expressed my view that this was a patronizing stance that still left uncertainty about the timing of the future status. Hence, it would play into the cards of radical rather than moderate forces on both sides. The formula reminded me of the colonial powers that tried to perpetuate their rule with the argument that the colony was not yet ready for independence. (When post-Second World War decolonization was rapidly cascading, Belgium still suggested fifty years of transition time for the then Belgian Congo …)

No doubt, this indefinite deferral policy provided fuel for the extremists that staged the serious riots in March 2004 when Kosovo Albanians went on a rampage, burning Serb houses and churches, and attacking internationals.

This traumatic event, which left nineteen people dead, basically shattered any fledgling confidence in multiethnic coexistence. It remains a rhetorical 'what if' question whether a fixed date for Status, with the admonition that Standards be met, would not have prevented much violence. I used to call this, with poetic licence, the 'Hong Kong scenario' in reference to the scheduled end of British rule over Hong Kong by a given date. Surely it could have persuaded the Kosovo Albanian leaders to be more forceful – and effective – in discouraging 'ethnic revenge'. It would also have removed the illusion on the part of Kosovo Serbs that reintegration in FRY/Serbia was a viable option, which the (northern) hardliners were so prone to exploit. Alas, such a scenario would have required political farsightedness and will on the part of Serbian political leaders in Belgrade, which was totally lacking.

Seeing the havoc created by uncertainty about the end goal, one cannot but conclude that international intervention in domestic affairs should not be 'open-ended'. What is minimally needed is a 'sunset clause' setting a deadline for its conclusion or, if the situation so warrants, a renegotiated mandate.

Lawlessness and impunity

The Albania and Kosovo interventions are examples of international response to crisis situations. Invariably, this involves putting an end to lawlessness and impunity. Basic democratic and human rights cannot be protected without the rule of law. Post-crisis or post-war reconstruction, rehabilitation and development vitally depend on effective law enforcement. In Kosovo this was a particularly pernicious problem. As the Serb-dominated police and judiciary had ceased to exist, the security void had to be addressed with urgency. An international UNMIK police force had to be deployed while a new, domestic Kosovo Police corps was being built up. The defunct judiciary was to be rehabilitated by appointing former judges and augmenting their capacity by training, upgrading and importing additional, foreign judges and expertise. All of this took an inordinate amount of time, which allowed the post-war climate of impunity to persist. It enabled the ethnic hostility – insufficiently restrained by the Kosovo Albanian leaders – to victimize innocent people and cause an unstoppable exodus of Kosovo Serbs and, smaller in absolute numbers, Roma.

The post-war ethnic violence in Kosovo, therefore, can, indeed, be seen as a major failure of the international intervention. The question, however, is how the 'international community' could have ever been expected to enforce law and order – in a chaotic post-war situation in an ethnically divided society, no less – when it had to rely on a wide variety of member states to provide the necessary means. Only an overwhelming law enforcement presence, virtually turning the place into a police state, could have made a difference. That scenario was a total impossibility in the given UN context, politically, financially and organizationally. As it happened, Kosovo was already quite generously treated in per capita terms, certainly compared to conflict situations in other (especially non-European!) parts of the world.[1] Combining various inputs from many different sources was bound to render any joint action cumbersome with a corresponding loss of efficiency and effectiveness. Apart from the poor timing, both the quantity and quality of these contributions – human and material – were not always up to the requirements. And thus, the only way to prevent the ethnic haemorrhage would have been to create political conditions that would effectively dissuade ethnic revenge. Carrots instead of sticks. Whether Goldstone's proposal of 'conditional independence', or 'Status with Standards' by another name, *by a pre-determined date* might have secured the desired outcome, is open to debate. My guess is that it would have made a difference.

Bernard Kouchner, in his slightly hagiographic book about his time in Kosovo, *Soldiers for Peace*, arrives at the conclusion that a massive international standby capacity of law enforcement is needed to better guide a post-war situation towards stability and peaceful coexistence. I share his idea, but do not believe in the international will to commit to such an instant multinational force. Weariness about supranational capacity building, prevalent at the time and even more so in the present day, seems to rule this out at the global level. It may stand a better chance of success at the (sub) regional level where interests could be more aligned. This would have the added benefit of cultural and ethnic proximity that would make such a standby capacity, under the auspices of a regional organization, more effective in deployment.

Ian King and Whit Mason, in their commendable *Peace at Any Price* go further than just lamenting the international laxity. They actually condemn the international community for failing to quickly restore law and order and prevent the ethnic killing and cleansing. They vastly overestimate, in my view, the feasibility of achieving international consensus on immediate and massive post-crisis funding and deployment. Not to mention the practical difficulties of recruiting the right types and numbers of internationals in a timely manner. It is simply impossible to create a legal state overnight. So, while I share all their misgivings, I am reminded of Bertolt Brecht's famous line when wishing for a better world: 'Doch die Verhältnisse, sie sind nicht so' (the conditions, though, they are not conducive). Which does not mean that the challenge should not be addressed, painstakingly yet ambitiously, issue by issue. But a healthy dose of realism helps against deception and despondency.

The human factor

The success of every international mission depends vitally on the human factor, the mission members who have to do the work, short- or long-term, supervisory or hands-on. Internationals joining a mission are a very motley crowd. Many have served in similar missions before and become professional mission-hoppers if not mission-junkies. They share any one or all of three main interests to varying degrees: challenge/adventure, outsize responsibility/prestige, and money. Invariably, over time the motivation shifts. When the pioneering adrenaline wears off and mission duties become more routine, the other incentives gain importance, money not being the least. The attractions of the job inevitably also lead to distortions, such as a tendency to perpetuate mission life as a goal in itself.

Apart from individual motives, geopolitical factors may distort the staffing of an international mission. The Kosovo Verification Mission was heavily dominated by Americans, some of whom were directly reporting to their intelligence masters in Washington bypassing the OSCE lines of communications. Similarly, Russia made sure it had its nationals near the centre of decision-making at UNMIK's headquarters and in field offices covering Serb-inhabited areas.

Most of the international staff – in Albania, Kosovo and many other places – serve with drive and dedication. I would not go as far, though, as attributing unselfish moral superiority, as implied in the hyperbolic motto of the UN Federal Credit Union: 'Serving the People who Serve the World'. There are certainly mission members who are less stellar and take advantage of – and liberties with – their international status. The number of four-wheel drives from Kosovo, with international logos, parked near seaside resorts on weekends in Greece – including my own, I must admit – could be quite staggering, confirming the perception of a hugely privileged work force. The worst performers, apart from the sheer incompetent ones, are those who combine arrogance with cynicism. With their unfounded notion of self-importance and basic lack of empathy, they compromise the standing of any mission among the local population. People are quick to recognize these flaws and start resenting the individuals, if not the whole mission. In the OSCE, where the bulk of the staff is supplied 'in kind' by donor countries, it was difficult to get rid of such dysfunctional staff. Voluntary departure was unlikely, for the reason that in their home countries they would be condemned to jobs far less glamorous and well-paying. Only a serious, proven breach of the code of conduct like theft or sexual harassment could be a ground for recall. The UN had a different problem insofar as their permanent contracts, with job security for life at pay scales often far above those back home, could lead to very routine, risk-avoiding job performance.

A greater problem than the occasional misfits in a mission, is frequent staff rotation. This creates a constant need for newcomers to go through the same learning curve and for the local people to get re-acquainted. When international staff is provided by participating states as in the case of the OSCE, much depends on the secondment policies of the individual countries. These can be quite restrictive. In Kosovo this was especially harmful in the case of the UNMIK police force, where rotations could be as frequent as every four or six months. A functional, minimum duration of contracts should be agreed upon to deal with this shortcoming.

A different but no less serious problem is the recruitment of local staff, ranging from security guards and drivers to interpreters, assistants and higher level co-workers. Local salaries paid by the international organizations are often multiples of what the local market can afford. As with other economic distortions, this has a serious, disruptive impact. It misallocates human resources, because qualified people go for the better-paying jobs even when these are far less commensurate with their qualifications. In Kosovo dentists became drivers, language professors interpreters, teachers security guards, lawyers simple clerks, nurses secretaries, etc. The language departments of the University of Pristina became seriously depleted because all of the qualified staff moved to international organizations to do translation and interpreting jobs.

Perpetuity syndrome

Given the material rewards and ego-inflation that come with mission assignments, there is a tendency on the part of internationals to overrate their role and overextend their stay. The mistaken notion of indispensability is a constant source of frustration for the local population. It explains why missions, over time, lose their popular appeal and support. People see the internationals performing jobs – with a pay and lifestyle way above local standards – that, in their opinion, could be done equally well or better by the local population. They see an inordinate amount of donor money ending up in the pockets of international staff, consultants, contractors and suppliers. This, by the way, often makes international pledges at donor meetings questionable because only a fraction of the promised funds – often inflated by rehashing earlier, unfulfilled pledges – flows directly to the recipient side.

Missions have an ingrained reluctance to scale down when possible. I have called this the 'perpetuity syndrome'. A famous example is the UNITAR in New York that kept extending its life line, although its *raison d' être* was far from clear. It was so appropriately nicknamed the UN Institute for the Tired and Retired that many people, including myself, forgot its real name. When by the end of 2001 the OSCE Mission in Kosovo (OMIK) had prepared the ground for democratic development and rule of law, including human rights guarantees, I considered the mission as basically completed. Of course, consolidation was still needed but that would require far less of an international presence than at the initial stages. It was a surprise and disappointment, therefore, to see ten, fifteen and twenty years later that OMIK was still massively present. This anomaly is, of course, also serving the local interests benefiting from an oversized international presence: real estate owners and agents, shops and restaurants, and, of course, the local employees who earn a multiple of the local pay. Then again, geopolitical reasons may be behind mission prolongation. The oversized OMIK, and UNMIK for that matter, are kept on artificial respiration because Serbia and the Russian Federation want to emphasize Kosovo's continuing need for international tutelage – and so keep its status unsettled.

Cultural imperialism

International interventions sanctioned by, or with concurrence of, the UN should reflect internationally agreed standards. Those may have been Western-inspired originally, but have since become UN-enshrined and globally subscribed: human rights, democratic principles, including the rights of minorities, and rule of law. In the case of Kosovo it was only logical that UNMIK was guided by these standards when rebuilding society. Hence the scrupulous efforts – sometimes to the chagrin of local politicians and other opinion makers – to create representative structures and involve all Kosovo constituencies in the governance, including ethnic minorities. Similarly, women were especially encouraged and enabled to assume responsibilities. Not just for democratic principles, because in my experience in conflict-ridden societies they have proven to be at least as apt as any man in lowering tensions and bringing about reconciliation. Our efforts in Kosovo to ensure their role in the police force (a minimum target of 20 per cent) and in politics (minimally 30 per cent in parliament) turned out to be hugely successful, also in the eyes of the local population. I have always found accusations that these efforts reflected 'cultural arrogance' or 'Western neo-colonialism' condescending towards the ordinary citizens, whether in Kosovo, Albania or elsewhere. Of course, there are cultural differences and sensitivities to take into account. International human rights do not imply cultural homogenization. Nonetheless, improving the prospects of individual lives by enhancing transparency in governance, tolerance, job opportunities and the rule of law is a rightful cause – to be pursued with not only respectful prudence but also determination.

Ethnic strife and nationalism

The decisive difference between the interventions in Albania and Kosovo was, of course, the ethnic factor. While there were distinct, cultural differences between the northern Ghegs and southern Tosks in Albania, also reflected in the political dimension, there was nothing comparable to the huge ethnic divide and enmity between the Serb and Albanian populations in Kosovo. For well over a century Kosovo had been a battleground of competing claims and ethnic strife, with the Serbs having the upper hand for most of the time, with international backing. The 1999 NATO-led military intervention was launched as a humanitarian intervention to restore land, livelihood and dignity to the Kosovo Albanian majority that had been subjected to gross violation of their human and democratic rights. The subsequent international rule was to end the vicious circle of ethnic strife and bring stability by establishing a multiethnic, democratic and open society. While the creation of a Balkan 'Switzerland' was far-fetched, the hope was that an interim international governance could provide, over time, ample provisions for minority rights and security for all inhabitants.

The utopian hope was as short-lived as unrealistic. There was total underestimation of the depth and width of the ethnic resentment that had been built up over the decades if not centuries. The Kosovo Serbs had become – overnight – a small, vulnerable minority in a separate Kosovo, instead of part of a large, dominant majority in Yugoslavia/Serbia. The Kosovo Albanians went through the exact reverse transformation, from a repressed minority in Yugoslavia/Serbia to an overwhelming majority in the new Kosovo. The underdog position was changed from one to the other community. This reversal of roles had happened before, albeit only briefly and under foreign occupation, when the Kosovo Albanians were empowered during the First and Second World Wars. It had ended with ruthless retaliation by the Serbian forces. Achieving peaceful ethnic coexistence in such historically loaded circumstances without clarity about the final status was a near-impossible task. It would require superhuman efforts, and probably several Nelson Mandelas, to contain the accumulated ethnic animosity, to clamp down on ethnic firebrands and to build a climate of tolerance, understanding, respect and cooperation. Moreover, economic progress for all to share and promising prospects for future generations would be an additional necessary condition (but 'not sufficient' by itself, in the old Marxist jargon).

These critical, contributing factors for ethnic peace were all wanting in post-war Kosovo. As a result, the ethnic hostility kept festering. As worldwide experience amply shows, there is nothing 'typically Balkan' about ethnic violence, just as there is no such thing as 'born hatred' between the Serbs and Albanians. What happened was that, like elsewhere in the world, ethnic identity as marked by linguistic, cultural and religious bonds got hijacked by nationalistic policies of unscrupulous individuals and elites vying for power and group dominance. Differences rather than the common good were magnified to the point of exclusion, xenophobia and demonization. Mythological self-aggrandizement and religious intolerance, most manifest on the Serb side, reinforced the mutual estrangement. Unfortunately, in multiethnic Yugoslavia, the nationalist fervour was not kept in check – after the Titoist lid was lifted with his death in 1980 – by timely economic reforms and enlightened domestic leadership. Incoherent and indecisive Western, especially European, policies did not help either. With the genie out of the bottle it was naïve if not highly delusional to think that international governance could lay the hard feelings to rest within a limited time span.

In our UNMIK and OMIK capacities, but also on the personal level, we went to extraordinary length in trying to keep the Kosovo Serbs on board in the new, separated Kosovo. However, with the mantra 'Kosovo je Serbija' (Kosovo is Serbia) kept alive by successive Belgrade governments and an uncompromising orthodox church, it was hard to convince them of the contrary. I have wizened to the conclusion that the long-lasting, man-made Serb–Albanian dichotomy in the Balkans can probably be overcome only by wholesale accession to a larger community of nations, in casu the European Union, in combination with shared economic progress and growing interdependence. Only then the physical and mental borders may become de-emphasized and ultimately fade away.

Final word

If there is one overall conclusion to be drawn, it is that international interventions, and by extension all international missions, cannot succeed without, first, cooperation from the host population and, second, a good dose of realism when setting goals and choosing means. The first pre-requires empathy with the plight of the common people rather than elites, the second, a simple realization that imperfect institutions, imperfect human beings and imperfect tools cannot create a perfect world. Lasting development has to come from within, it will come with ups and downs and it will take many years in coming. To use my favourite quote from a wise, old man I met in the Sahel when I was promoting the work of the UN Development Program: 'on ne developpe pas, on se developpe' (one cannot develop people, people develop themselves). What international action can do – with ambitions as well-tempered as Bach's *Well-Tempered Clavier* – is initiating and supporting progress in the direction of transparent, accountable governance and rule of law while minimizing negative side effects also known as 'collateral damage'. Empathetic realism for short.

Note

1   The former Egyptian UN Secretary General, Boutros Ghali, had a case when he complained, at the time of the Bosnian war, about the preoccupation of the dominant powers with the war and suffering in Yugoslavia as compared with calamities elsewhere in the world.

Abbreviations

AKK	Alliance for the Future of Kosovo, created in 2001 by Ramush Haradinaj
CEC	Central Election Commission
CIA	Central Intelligence Agency, Washington
COE	Council of Europe, headquartered in Strasbourg
DP	Democratic Party (in Albania)
EBU	European Broadcasting Union, based in Geneva
ECMM	European Commission Monitoring Mission, later renamed EUMM (EU Monitoring Mission), initially based in Zagreb, in 1997 moved to Sarajevo
EU	European Union, headquartered in Brussels
FARK	Armed Forces of the Republic of Kosovo, created by the LDK-led government-in-exile
FRY	Federal Republic of Yugoslavia, comprising Serbia and Montenegro, successor of (Tito's) Socialist Federal Republic of Yugoslavia
HOM	Head of Mission
IAC	Interim Administrative Council, UN-led executive council in post-war Kosovo
ICTY	International Crimes Tribunal for the former Yugoslavia, The Hague
IDP	Internally Displaced Persons

JIAS	Joint Interim Administrative Structure, created in November 1999, operational from January 2000
KTC	Kosovo Transitional Council, created in July 1999, predecessor of the elected Kosovo Parliament
KVM	(OSCE-led) Kosovo Verification Mission, late 1998–June 1999
KFOR	(NATO-led) Kosovo Forces in Kosovo
KLA	Kosovo Liberation Army (UCK in Albanian)
KP	Koalition Povratak (Coalition Return), Kosovo Serb political party created in 2001
KPC	Kosovo Protection Corps (TMK in Albanian)
KPS	Kosovo Police School
LBD	United Democratic Movement, created in 1998 by Rexhep Qosja
LDK	Democratic League of Kosovo, created in 1989 with Ibrahim Rugova invited to become its president soon thereafter
LPK	Popular Movement of Kosovo, new name (1987) of the Popular Movement of the Republic of Kosovo (LPRK) created in Switzerland in 1981
NATO	North Atlantic Treaty Organization, headquartered in Brussels
ODIHR	Office for Democratic Institutions and Human Rights, Warsaw
OMIK	OSCE Mission in Kosovo
OSCE	Organization for Security and Cooperation in Europe, headquartered in Vienna
PDK	Democratic Party of Kosovo (new name of PPDK, Party for Democratic Progress in Kosovo), co-founded by Hashim Thaci in October 1999
PGOK	Provisional Government of Kosovo, KLA-led government created in April 1999 after Rambouillet
PISG	Provisional Institutions for Self-Government, created by UNMIK and operational as of 31 January 2001

PPK	Parliamentary Party of Kosovo, founded in 1990 as opposition party alternative to LDK
RTK	Radio Television Kosovo, successor to RTP
SHIK	(Sherbimi Informativ i Kosoves) Secret Service of the KLA
SNC	Serb National Council
SP	Socialist Party (in Albania)
TMC	Temporary Media Commissioner
UNHCR	UN High Commissioner for Refugees, headquartered in Geneva
UNICEF	United Nations Children's Fund, headquartered in New York
UNMIK	United Nations Mission in Kosovo
UNSC	United Nations Security Council, New York
UN SRSG	Special Representative of the UN Secretary General

Sources consulted

Albania/Kosovo

OSCE Archives, Weekly-, Spot-, Monthly- and Special Reports, 1997–2001, OSCE Archives, Prague.

Albania

Abrahams, Fred. *Modern Albania*. New York: New York University Press, 2016.
Durham, Edith. *Albania and the Albanians, Articles and Letters 1903-1944*, edited by Bejtullah Destani. London: Centre for Albanian Studies, 2001.
Elsie, Robert. *Historical Dictionary of Albania*. Lanham: Scarecrow Press, 2010.
Fabius, Jan. *Zes Maanden in Albanie*, Tjeenk Willink and Haarlem, 1918. Amsterdam: Arbeiderspers, 1991.
Marchio, Riccardo. 'Operation Alba': a European approach to the peace support operation in the Balkans. Carlisle, PA: US Army War College research paper, April 2000.
Vickers, Miranda. *The Albanians*. London: I.B.Tauris, 2006.
Zonne, Joep. *Lodewijk Thomson – De Mediamajoor*. Utrecht/Tirana: Skanderbeg books, 2019.

Yugoslavia/Kosovo

Anstadt, Milo. *Scheuren in de heksenketel*. Amsterdam: Uitgeverij Contact, 1993.
Baudouin, Jacques. *Naissance d'une Democratie*. Editeur: Nouveau Monde editions, 2018.
BBC. Moral Combat: NATO at War. BBC2 Special, March 2000.
Boyes, Roger and Suzy Jagger. *New State, Modern Statesman*. London: Biteback Publishing, 2018.
Brown, Michael E.A. ed. *Nationalism and Ethnic Conflict*. Cambridge: MIT Press, 1997.
Cubrilovic, Vasa. *The Expulsion of the Albanians, Memorandum Presented in March 1937 in Belgrade*. Belgrade: V. Čubrilović, 1937.
Djilas, Milovan. *Conversations with Stalin*. New York: Harcourt, Brace & World, 1962.
Elsie, Robert. *Historical Dictionary of Kosovo*. Lanham: Scarecrow Press, 2011.

Glenny, Misha. *The Fall of Yugoslavia*. London: Penguin Paperback, 1996.
Glenny, Misha. *The Balkans, Nationalism, War and the Great Powers, 1801–2012*. New York: Granta Books, 2012.
Hamzaj, Bardh. *A Narrative about War and Freedom (dialogue with the commander Ramush Haradinaj)*. Pristhtina: Zeri, 2000.
Heraclides, Alexis. 'Ethnonational and Separatist Conflict Settlement and the Case of Kosovo', in *Kosovo: Avoiding Another Balkan War*. Athens: University of Athens, 1998.
Herscher, Andrew and Andreas Riedmayer. *The Destruction of Cultural Heritage in Kosovo, 1998-1999: a Post-War Survey*. Cambridge: Kosovo Cultural Heritage Survey, 2001.
Independent International Commission on Kosovo. *Conflict, International Response, Lessons Learned*. Oxford; New York: Oxford University Press, 2000.
Judah, Tim. *Kosovo: War and Revenge*. New Haven, CT: Yale University Press, 2002.
Judah, Tim. *Kosovo: What Everyone Should Know*. Oxford; New York: Oxford University Press, 2008.
Kadare, Ismail. *Drie rouwzangen voor Kosovo (Three elegies for Kosovo)*. Amsterdam: van Gennep, 1999.
King, Ian and Whit Mason. *Peace At Any Price*. London: Hurst & Company, 2006.
Kouchner, Bernard. *Les Guerriers de la Paix*. Paris: Editions Grasset, 2004.
Krstic, Branislav. *Kosovo – Causes of the Conflict, Reconciliation of Rights*. Belgrade: Liber press, 2001.
MacLean, Fitzroy. *Eastern Approaches*. London: Penguin Books, 1991.
Malcolm, Noel. *Kosovo, a Short History*. London: Macmillan, 1998.
Maliqi, Shkelzen. *Kosova, Separate Worlds*. Prishtina: Dukagjini PH, 1998.
OSCE. *Kosovo, As Seen, As Told*, Vol I and Vol II. OSCE Office for Democratic Institutions and Human Rights, 1999.
Qosja, Rexhep. *Die ogen en de dood*, with postface by Ismael Kadare. Amsterdam: Van Gennip-Novib-Ncos, 1997.
Reuter, Jens. 'Serbien und Kosovo – Das Ende eines Mythos', in *Der Kosovo Konflikt*. Munchen: Bayerische Landeszentrale fur politische Bildungsarbeit, 2000.
Sans, Anne-Laure. L'Intervention de l'OSCE dans les Balkans. Heurs et malheurs de la Mission de verification au Kosovo, *PSIO Occasional Paper*, 2004.
Schwartz, Stephen. *Kosovo: Background to a War*. London: Anthem Press, 2000.
Veremis, Thanos and Evangelos Kofos, eds. *KOSOVO: Avoiding Another Balkan War*. Athens: University of Athens, 1998.
Zimmerman, Warren. *Origins of a Catastrophe*. New York: Random House, 1996.
Zlatko, Pakovic in collaboration with Jeton Neziraj. *Encyclopedia of the Living*. Belgrade: The Center for Cultural Decontamination, 2016.

Index

Abnori, Pjeter   21, 28, 164
Agani, Fehmi   37, 85
Albright, Madeleine   42, 47, 48, 86, 88
Amanpour, Christiane   56
Anastasijevic, Dejan   55
Andjelkovic, Zoran   85
Andric, Ivo   71
Annan, Kofi   75, 117, 189, 193
d'Ansembourg, Jan   3
Ardian   85
Artemije, Bishop (Radasavijevic)   91, 92, 113, 115, 129, 131, 146, 155, 157, 164, 177
Athisaari, Matti   54

Bakalli, Mahmut   43, 110, 188, 195
Bennet, Steve   99
Berisha, Kole   91
Berisha, Sali   2, 3, 5, 11, 20, 27, 29, 30, 38, 44, 88
Beshiri, Ismije   13, 23, 55, 56, 84, 88, 116, 163
Biegman, Niek   56
Bimo, Roland   20
Brovina, Flora   119, 147, 187
Buja, Ram   48
Bukoshi, Bujar   37, 38, 44, 85–7, 122
Burim   85
Bush, George W.   60(f), 171, 192

Carlson, Scot   26
Ceka, Nerita   2
Ceku, Agim   48, 75, 102–5, 170
Ceku Ethen   105

Cernomyrdin   54,
Cerovic, Stojan   55, 159
Chomsky, Noam   53
Clark, Wesley   58, 100
Clinton, Hillary   163
Cosic, Dobritsa   82(f)
Covic, Nebojsa   157, 160, 172, 174, 176, 177, 181, 191, 193, 196, 200
Cubrilovic   71, 82(f)
Curuvija, Slavko   55

Dacic, Ivica   50, 160
Demaci, Adem   21, 37, 40, 44, 47, 48, 73, 74, 82(f), 87, 112, 132, 147, 164, 186
Djilas, Milovan   21, 31, 73, 82(f), 164
Djindjic, Zoran   113, 128, 147, 159, 160, 163, 168, 177, 179(f)
Dobruna, Vjosa   87, 102, 122, 186
Drake, Martin   174
Draskovic, Vuk   49
Dugi   85
Durham, Edith   69

Eide, Kai   59
Erben, Peter   126, 158

Fehmiu, Bekim   80
Fino, Bashkim   3
Fisher, Jeff   126
Frederiksen, Sven   77
Frowick, Robert   16

Gelbard, Robert   39
Geoana, Mircea   171

George, Bruce   198
Geremek   11
Ghali, Boutros   220(f)
Godo, Sabri   10, 26, 43, 48
Gorani, Dukagin   59(f), 109, 190

Haekkerup, Hans   151–3, 156, 159, 166, 173, 184, 193, 194, 198
Hajdari, Azem   21, 22, 44
Hajrizi, Mehmet   86
Haliti, Xhavit   44
Haradinaj, Daut   105, 162
Haradinaj, Ramush   42, 75, 82(f), 104, 105, 127, 162, 170, 177, 184, 188–91, 194, 195
Haxhiu, Baton   59(f), 109, 129, 156
Holbrooke, Richard   40, 41, 49, 142
Hoxha, Enver   xv, 1, 7, 13, 18, 28, 73
Huys, Twan   15
Hyseni, Hydajet   86

Imami, Arben   26
Isidora   174
Islami, Kastriot   56
Isles, Tim   174
Ivanovic, Milan   114, 153, 170
Ivanovic, Oliver   114, 120, 131, 133, 154, 157, 160, 168, 170, 176, 196

Jackson, Michael   58, 62, 90, 103, 104
Jaksic, Marko   114, 131, 170, 176
Jashari, Adem   39, 112
Jocelyn, Andrew   174
Judah, Tim   68

Kadare, Ismael   66, 68, 79, 115
Keller, Gabriel   53
Kelmendi, Bajram   87, 121
Kelmendi, Nibike   121
King, Ian   214
Kostunica, Vojislav   139, 160, 174, 177, 192, 193, 200
Kosumi, Bajram   44, 79, 86, 87
Kouchner, Bernard   77, 90, 92, 102, 106, 108, 116, 120, 129, 132, 135, 137, 143, 144, 151, 213

Krasniqi, Jakup   112
Kurti, Albin   119, 147

Lavrov, Serge   163
Leci   85
Legisi, Ndre   23
Leroy, Alain   128
Lindh, Anna   162
Luci, Rexhep   89, 139
Lustaku, Sami   104, 140, 162

Mahmuti, Bardyl   112, 187
Majko, Pandeli   24, 27–30, 56, 88
Malcolm, Noel   82(f), 188
Maliqi, Shkelzen   109
Maloku, Naim   127, 146, 195
Marty, Dick   66
Mason, Whit   214
Meidani, Rexhep   2, 5, 19, 22, 26, 33, 44, 48, 87, 88
Melo, Serge Viero de   62, 77, 90, 91, 108
Meta, Ilir   19, 24, 30
Michel, Louis   162
Mierlo, Hans van   2
Milo, Pascal   48
Milosevic, Slobodan   36, 37, 39–43, 50, 51, 54, 74, 81, 87, 113, 164
Mitchell, Sandra   63
Montgomery, Wes   182, 183
Mustafa, Rrustem   104, 162
Mustafa, Xhemajl   145

Nano, Fatos   2, 3, 5, 12, 19–24, 27, 31, 43
Nedic, Milan   71
Nokic, Randel   194, 196
Noli, Bishop Fan   9
Novicki, Marek   102

Obama, Barrack   79
Ogatha, Sadako,   56

Pardew   163
Patten, Chris   162
Pavle, Patriarch   177
Ponte, Carla del   66

Potovski, Petar   129
Pulver, Rob   2, 6, 122
Putin, Vladimir   xvii(f), 171

Qosja, Rexhep   36–8, 44, 49, 75, 86, 88,
    91, 115, 117–18, 127, 131, 132, 146

Radosavlevic, Nenad   176, 195, 196
Ralston   163
Rankovic, Alexandar   73, 82(f)
Raskovic-Ivic, Sanda   160, 172, 193
Raznatovic, Zjelko (Arkan)   174, 179(f)
Reka, Blerim   158, 165, 186
Rexha, Ekrim (Commander Drini)   123
Rexhepi, Bajram   120
Rice, Condoleezza   172
Ristic, Dustan   91
Rowland, Jackie   192
Rubin, James   51, 124
Rugova, Ibrahim   12, 37–41, 44, 47, 48,
    50, 75, 85–8, 92, 99, 115–18, 121–2,
    127, 132, 140, 153, 154, 162, 167,
    177, 186–91, 194, 199
Ruka, Ethem   30

Sarqini, Aferdita   109
Sava, Father (Janjic)   91, 113, 120, 129,
    132, 148
Sejdiu, Fatmir   194
Selimi, Sylejman   104
Selimi, Rexhep   104
Sesjel, Vojislav   113, 128
Shala, Blerim   59(f), 91, 109, 156, 159, 165
Shehu, Tritan   29
Solana, Javier   128, 162, 163
Stojanovic, Lazar   92
Surroi, Veton   37, 38, 44, 48, 59(f), 66,
    86, 87, 92, 108, 132, 141, 165, 190
Svilanovic, Goran   160

Tadic, Boris   113, 114, 173
Thaci, Hashim   37, 41, 44, 47, 48,
    50, 64, 75, 82(f), 85–8, 91–2, 102–5,
    112, 115–18, 121, 122, 126, 127,
    131, 132, 153, 154, 162, 168,
    170, 177, 179(f), 187, 189–91,
    194, 200
Thomson, Lodewijk   8, 9
Tito, Joseph Broz   xv, 72, 73
Toptani, Essad Pasha   7
Traavik, Kim   106
Trajkovic, Momcilo   91, 92, 118,
    124, 129, 131, 154, 168, 177,
    195, 196
Trajkovic, Rada   128, 138, 148, 155,
    168, 189, 194, 195
Trotsky, Leon   69
Tucovic, Dimitrije   69
Tudjman, Franjo   74

Valentin, Marcel   198
Vejsiu, Ylli   29
Vlasi, Azem   36
Vollebaeck, Knut   85
Vranicki, Franz   2, 4
Vucic, Alexander   160
Vukicevic, Stanimir   145

Walker, William   46, 53, 57
Watson, Fiona   108
Wied, Wilhelm zu   9

Younes, Nadia   108

Zatriqi, Agim   185
Zimmerman, Warren   80
Zivkovic   160
Zog(u), Ahmet   6, 9, 71
Zog(u), Leka   5, 6

www.ingramcontent.com/pod-product-compliance
Ingram Content Group UK Ltd.
Pitfield, Milton Keynes, MK11 3LW, UK
UKHW021906220326
469204UK00008B/225